"The Relationship Model helped the board of Grace International School develop the change strategy required to move from a Managing board to a Governing board."

Nancy Benham, MBE
Chair of Board of Governors 2000-2002, Grace International School
Dhaka, Bangladesh

"The process of transforming from a managing board to a governing board using the Relationship Model was a paradigm shift. However, it resulted in making Pro Coro Canada a more stable organization, increased morale, better leadership in every sense, and an encouraging positive future outlook."

Trent Worthington, Minister of Music
St. Albert Alliance Church
Associate Conductor, Pro Coro Canada, Edmonton, Alberta, Canada

"Finally, a light is shone on the path out of the chasm of non-profit organizational planning. Thanks, Les Stahlke!"

Gary R. Burkee, President
The Burkee Group
Chairman of the Board, Star of Hope Foundation
Milwaukee, Wisconsin, USA

"The Relationship Model of governance and management helped us clearly define how to properly plan to respond in almost any future situation."

Ed and Rhoda Kirk, President and Vice President/Secretary
AA Electric S.E., Inc., Lakeland, Florida
Members, Board of Directors
Hope Seeds, Inc., Palmetto, Florida, USA

"Recently The Edmonton Academy governing board adopted the relationship model. It has made a big difference in terms of how we operate. It has certainly empowered the staff to handle the day to day operations and running of the school while allowing the Board to concentrate on strategic direction. Recently our Executive Director said, 'We have made more progress in the last two years than the ten previous years. The board is able to concentrate on strategic direction rather than spend their meetings talking about details in the management of the school.'"

Joyce Johnson, Chief Operating Officer, The Good Samaritan Society
Board Chair, The Edmonton Academy, Edmonton, Alberta, Canada

This book is dedicated to the memory of

Paula Jeanne Stahlke

October 11, 1938 - October 29, 2001

without whose affirmation, involvement and servant leadership
this book would never have been written.

GOVERNANCE
MATTERS

Relationship Model™ of Governance, Leadership and Management

Les Stahlke
with
Jennifer Loughlin

Balancing Client and Staff Fulfillment in
Faith-based Not-for-profit Organizations

ISBN 0-9733685-0-0 Governance Matters - Balancing Client and Staff Fulfillment in Faith-based Not-for-profit Organizations

Production Credits: Cover Design: Mike Lee Text Design: Ronda Petersen Layout: Lori St. Martin Printer: Imperial Printing Ltd., Edmonton

Printed in Canada

10 9 8 7 6 5 4 3 2 1

Governance Matters

Table of Contents

Acknowledgements

Prologue

Part 1 The Relationship Model™ – Finding Good Soil

**Part 2 From the Roots Up –
Governance, Leadership and Management**

Part 3 Appendices

Jennifer Loughlin

Following a childhood commitment to world mission, Jennifer served in a mission hospital in Nazareth. While at a major London hospital, Jennifer was invited to serve with TearFund, a Christian Relief and Development Agency. For 16 years, she was responsible for selecting and supporting people who served throughout the developing world, initiating a unique program for new graduates to gain cross-cultural experience.

With a Master's degree and as Director of Human Resources, Jennifer served with Mission Aviation Fellowship Europe, a mission flying into some of the world's most inaccessible places.

Jennifer maintains her commitment to international mission as a trustee of People In Aid, an organization establishing and maintaining standards of good practice for international aid workers. Today, she supports non-profit boards in their governance responsibilities through her organization, Creative People Solutions.

Jennifer lives in Cobham, Surrey, United Kingdom.

About the Authors

Les Stahlke

Les Stahlke has spent his entire 40-year professional career in leadership positions in not-for-profit organizations. Following six years as a parish pastor in Alberta, Canada, Les led in the founding of the Lutheran Association of Missionaries and Pilots (LAMP). During his 25 years as CEO, LAMP became an international organization with two boards and expanded to serve people scattered over more than one million square miles of northern Canada and Alaska.

In 1995, he accepted an appointment to serve as the CEO of Mission Aviation Fellowship Europe, a consortium of ten European national MAFs, providing air transport services in four east African countries plus Chad, Madagascar, Bangladesh and Mongolia.

Les has served on numerous not-for-profit boards as a director and chair. The Relationship Model™ is supported by many years of leadership experience, personal observation, theological study, research and analysis.

Since 1999, Les' company, GovernanceMatters.com Inc., has offered the Relationship Model™ to churches, faith-based and secular not-for-profit organizations in North America, Europe and Asia. He presents the model in person and via the Internet.

Les Stahlke lives in Edmonton, Alberta, Canada.

Acknowledgements

I think of writing this book as a process of downloading information from my brain. It has been a long and complex process. Without the encouragement and support of others it would not have been possible. I want to acknowledge the people who helped make it happen.

First, I want to acknowledge the many years of support that my late wife, Paula, my soul-mate for forty-three years, gave so generously. Her common sense and intuition, her insights and encouragement shaped the way I worked and learned. Her gifts and insights are inseparable from the words of this book.

Co-workers and clients in Canada, the United States, Europe, Africa and Asia provided a broad exposure to governance, leadership and management issues in many cultures. I could list hundreds of people who have helped me develop this model.

My sons, Thom and Paul, made significant contributions to this effort. Thom designed the prototypes of most of the illustrations in this book. Paul provided endless hardware and software support, enabling me to benefit from the technology vital to this process.

My colleagues, Jennifer Loughlin in the United Kingdom and Ron Schlegelmilch in Canada, provided more than an important sounding board. They added their own experience in working with not-for-profit organizations and many ideas that enhanced this work.

Mike Lee is the gifted artist who designed the cover and the organizational chart in the form of a tree that has become the logo for the Relationship Model™. He also drew the three caricatures, which look more like me than I do.

Neil Sawers provided the professional style editing to every chapter. His expertise is documented in his own book on writing, *Ten Steps to Help You Write Better Essays & Term Papers*. This book is much more readable because of his highly-tuned gifts.

Judy Bauer's eye for detail, trained by four years of work in the educational publishing industry, found opportunity for more correction and polishing than I thought possible. She systematically reads for meaning, grammar, spelling and punctuation.

Ronda Petersen and her team at Imperial Printing Ltd. put the final touch to all this effort by producing the beautiful volume you are holding now. Their knowledge of publishing and printing was invaluable in putting this downloaded information on to a printed page.

Other friends, co-workers and members of my family provided the ongoing encouragement that I needed to keep at the task. Whatever benefit that you receive personally and in your organization is the result of a complex team effort.

Les Stahlke
August 2003

Prologue

"Who is your audience?" people ask me. Personal friends and colleagues have suggested that I write this book for four different types of organizations:

- faith-based not-for-profit organizations
- secular not-for-profit organizations
- Christian churches
- for-profit corporations.

The Relationship Model™ of governance applies to all, but I am writing primarily for the first of these four. In this book I have chosen to emphasize the source of the Relationship Model™—the Bible. I believe that the Relationship Model™ follows God's design for healthy, balanced relationships.

Other holy books contain the same insights. For example, the Koran makes 67 uses of the word "limitations" in the same context as it appears in the Relationship Model™.

Even people for whom holy books may have no particular value may benefit from the Relationship Model™. Common sense is at the heart of this model of governance, leadership and management. I believe that common sense is another of God's creations. Why would there be any conflict between what we read in the Bible and what we know from common sense?

I suggest that the best way to read this book is by starting at the beginning in order to introduce yourself to the conceptual basis of healthy, balanced working relationships detailed in the Relationship Model™. Once you have done this, feel free to move to the section most applicable to you, perhaps the role you have in your organization. There is something here for boards, board chairs, CEOs, managers, paid and volunteer staff.

Two of us have had a role in writing this book. Jennifer Loughlin, my colleague who lives and works in the United Kingdom, has written the sections that deal with competencies of board members, board chairs, chief executive officers and managers. Her research and expertise in competencies, vital components to healthy working relationships, is a major part of the Relationship Model™.

Many of the common English words in the text are used as technical terms. They have specific meaning to give the model clarity. For example, words like *strategic* and *tactical* can have several meanings. Other words, like *power*, *hierarchy* and *accountability* have been "abused" over the years. Each carries baggage that changes the meaning for many of us. In this book these words have only one meaning. All words to be taken as technical terms are included in the Definition of Terms in Part 3, Appendix A. Referring to these definitions may help you to understand the model more clearly.

You will also find in the appendices a bibliography of the work of other people on this journey towards knowledge. The development of their themes and concepts is, I believe, worthy of your consideration. Their works are foundational to this practical application of governance to not-for-profit organizations. I have quoted from some of their works, as I considered appropriate and valuable.

Life is a journey of learning, a journey that appears to have no destination of complete wisdom in this life… only milestones of "aha" experiences and discoveries. My purpose is to add value to your own journey by building on what is already available to you.

I believe that from your own experience and common sense, you are already acquainted with the many pieces that make up the "puzzle" of healthy, balanced working relationships. My hope is that this book will help you find clarity in seeing how the many pieces can fit together to form the big picture of a healthy not-for-profit organization.

Les Stahlke

The Relationship Model™ - Finding Good Soil

PART *1*

What's the Difference?

Genesis

Is there a balance between the fulfillment of the clients and the fulfillment of the staff in your organization? The most important principle contained in this book is that for an organization to be healthy, both staff and clients must be equally fulfilled.

This book, detailing the Relationship Model™, is a simple yet compelling result of examining the design of healthy relationships in the Old and New Testaments so as to demonstrate the principle in action.

The most important principle contained in this book is that for an organization to be healthy both staff and clients must be equally fulfilled.

The entire Bible teaches in stories. We can put the lessons of these stories into a logical sequence in order to learn from them. That is what this book does. I want to assure readers who may not regard the biblical literature as the definitive word of God, that the Relationship Model™ deals with universal truths. There is nothing in this book that is not also supported by other holy books, common sense, and many excellent authors. Thus, while this book is written specifically for board members, CEOs and staff of Christian, faith-based, not-for-profit organizations, there is no reason why any organization cannot benefit from the insights that follow.

What's the Difference?

So what's different about the Relationship Model™ from other models that deal with board governance, leadership and the management of organizations? Why should you expect to gain something from this book that you don't already know? The answer to both questions has to do with common sense and clarity.

Common Sense and Clarity

I've been told repeatedly by those who use the Relationship Model™ that it brings familiar, common sense, every-day themes into harmony with one another. Because you already have a measure of common sense from your own life experiences, I doubt that you will be introduced to any concepts you don't already use in some aspect of your life and work.

The most significant benefit of this model of governing, leading and managing your organization, however, is clarity. Clarity, as you will see when we discuss the diverse elements of the Relationship Model™, leads to dramatic shifts in our abilities to build relationships that work, as opposed to those that don't.

To begin to appreciate the extraordinary difference the Relationship Model™ can make, let's review the most widely accepted model in use throughout the world today—the Default Model.

The Default Model

The Default Model is the most common model that I have seen in the world of not-for-profit organizations. Of course, it's not a model at all—it's the lack of a model. It's just that some characteristics are so common to organizations around the world that you would think someone wrote the book and everyone bought it. You would think that the Default Model was a best seller, translated into many languages.

There are two main characteristics of the Default Model:

1. It encourages people to bring whatever values they hold into the organization.

The problem with this characteristic is that no attempt is made to identify which of those values are worthy of becoming the core values of that organization.

Values drive all human behaviour, including governance, leadership and management. Yet how many organizations take the time to decide and to agree what values will form the basis of relationships in the workplace? In my experience, precious few. The result is that you can find a board whose chair is power-oriented, perhaps even abusive, but who won't be challenged by any board members whose value system happens to be *laissez faire*.

The resulting process may be dysfunctional, not only in the governance that flows from it, but in the cycle of damaging, self-perpetuating behaviour it generates.

All too often we assume (and we'll talk about assumptions in a moment) that everyone is going to use "Christian" values. When not everyone does, we try to forgive and forget. Meanwhile, people are unhappy and unfulfilled and the quality of the services they offer frequently suffers.

2. It lacks a clear structure of working relationships.

Did you ever wonder whether or not you had the authority to do something? Or know already that you don't? Do you have to get permission or at least "double check" to be sure? I have found that it is *more common* for people to hesitate to act because they're uncertain about how much authority they have, rather than from a lack of confidence.

Did you ever have the feeling that you didn't know what was expected of you? Or if you did that it wasn't realistic? In my experience it is *more common* for people to assume what is expected of them rather than to actually know. They rarely have negotiated goals that are clear and specific.

And now, to *assumptions*. The Default Model specializes in assumptions and in using words that have different meanings to different people. Defining them would be to impose your values on others. The Default Model moves from assumption to confusion, from confusion to conflict and from conflict to brokenness.

From values to structure to assumptions, the Default Model is the pathway so many organizations follow—by default. The Default Model affects some other major areas. In particular:

- forgiveness versus accountability
- reversing roles
- managing or parenting
- productivity and fulfillment in balance.

Forgiveness vs. Accountability

Accountability in the Default Model is usually looked upon as discipline, punishment, or judgment. Many organizations consider it undesirable, something to be avoided—and avoid it they do.

Forgiveness, in the Default Model, is open to misinterpretation. Fail to do something that you agreed upon, and you're forgiven because of the "circumstances," or other appropriate justification. The result is that forgiveness and accountability are confused. We replace one with the other.

People in organizations using the Default Model would never relate accountability to receiving a bonus or promotion, an official commendation or award.

We will show later on that forgiveness is a strong value and accountability a neutral process. Both are vital. They are apples and oranges, not good apples and rotten apples. Confuse the two and the results are usually painful and sometimes disastrous.

Reversing Roles

Organizations that govern, lead and manage by default—without a model— usually reverse the roles of governance and management. We find boards that manage and CEOs and managers that do the strategic planning. Boards get into the detail of financial management in the absence of policy that would authorize the CEO and staff to do that work. They receive endless reports about how programs are doing. They are so conscientious about managing and shadow-managing and advising management that they don't have time to interact with clients or plan the future priorities of services and target groups.

Thus, strategic thinking and planning, the single most important governance process, defaults to the CEO and senior managers. Because of their close relationship to clients and their needs, managers develop the strategic direction for the board to approve. They do a good job. The board examines the management implications of the strategic plans and approves them. After all, the staff members know better what the clients need. Besides, says the board, "We trust our CEO to lead us in the right direction."

The strategic and tactical (technical terms) are reversed. Governors manage and managers govern—by default, not by design.

Governance—Is It Managing or Parenting?

By default board members, who may never have been on a board before, come to their new responsibility loaded with management experience. They have managed their finances. They have managed at work. They have accumulated a lot of experience and wisdom and are eager to share it with an organization that has invited them to serve by joining the board. It's flattering. It's compelling. It's serious business, and they want to do it well.

Unfortunately, few have learned the difference between governance and management. They join the board with the wrong paradigm, the wrong orientation. They assume that to be good board members they must be good managers.

It would be much better for the quality of governance, if the new board member would join with a paradigm of parenting. Every adult person in the world has experience in parenting or memories of being parented. Governance has more in common with parenting than with management. That's what the term "governess" implies.

Parenting consists of setting boundaries for children in which they can learn to manage themselves as adults. If parents didn't give as much authority to their children as the children can handle—more and more as they grow older—the children would never become functional adults. It's the delegating of authority and responsibility with loving accountability that makes parents successful in raising healthy children.

That parenting paradigm, as we shall see more fully, is what good governance is about. It is why this book is designed to assist boards to move from management to governance. We will do that by leaving the Default Model behind and learning to apply the Relationship Model™. Boards will be enabled to lead the organizations they govern into new visions of growth and service.

At the same time, however, they will maintain control of the health of the organization and its productivity, with governance instead of management. They will also do it with greater fulfillment and satisfaction, well aware of the important contribution they provide to their organization and their community.

Productivity and Fulfillment in Balance

At the very beginning of this chapter I said that the most important principle in the Relationship Model™ was that "for an organization to be healthy there must be a balance between the fulfillment of the clients and the fulfillment of the staff." Another way of saying this is that the productivity of the organization and the enrichment of the staff must have the same priority.

As the Default Model comes into play, however, what actually happens in not-for-profit organizations is often quite different. On one hand, there are organizations in which staff are too comfortable and clients not properly served. Inefficiency, waste and abuse abound. The donors who support such organizations are often ignorant of what is really happening. They trust what they read and have no accountability process to know that the truth is very different.

More common and just as sad is the opposite situation. People working within the organization burn out, leave and are replaced by people who struggle as long as possible before burning out themselves. Sometimes this is due to callous and insensitive management coupled with a board that doesn't consider staff satisfaction worthy of its scrutiny. A manager may say, "If you don't like your job, there are ten people looking for work and waiting to take your place. If you don't like it, leave!" The bodies of former employees are left in the wake of managers like this. The things they care about don't include the fulfillment and enrichment of the very people who provide clients with services.

Sometimes, however, the lack of fulfillment is a problem that people bring with them into the workplace, particularly in Christian faith-based organizations. Such people are their own worst enemy. I have often said that if we could get rid of "the devil, the world and our flesh" but retained "the Protestant work ethic," we would still be in deep trouble.

Why is this? Because people sometimes try to give back to God more than they have been resourced to give. A desire to please goes beyond what is available, resulting in pain and failure that often continues for far too long. I have spoken to many beautiful people who choose to deny themselves the very fulfillment that God has promised. They have the misguided notion that God is demanding something of them in an area where, in fact, God has given them the freedom to choose. People "on fire for the Lord" too often burn out doing the work in which they should be most fulfilled. We will examine later in more detail the relationship between God's will and our freedom to choose.

▶ *People "on fire for the Lord" too often burn out doing the work in which they should be most fulfilled.*

From Whence the Relationship Model™

You may wonder just where the Relationship Model™ originates. How could it be that there would be a model that seems to put the pieces together that wasn't written centuries ago—a model that would have replaced the Default Model long before we could even read?

I have asked the same question. Had I come across such a book, I would sell it, not write one that contains information that appears so obvious that it is already well known to us.

▶ *What we haven't done is put the pieces together to form the big picture.*

So, what is the answer? I believe that all of us possess the unique pieces of knowledge that make for healthy, balanced relationships. We practice the elements set out in this book in most, if not all, of our relationships. What we haven't done is put the pieces together to form the big picture. That's why we can't always analyze why a relationship is going wrong, even if we can identify the specific dysfunction.

The Relationship Model™ is not rocket science. It is a very simple result of examining the design of healthy relationships in the Old and New Testaments. As I mentioned earlier, the entire Bible teaches in stories, both in the Hebrew culture and also the Greek and Roman cultures. It is the modern western mind that insists on putting the lessons of stories into a logical sequence and making an outline of the lessons contained in those stories. That is what this book does.

Reality Check – Common Sense Takes Forever to Apply

I must admit that while the concepts in this book are easily understood, they seem to take a lifetime of practice to learn, because they apply to all relationships. The Relationship Model™ could as easily be a book about marriage or parenting as about governance. It could discuss the teacher/student relationship as easily as the employer/employee relationship. For this reason, you can expect that what you choose to learn here will support your efforts to make all your relationships healthy and fulfilling, not just for you, but for the people you know, love, live with and work with.

Let the journey begin.

Notes

Values
and Power

Values

Imagine that you are having a problem in one of your relationships at work. If your experience is normal, you won't have to think very hard before coming up with an example. "I wonder what drives that person to behave like that," you ask yourself. "We're definitely not on the same wave length."

In this chapter, we deal with the connection between values and relationships in the workplace. We explore the common value systems we encounter. In particular, we identify what goes wrong when these systems fail the organization and its people.

We begin by identifying what we mean by values. Next, we move to the "values continuum"—the range of values that can exist in organizations. We then examine how those different value systems impact an organization's six core processes. Finally, we review The Seven Deadly Sins, seven classic examples of values that can cause extraordinary damage to an organization and its people.

What are values?

In the context of working relationships, values are "any beliefs or strongly-held concepts that guide or determine our behaviour" in that relationship.

There is almost no end to the list of values. Try these:

Honesty, integrity, loyalty, transparency, truthfulness, industry, effectiveness, efficiency, planning, evaluation, trust, friendliness, listening, communication, consensus, etc.

In my study of the Bible, plus observations and analysis of the workplace, I have identified three core values that are essential to healthy working relationships. They are:

- affirmation
- involvement
- servant leadership.

To understand and appreciate everything that follows, we need to be clear on what we mean by these core values.

Affirmation

Affirmation is another word for love. God is love. To be accepted by God in Christ is the most treasured possession of every Christian. It's no stretch to see that affirmation is the single most powerful motivation for good that we can possibly introduce into our relationships—at home, in church, at work and at play.

Affirmation takes many forms. When we need help and support, it is expressed as compassion. When we hurt someone with our words or actions, it takes the form of forgiveness. Affirmation can show up as patience, a willingness to listen and understanding. It is often expressed by a smile, a handshake or a hug.

Involvement

Involvement means that people are not left out of the decision-making processes that affect them. They are included. Another word for involvement, therefore, is inclusion. Another is engagement.

When we involve the people in our organizations—and even outside our organizations—who are affected by our decisions and plans, a marvelous thing happens. Their sense of commitment and ownership increases.

The outcome matters to them, making success and fulfillment much more likely.

Synergy is also at work here. By allowing everyone to participate, the result is far superior to that which anyone in the group could produce alone, including the leader! The sum is greater than many parts working on their own.

Servant Leadership

The essence of servant leadership is the power of being lifted up by our *source of authority* rather than being put down. Instead of being overpowered, we are empowered. Instead of being oppressed by rules, we are given freedom to excel. Instead of being afraid to take risks for fear of failure, we are encouraged to risk and learn from our mistakes.

Servant leadership is the lesson Jesus taught the disciples by washing their feet. It is a lesson that can make a major difference in an organization.

The Values Continuum

Laissez-faire Values	Relationship-oriented Values	Authoritarian Values
▽	▽	▽

How authority is used in an organization can be displayed as a continuum of values. It spans a spectrum from complete abdication of authority at one extreme to lust for power at the other. The three value systems that flow into each other, as illustrated above, are:

- *laissez-faire* values
- relationship-oriented values
- authoritarian values.

◄

It's no stretch to see that affirmation is the single most powerful motivation for good that we can possibly introduce into our relationships.

Laissez-faire Values

We may be drawn to the left by a *laissez-faire* value system where we tend to avoid conflict and dealing directly with issues. To varying degrees, this value system exhibits lack of clarity on roles and responsibilities. Traditions and assumptions are more common than policies and goals. In its extreme form, *laissez-faire* is identified by a complete abdication of authority.

Relationship-oriented Values: Affirmation, Involvement and Servant Leadership

This value system is at the center of the spectrum. It is the foundation, or perhaps the fulcrum, of organizations that succeed in their mandates. This value system insures a balance between client and staff fulfillment, fully incorporating the core values of affirmation, involvement and servant leadership.

Authoritarian Values

We may be drawn to the right by an authoritarian value system where "might is right" and where obedience produces rewards. More extreme is the system where someone in authority is motivated by a desire or lust for power. "My way or the highway," comes from this value system. This system produces abuse of power and real harm to healthy relationships.

Individuals and their organizations may be pulled towards either end of the continuum, leading to problems that are all too common. By understanding these value systems we can:

- comprehend the symptoms that we are observing
- identify the causes behind any problems we encounter
- learn how to change those underlying causes so as to improve the work we do and better fulfill those who carry it out.

Keep this continuum in mind during the rest of this chapter as we show you how an organization's value system impacts each of its core processes.

It was a sultry August day in the Midwestern U.S. community, but inside the boardroom the atmosphere was even more stifling. The board of 18 and the complement of staff and guests brought the number of people to nearly 30.

The board chair had just interrupted a director in mid sentence and began a tirade against him. It went on for five minutes, but to those who watched in stunned silence the tirade felt like 20. It seems the director was expressing a view that opposed the direction that the board chair had in mind.

The director was a retired professional educator. He was a long-time member of this board of directors that governed a highly-respected private Christian secondary school. He had the admiration of the rest of the directors, the staff, and many alumni. But this was not going to be his best day. Before the meeting was over he would be derided, humiliated and would finally walk away in tears.

The board chair began to berate the director for his disrespect of the chair in insisting on making his views known despite the chair's insistence that he stop talking. Then the chair proceeded to rail against the quality of the director's thinking and even his commitment to the organization. Finally, he expressed his disappointment that the director was on the board at all.

The other directors were stunned into silence. The staff members and the guests were shocked and afraid. No one had the courage to speak up on behalf of the beleaguered director for fear of having the chair's wrath descend on him or her.

Mercifully, it was time to break for lunch. It gave opportunity for the director to go to his room to "lick his wounds" and regain his composure for the rest of the meeting.

Where would you place this board chair on the continuum of values?

Where would you place the other directors who watched with embarrassment and silence?

How the Continuum Impacts the Six Core Processes

An organization has six core processes. Each one is affected by the organization's dominant value system. The core processes are:

1. communication
2. decision-making
3. conflict resolution
4. planning
5. delegating
6. accountability (measuring and monitoring)

We'll discuss the effect of each value system on each process, particularly the weaknesses. Then, in later chapters we will deal with each process in greater depth.

1. Values and Communication

Laissez-faire Values	Relationship-oriented Values	Authoritarian Values
Sporadic & Unclear Information	*Accurate & Timely Information*	*Controlled Information*

Communication is perhaps the key core process, since it is an inseparable part of every other process. We define communication as the sharing of thoughts and feelings (information and values) by written, spoken, and non-verbal means.

A manager's ability to communicate effectively is vitally important because that's how information is transferred, information being one resource that people must have for successful and fulfilling work. (The others are human resources, financial resources and time.)

Communication expresses the underlying values that a manager holds towards those who look to him/her for authority. Those values will determine whether his/her staff members receive the information they need when they need it. How those values are expressed is decisive in whether the staff is successful, fulfilled, both or neither.

Laissez-faire Values

Communication driven by this value system will usually be inadequate as it tends to abrogate the authority to provide staff with information. It's not because the manager is controlling or manipulative, but rather that s/he has a tendency to shy away from the impression of being in control. The manager mistakes "distance" from staff, as staff empowerment. The critical importance of information is misunderstood, leaving staff members to obtain what information they can on their own. The result is an organization where staff feels neither empowered nor valued.

Authoritarian Values

When communication is driven by a value system where the manager espouses power, control, manipulation and/or abuse, the resulting communication process is often one in which:

- information is deliberately withheld
- staff members have to keep coming back for permission before feeling confident enough to act.

In this system the source of authority has, or takes, more power than needed to handle his/her responsibilities. This deliberate metering out of information inevitably reduces an organization's success as well as the fulfillment of its staff.

Relationship-oriented Values

When affirmation, involvement and servant leadership are the values that drive the communication process, the manager's information is generous, accurate, and matched to staff requirements. They are affirmed in their need to know, involved in determining what information is communicated, and supported in putting that information to work.

Observation

"Live and let live" and "might is right" value systems are equally dysfunctional. Incompetence or abusive power in the communication process have the same effect—the loss of productive and satisfying work.

To manage effectively, managers must recognize the characteristics of *laissez-faire* or authoritarian value systems, in their own communications. Is the information incomplete, sparse, inaccurate, controlled, manipulated or false? In healthy working relationships managers are accountable to staff for providing key information. In turn, recipients can support managers by holding them accountable for a communication process that is committed to success and personal fulfillment.

Being aware of one's own value system, including a commitment to affirming, involving and providing servant leadership, helps ensure that the communication process does lead to effective change management. In turn, this paves the way for organizational growth and deep, personal fulfillment for staff.

2. Values and Decision-making

Laissez-faire Values	Relationship-oriented Values	Authoritarian Values
▼	🤝	▼
Unclear Parameters	*Freedom Within*	*Permission*
Uncertainty	*Clear Limits*	*Mentality*

Successful decision-making requires a balance between authority and responsibility. When that balance is in place, an organization's staff and the clients they serve will be equally fulfilled. The quality of the process by which decisions are made, however, is determined more by the underlying values than by any other factor.

Laissez-faire Values

This value system has a negative impact on relationships and the decision-making process. The absence of clear direction is a prime indicator that *laissez-faire* values are predominant. Left alone or even abandoned, decision makers are disempowered because they don't know either the extent of their authority or their responsibilities. The result can be a decision-making process where:

- decisions fail to meet the organization's overall needs
- the process is stalled
- the process is stopped, and no decision made.

Authoritarian Values

◄

To manage effectively, managers must recognize the characteristics of laissez-faire or authoritarian value systems in their own communications.

The dominance of this value system can also be harmful to relationships and the quality of decisions. The most obvious indication is the failure to involve those directly affected by the decision. When someone in authority makes an arbitrary decision without including the talents, experience and wisdom of those affected, here's what can happen:

- The decision is rarely the best it can be.
- Expectations are unrealistic.
- The resources—people, finances, information or time —are insufficient.
- Good people become resentful.

Unfortunately, the "might is right" mentality of authoritarian management fails to see the need for involvement. Damage to relationships, reduced fulfillment and drops in productivity are the inevitable result.

Relationship-oriented Values

When affirmation, involvement and servant leadership form the basis of the process, decision-making operates from a healthy set of values. In particular, those affected by a decision know whether:

- the decision is being delegated to them to make
- their source of authority wants input so as to make the best possible decision.

In either case, the involvement of those affected is significant to the process, affirming their importance. People quickly sense the support of the servant leader who is the source of authority. Instead of "lording it over" or abandoning them, the servant leader ensures that decision makers have both the authority and the resources to make quality decisions.

3. Values and Conflict Resolution

Laissez-faire Values	Relationship-oriented Values	Authoritarian Values
Avoidance & Denial	*Forgiveness, Justice, Amends, Reconciliation*	*Unilateral Judgement*

Along with communication and decision-making, conflict resolution is often a component of all other organizational processes.

Conflict is part of life. Where difficulties arise, it's usually because any efforts to resolve conflict are sabotaged by the existing value system.

Laissez-faire Values

Many of us have a strong desire to get along and have all our interactions be peaceful. The hallmark of this system is discomfort with conflict. To some, it's indicative of sin in our lives. Thus, if conflict raises its head, we react by:

- trying to avoid it
- downplaying its importance
- denying it, even when it's obvious to a third party.

With *laissez-faire* values controlling our behaviour, we won't experience the healthy interaction and debate that conflict generates. More importantly, we will miss out on the opportunity to synthesize any benefits.

When conflict is destructive, our unwillingness to deal directly with it allows conflict to fester, smoldering like an underground fire that never goes out.

In another vein, our tendency to apply forgiveness to deal with conflict is yet another indicator that we consider conflict to be wrong. Using forgiveness in this way, without directly confronting and dealing with those responsible, remains a sign of *laissez-faire* values, and is, therefore, untenable.

Authoritarian Values

The authoritarian has little patience with those who disagree with his or her point of view. "It's my way or the highway," or so the story goes. "I have the

authority in this relationship, and that's the end of it."
With authoritarian values dominant, no healthy
challenge of ideas can take place, or even be heard. Such
ideas challenge the source of power, depriving the organization of any potential benefits.

In its extreme form, people suffer for even suggesting
alternate views. In the political arena the GULAGS are
evidence of this sad reality. In our arena good people who
attempt to add value to organizations to whose mission
they are committed, not only risk abuse, but possibly the
loss of employment.

Relationship-oriented Values

◄

*A senior
manager of one
of my client
organizations
has the slogan
"Embrace
conflict!" in her
office, inviting
her staff to
challenge
assumptions,
ideas and
decisions.*

This value system is comfortable with conflict and
encourages healthy debate. It recognizes that good ideas
become purified when tried by fire. If unhealthy
behaviour creates havoc within an organization, the
relationship system will not hesitate to confront any
person or group responsible. It does so, however, in a
manner that seeks to maintain healthy relationships, and
restore them where fractured.

When processed with affirmation, involvement and
servant leadership it will benefit any organization. A
senior manager of one of my client organizations has the
slogan "Embrace conflict!" in her office, inviting her staff
to challenge assumptions, ideas and decisions.

Specifically, *affirmation* takes the form of forgiveness if
the relationship is negative. *Involvement* invites the
exchange of ideas and listens to expressions of dissent.
Servant leadership seeks to support individuals even
during conflict. A relationship-oriented organization,
therefore, enjoys the fruits that healthy dissent can
produce while dealing directly and fairly with any conflict
that threatens its welfare.

Observation

The conflict resolution process is often a part of the accountability process. We will be dealing more fully with both conflict and accountability in Chapters 5 and 6.

4. Values and Planning

Laissez-faire Values	Relationship-oriented Values	Authoritarian Values
▼	🤝	▼
Vague Direction	*Freedom Empowerment*	*Unilateral Orders*

Planning is the fourth core process of an organization. Both strategic planning (what the organization does) and tactical planning (how the organization does it) are vital to the success of the organization's mission.

Laissez-faire Values

On the "live and let live" end of the continuum, planning tends to get dropped out as we let our organizations choose, by default, the path of least resistance. In strategic planning this results in bumping into the future and tripping over our mission and its priorities. Sometimes this is described as "following the Lord's leading" or "surrendering to God's will." Actually, it is more an abrogation of the authority and responsibility that God gives us, i.e., choosing how best to use our personal and collective gifts.

Authoritarian Values

At the other extreme, there is a one-sided planning process, often led by an individual founder, CEO, board chair or an "executive committee." This can occur only when the organization's members or board share a *laissez-faire* system. By default, they allow planning to be driven by whoever wants to take the organization in a certain direction. This process reflects the desires of a few. There is no listening to the needs of stakeholders or the insights of staff. As such, it is an unaffirming, non-involving and non-supportive approach to planning.

It's not uncommon for members and employees, even whole boards, to believe that the strategic direction should be determined by the "leader,"

◄

*Both strategic
planning (what
the organization
does) and
tactical planning
(how the organi-
zation does it)
are vital to the
success of the
organization's
mission.*

usually referred to as "following the leader's vision." Apparently the leader has a more valuable vision than the collected wisdom of all stakeholders combined! Which just shows that even a mildly authoritarian leader can be tempted to fill a planning vacuum left by the majority.

Relationship-oriented Values

This is the value system open to change. It encourages all stakeholders to propose, debate, create and manage any change necessary to adapt to a changing world. In so doing, it affirms, involves and supports change agents, enabling the best possible solutions to come to the forefront of the planning process.

5. Values and Delegating

Laissez-faire Values	Relationship-oriented Values	Authoritarian Values
Unclear Expectations	*Attainable Expectations*	*Unrealistic Expectations*

Delegating authority and responsibility is the fifth core process of an organization. Within this process we see different but equally unsatisfactory experiences at either end of the continuum.

Laissez-faire Values

The manager fails to provide clear boundaries when delegating authority to others. To compound the situation, expectations are not made clear either. This leaves recipients confused as to their responsibilities. Such managers prefer to avoid conflict or accountability because they don't want to either be demanding, or to hurt people's feelings.

In its extreme form, authority is abdicated completely. The manager seldom sees the recipient and interaction is minimal. This can leave recipients:

- feeling disempowered – *"What authority do I have?"*
- ineffective and inefficient – *"I'm not clear what my responsibilities are."*
- abusing their power – *"No one's watching me, and they don't care anyway. I'll do what I want."*

Authoritarian Values

Recipients are not given clear limitations to their authority. They, therefore, experience a "permission mentality," constantly checking with those in charge to make sure that they have authority to act.

When it comes to responsibility, since they've not been involved in negotiating expectations, they're scared that more work is expected of them than they can handle. And since the source of power has a strong need to retain power, these recipients can also count on being disempowered.

In its extreme form, the lust for power results in complete disempowerment, i.e., enforcing impossible expectations that were never negotiated or likely discussed.

Relationship-oriented Values

The delegation of authority is experienced as freedom and empowerment when founded on affirmation, involvement and servant leadership. Full responsibility is experienced as the ownership of clear goals.

6. Values and Accountability

Laissez-faire Values	Relationship-oriented Values	Authoritarian Values
Frustration & Uncertain Performance	*Client & Staff Fulfillment*	*Disappointment & Defeat*

Accountability is the monitoring of performance and the measurement of results. For a number of reasons, *lack of accountability* is the most difficult problem faced by Christian organizations—an odd paradox given that, in fact, accountability ought to be the gift we give one another.

The problem lies partly in the word itself. A common word, accountability frequently appears in front page headlines, but almost always in a negative context. Someone's done something wrong, or they haven't kept their word. Whatever it is, the consequences mean some kind of punishment.

As Christians, we're taught that if someone fails or does something wrong, we forgive them. Accountability, therefore, is something that forgiving people have difficulty in coming to terms with, or find unacceptable. It certainly isn't considered a gift.

Laissez-faire Values

In working with many organizations over the years, I've found that *laissez-faire* is the most common value system when it comes to lack of accountability. Many people simply don't understand what accountability means especially in Christian-run organizations. To emphasize the point in the previous two paragraphs, they associate accountability with words like punishment, discipline, or being fired. So they replace it with forgiveness and thus avoid holding people accountable for the commitments they make and the results they produce.

Authoritarian Values

◄

Lack of accountability is the most difficult problem faced by Christian organizations.

We all know of situations where accountability was punishing and unfair. It's what can happen when the source of authority assumes a position of unilateral power. A "boss" may bully, blame, discredit, humiliate, embarrass and emotionally abuse a person whose productivity doesn't meet expectations. You can bet that the expectations were never negotiated. The person in charge probably "presented some goals" without being sensitive to either the available resources or the recipient's ability to carry them out.

Relationship-oriented Values

Success and personal fulfillment are the results when affirmation, involvement and servant leadership are the foundation for an understood, agreed upon and fairly applied process of accountability.

Laissez-faire Values at Work

Richard was the founder of a successful Canadian charity. Charismatic beyond what you experienced anywhere else you worked, he was a visionary, a good listener, an effective fundraiser, dependable, honest. Did he lack anything? Did he have any flaws at all? Well, yes, in your view he did. He had a wonderful sense of humour, a dry wit that often surprised you into instant laughter. Unfortunately, he had a bad habit of teasing people with humour that was insensitive, that made people feel devalued and embarrassed. No one ever said anything, of course. He was successful, and he was the CEO. Years went by without his ever knowing that he hurt people's feelings with humour. How could he know? People always laughed.

Dennis was a square peg in a round hole. It was a real shame that he lasted in the job so long. Unsuccessful and unproductive, he was also unfulfilled. Sylvia was his immediate supervisor. She always tried to help. She was a kind, forgiving person. Very supportive, the kind of source of authority anyone would love to have. She thought that people should be left alone to do their job. She thought of performance reviews as untrusting. Besides, she found it difficult to talk to Dennis about his lack of competencies for the job he held. His failure and unhappiness went on and on.

Observation

Accountability is a neutral process of monitoring and measurement. Unfortunately, many of us don't see it that way. We misunderstand its role, are uncomfortable with it and therefore avoid it. And even when we're affirming, involving and supportive of our staff in most matters, we often slip into *laissez-faire* values when dealing with accountability.

Authoritarian Values at Work

John worked for a CEO who was simply abusive of power. The CEO was very personable but never transparent. He always seemed to have another surprise to take John off guard. When John didn't support his direction, he was criticized for being disloyal and for not trusting as he should in a Christian organization. People would leave the organization demoralized. Even board members would give up when they realized they weren't going to be able to change the pattern and certainly couldn't live with the damage it was causing. Morale was terrible, but no one seemed to be willing or able to do anything about the situation.

The Seven Deadly Sins of Organizations

We have taken you through the continuum of values and shown how those values affect the core processes of our organizations. Some problems tend to have a greater impact than others in causing organizational breakdown. I call them **The Seven Deadly Sins.**

The good news is that they are not always deadly. They are often subtle and chronic rather than obvious and fatal. All organizations live with them to some degree. The degree varies with the values of those who influence the organization. One thing is certain: dysfunctional values tend to be passed on from one "generation" to the next.

▶

Six of the seven deadly sins are on the laissez-faire side of the continuum.

The bad news is that there are more than seven, because the mistakes and weaknesses of organizations can take many forms. These seven, however, seem to me to be the most common.

What seems surprising is the common pattern into which most of these Deadly Sins fall. Look at the bar charts. Six of the seven deadly sins are on the *laissez-faire* side of the continuum. This indicates, and it's our experience, that the most common problems in Christian or Christian-run organizations stem from a *laissez-faire* value system.

The seven Deadly Sins and the core processes in which they appear are:

Values Determine Working Relationships

Laissez-Faire Values	Relationship-oriented Values	Authoritarian Values
▼ ❶	🤝	▼ ❷

Planning

Vague Direction	*Freedom & Empowerment*	*Unilateral Orders*
❸		

Delegating

Unclear Roles & Expectations	*Attainable Expectations*	*Unrealistic Expectations*
❹ ❺ ❻		

Accountability

Uncertain Performance	*Client & Staff Satisfaction*	*Judgement & Failure*
❼		

Deadly Sin #1
Weak Governance, Leadership and Management

Symptoms:

- How authority flows is not defined or clearly understood.
- Decisions are not documented clearly.
- Little or no monitoring of performance or measuring of results happens.

Result:

- Staff and volunteers are frustrated at lack of clarity.
- Quality and effectiveness of service delivery suffer.
- Personal fulfillment of staff and volunteers is lacking.
- Good people leave and aren't missed.

Deadly Sin #2
Abusive Leadership and Management

Symptoms:

- Overconfidence.
- Meddling in the work of others.
- Staff/volunteer discouragement.
- Broken relationships.
- Manipulation.
- Personal agendas are forced on the entire group.

Result:

- Individual rights are violated.
- People are abused, discouraged, unfulfilled.
- Good people leave.
- Effective ministry suffers.
- Without accountability abuse increases and becomes chronic.
- Culture is damaged.

Deadly Sin #3
Vague Strategic Direction

Symptoms:

- The organization has no statements of Values, Vision or Mission or they exist but are outdated, unknown and/or without ownership.
- Future is based on "faith" instead of careful planning.

Result:

- Strategic direction is assumed by the CEO instead of being led by the board.
- Confusion and/or disagreement of purpose and priorities lead to unfocused ministry and ineffective and inefficient use of resources.

Deadly Sin #4
Unclear Roles and Responsibilities

Symptoms:

- Who has authority, and for what, is unclear.
- Few or no current job descriptions exist.
- There is a reliance on precedent and tradition.
- Assumptions differ.

Result:

- There is a significant duplication of effort.
- Some responsibilities are not covered.
- Confusion leads to disagreement and strained or broken relationships.
- Volunteers are frustrated and unfulfilled.

Deadly Sin #5
Unclear Expectations

Symptoms:

- Goals are not established for strategic outcomes or tactical outputs.
- Goals are established by the source of authority but not negotiated with staff in proportion to available resources.
- Expectations are assumed but not expressed.

Result:

- Differing assumptions are made.
- Staff and volunteers have no way of knowing when they have succeeded.
- Differing expectations lead to misunderstandings, a sense of failure and breakdown of relationships.

Deadly Sin #6
Square Pegs, Round Holes

Symptoms:

- First available warm body willing to accept staff or volunteer position is accepted.
- Inadequate training or orientation are provided.
- Skills are not matched with needs of the positions.

Result:

- Service quality is limited by lack of ability of the staff/volunteer assigned.
- Work is unfinished.
- Staff and volunteers are unfulfilled and demoralized, wanting to make a positive contribution but without "the right stuff."

Deadly Sin #7
Forgiveness Confused with Accountability

Symptoms:

- Accountability mechanisms are poorly defined, not used or don't exist.
- Poor performance or behaviour is tolerated, treated with understanding and forgiveness.
- Annual performance reviews are rare or non-existent—especially at the board level.

Result:

- Successful staff and volunteers are not affirmed.
- Weak staff and volunteers are not supported or redirected.
- When forgiveness fails to produce change in unacceptable performance and behaviour, judgement and unfair dismissal may follow with accountability and redirection never happening.

Fortunately, many organizations work from the values of affirmation, involvement and servant leadership. People who work in these organizations are generally enriched and productive. It's only when productivity and fulfillment break down that a tendency towards sloppy governance, leadership and management is seen more often.

Less frequent, but still disturbing, is abusive power (see Deadly Sin #2) in the workplace. Ironically, the main reason abusive behaviour continues is the *laissez-faire* value system. Many people don't know how to deal with the abusive power. Or, they have a tendency to "forgive" any behaviour-causing stress.

Summary

The values that guide governance, leadership and management will determine the degree to which work is successful and productive, enriching and fulfilling. No single factor will have a greater effect on the core processes than these values.

A continuum of value systems determines our behaviors. With *laissez-faire* values we witness a "live and let live" culture and sometimes even an abrogation of power and authority. People are disempowered by default and neglect.

With *authoritarian* values we witness a "my way or the highway" tendency. Too much power is retained by the source of authority. People are again disempowered—this time by intent, not neglect.

The *relationship-oriented* value system produces healthy relationships within organizations. Its values of affirmation, involvement and servant leadership enable the source of authority to balance authority and responsibility. The result is effective and efficient work and workers who find enrichment and fulfillment in their success.

No healthy relationship is found without the values of affirmation, involvement and servant leadership. They are explored more fully in Chapters 3 and 4.

Relationships – the Original Design

"I will show you what he is like who comes to me and hears my words and puts them into practice. He is like a man building a house, who dug down deep and laid the foundation on rock. When a flood came, the torrent struck that house but could not shake it, because it was well built."
(Luke 6:4 – 48)

Introduction

To build an organization we need to start with a solid foundation. God's design of healthy relationships is that foundation, giving us a practical, empowering base for the Relationship Model™ and a healthy organization.

The purpose of this chapter is to identify those values and components common to what we understand to be God's design for healthy relationships between God and people and between the people themselves. Notice that we say "what we understand to be" God's design. There has been a tendency over the centuries to search for evidence in the Bible to support whatever we want to believe. The objective is to give divine stature to a purely human concept. Even theologians are not immune to manipulation.

It is important for you to test the validity of this chapter by measuring its contents against your own beliefs, theological framework and research. If you have chosen to read this book in spite of its biblical orientation rather then because of it, you will be able to put the Relationship Model™ to an important test—that of common sense. You can satisfy yourself that this material is worth your time and effort, enabling you to build working relationships that produce value and enrich lives.

What we have seen is a consistent pattern in successful relationships from the Hebrew, Greek and Roman cultures, as well as in other biblical cultures. In the Old Testament we will focus primarily on the relationship between God and Adam and Eve as well as God and Joshua. The New Testament presents the rich relationship between the Father and the Son and that between Jesus and his disciples. These relationships are filled with teachings that apply to the design of healthy relationships today.

Not surprisingly, we can learn just as much from biblical examples of unhealthy relationships where mistakes, problems, abuses, and brokenness abound. How these issues were addressed teaches us a lot on how to diagnose and cure our own unhealthy relationships.

Wouldn't it be great if we could check a biblical index and get our answer under "Relationships, Theology of"? It isn't that easy. Beginning in Genesis and throughout the Old Testament, the truths and mysteries of God are told in story form. Jesus continues the tradition in the New Testament by teaching through stories and parables.

Our western minds have a deep need to synthesize the truths that we glean from stories. We do this in order to create a model, an analytical and theoretical blueprint, which will allow us to build our own definition of healthy relationships. We work with the Relationship Model™ in a similar way so as to reduce a very large body of material from several cultures, written over many centuries, to a few simple and clear guidelines.

Almost everything written about the Word and work of God is about relationships. However, you're unlikely to find books and articles about a theology of relationships. For us to uncover the principles that might form such a theology, we must work our way through the Bible to uncover threads common to the design of all relationships.

By putting the principles in God's design of these relationships at the heart of our model, we will be able to build relationship-centred organizations. We can then apply these principles to our understanding of governance, leadership and management.

It's About Power

Genesis 1:1 contains a major claim of divine power:

"In the beginning God created the heavens and the earth."
(Genesis 1:1)

Most of what follows is about how God:

- handles God's own authority
- delegates that authority
- wants us to use authority.

In the New Testament, the Son of God makes another very significant claim:

"All authority in heaven and earth has been given to me."
(Matthew 28:18)

◄

Almost everything written about the Word and work of God is about relationships.

Authority (power in its neutral sense is simply a synonym) is one of the most important and common subjects of the Bible. No relationship is mentioned without some indication of how authority flows in that relationship. At the very least, we will always know the direction of flow, i.e., who has more power in the relationship. Perhaps the parties about whom we are reading don't agree, but we can usually tell whether one has more power than the other, or whether they are peers.

Where the Values Fit

It may seem odd that we begin this chapter with a focus on God's authority. Why not God's love? God is love, and the entire purpose of the Bible is to assure us of God's love—in all the circumstances of life and for all time and eternity.

The values that God displays are essential to understanding God's design for healthy relationships. We will now put those values into a context that forms the structure of the relationship:

- God gives each of us human beings some of God's authority, but that authority is always limited in very specific ways.

- God gives each of us responsibility, and that responsibility is always accompanied by expectations.
- Every one of us is accountable to God for our performance and behaviour.

What gives our relationships such effectiveness and enrichment is the set of values that we enjoy as God's creatures. It is in understanding these values, well documented throughout the Scriptures that God's design takes on its meaning. These values, as we discussed in the last chapter, are:

- God's affirmation
- God's involvement of us
- God's servant leadership.

These values are foundational in that they encompass all other values within them. In Chapter 2, we defined those values. In this chapter, we show by example from the Bible how God demonstrates and solidifies these values.

God Affirms Us

Affirmation is the first and most awesome of God's values. God is love. There is no clearer or more repeated message in the Bible. Affirmation is the value that caused God to:

- create the world
- promise the Messiah
- keep that promise in Jesus
- take us back to God for all eternity.

Affirmation is first expressed in Genesis Chapter 1 when God announces the decision to create man and woman:

"Then God said, 'Let us make man in our image, in our likeness, and let them rule over the fish of the sea and the birds of the air, over the livestock, over all the earth, and over all the creatures that move along the ground.'" (Genesis 1:26)

It's difficult to think of a more awesome example of love than to be created in the image of God.

Throughout God's relationship with Israel, God repeats the promise of love and faithfulness, continually renewing the people's hope for a land of their own. Through Jeremiah, the Lord declares:

"When seventy years are completed for Babylon, I will come to you and fulfill my gracious promise to bring you back to this place. For I know the plans I have for you…plans to prosper you and not to harm you, plans to give you hope and a future." (Jeremiah 29:10)

Another powerful reference to the eternal plan of God's affirmation is found in Paul's letter to the Christians in Ephesus:

"Praise be to the God and Father of our Lord Jesus Christ, who has blessed us in the heavenly realms with every spiritual blessing in Christ. For he chose us in him before the creation of the world to be holy and blameless in his sight. In love he predestined us to be adopted as his sons through Jesus Christ, in accordance with his pleasure and will—to the praise of his glorious grace, which he has freely given us in the One he loves." (Ephesians 1:3 – 6)

It seems that the people of God have always had difficulty holding on to God's promises. As a result, God has found it necessary to reassure us time and again. The Scriptures constantly remind us of God's unilateral decision to bring us into a relationship with God in Christ. First, from Isaiah:

"But you, O Israel, my servant, Jacob, whom I have chosen, you descendants of Abraham my friend, I took you from the ends of the earth, from its farthest corners I called you. I said, 'You are my servant; I have chosen you and have not rejected you.' So do not fear, for I am with you; do not be dismayed, for I am your God. I will strengthen you and help you; I will uphold you with my righteous right hand."
(Isaiah 41:8 – 10)

◀

It's difficult to think of a more awesome example of love than to be created in the image of God.

Second, the words of Jesus from St. John's Gospel:

"I no longer call you servants, because a servant does not know his master's business. Instead, I have called you friends, for everything that I learned from my Father I have made known to you. You did not choose me, but I chose you and appointed you to go and bear fruit—fruit that will last. Then the Father will give you whatever you ask in my name." (John 15:15 – 16)

Perhaps our difficulty is that we tend to create God in our image and forget that God has created us in God's image. Our image is one of brokenness and finality. We have all experienced giving up on people after a certain point in a broken relationship. We then assume that God, too, has His limits, beyond which God will give up on us and let us slip from God's grasp. How eloquent and affirming, therefore, is this passage from Isaiah:

"Can a mother forget the baby at her breast and have no compassion on the child she has borne? Though she may forget, I will not forget you. See, I have engraved you on the palms of my hands." (Isaiah 49:15 – 16)

In the New Testament, Paul repeats the certainty of God's love in Christ when he asks the Romans:

"Who shall separate us from the love of Christ? Shall trouble or hardship or persecution or famine or nakedness or danger or sword? No, in all these things we are more than conquerors through him who loved us. For I am convinced that neither death nor life, neither angels nor demons, neither the present nor the future, nor any powers, neither height nor depth, nor anything else in all creation, will be able to separate us from the love of God that is in Christ Jesus our Lord." (Romans 8:35 – 36, 38 – 39)

Praise God for our eternal security. That conviction of being in the family of God forever gives us the freedom to concentrate on giving thanks to God with the rest of our lives, as individuals and as organizations:

"For Christ's love compels us, because we are convinced that one died for all, and therefore all died. And he died for all, that those who live should no longer live for themselves but for him who died for them and was raised again." (2 Corinthians 5:14 – 15)

God Involves Us

God's decision to involve the people whom God created and who are affected by God's decisions is a hallmark of God's relationship with us…it was part of God's plan from the very beginning:

"The Lord God took the man and put him in the Garden of Eden to work it and take care of it." (Genesis 2:15)

T.R. McNeil writes in Holman's Bible Dictionary:

"God's people work because they are made in His image. The Bible opens with a picture of a working God. God worked in creating a universe. He has been at the job of sustaining creation since He fashioned it.

To be created in God's image means, in part, that people have the capacity to work, to fashion, to create. The notion that labour came into being as a result of

humanity's fall does not reflect biblical truth. Sinless humanity was placed in the garden to cultivate it."
(Holman's Bible Dictionary)

◀

That conviction of being in the family of God forever gives us the freedom to concentrate on giving thanks to God with the rest of our lives.

The whole of the Scriptures is the story of how God involved His people in God's work. Throughout the history covered by the Old Testament, God called political, military and spiritual leaders. God called judges and prophets, priests and kings. In the New Testament period God involved Mary in bringing the Son of God into the world. He commissioned the apostles and sent out the 70. He involved Paul in bringing the Gospel to the Gentiles.

In fact, God has been involving common people from the beginning of time, encouraging us to take the Gospel to the ends of the earth in our words and actions.

Surely the most powerful example is God's decision to involve us in creation itself in which people, animals and even plants are empowered to reproduce themselves. When we consider how easy it would be for God to continue to create perfect Adams and Eves, it seems ironic that God would entrust procreation to us. After all, we know there are thousands of genetic errors that can be passed on to future generations in humans alone.

▶

It seems ironic that God would entrust procreation to us. After all, we know there are thousands of genetic errors that can be passed on to future generations in humans alone.

Why would God even think to involve us in creation when God knew that the fall would result in an imperfect procreation process? Was it simply poor planning or bad judgment? Is it another one of those paradoxes that goes beyond our ability to understand?

This decision to involve us delivers an obvious and very powerful result. Involvement produces ownership. We have a sense of ownership that knows no bounds. Consider the relationships between Abraham and Isaac, between Hannah and Samuel, between David and Solomon, between Mary and Jesus, and between the prodigal son and his father. Every one of these relationships speaks volumes about the intense bond that develops between parents and children. What a contrast there is between the sense of ownership of a child we created and the sense of ownership of something we purchased.

God's involvement extends also to our planning and decision-making. Involving Adam and Eve in the work of tending the garden was part of God's plan, not a result of the fall.

God involves us in the planning and decision-making involved in fulfilling our basic human responsibilities—to love God and to love our neighbor. "Love your neighbor as yourself." God advises us that since we're aware of our own needs, we have the pattern we can use in meeting the needs of our neighbour.

Another compelling example of the value that God places on involvement is the Great Commission of Matthew 28. Undoubtedly, God could have done a better job of preaching the Gospel without our involvement. The message that Christians have preached on God's behalf has hardly been a model of clarity and effectiveness, despite the extraordinary advances in communication technology at our command. While God could speak to everyone in his or her own language simultaneously, the best we can do is have 25% of the world's population watch the world soccer finals live!

Yet, despite our track record, God gives us the freedom to choose our own role in the Great Commission. We are challenged by that involvement and are committed to sharing the message of God's love in Christ, constantly searching for new and creative ways to do so. Imagine what would happen if we were to bring the value and benefit of involvement to all our relationships.

God Leads with a Servant Heart

The use and abuse of power is a common theme in the Scriptures, as it is in today's organizations. In his teachings and example, Jesus reversed the role that power often has in relationships. In Matthew's Gospel, Jesus delivers a scathing denunciation of the Pharisees' abuse of power. However, Jesus does not leave it at that. Instead, he goes on to teach how power should be used in relationships.

"The greatest among you will be your servant. For whoever exalts him will be humbled, and whoever humbles himself will be exalted." (Matthew 23:11 – 12)

The Pharisees were not the only ones who abused power. Jesus called together the non-Jewish rulers of the day, pointedly telling them:

"You know that the rulers of the Gentiles lord it over them, and their high officials exercise authority over them. Not so with you. Instead, whoever wants to become great among you must be your servant, and whoever wants to be first must be your slave—just as the Son of Man did not come to be served, but to serve, and to give his life as a ransom for many." (Matthew 20:25 – 28)

The disciples were not immune to the temptations of power either. Imagining themselves with Jesus after he finally established his kingdom, they began to argue among themselves as to who would be the greatest. Immediately, Jesus put power in its proper perspective:

"Jesus knowing their thoughts, took a little child and had him stand beside him. Then he said to them, 'Whoever welcomes this little child in my name welcomes me; and whoever welcomes me welcomes the one who sent me. For he who is least among you all—he is the greatest.'"
(Luke 9:46 – 48)

◀

God gives us the freedom to choose our own role in the Great Commission

In all his teaching and especially by his example, Jesus supported his followers. When the sick were brought, Jesus healed them. When he arrived late and found Lazarus dead, he raised him to life again. When the crowds followed him without thinking of their need for food, he fed all 5,000 of them.

Jesus taught his disciples that servant leadership was a necessary part of what he was doing for them and should be a mark of their ministry. In John's Gospel, Jesus demonstrates this by washing the disciples' feet. He then informs the disciples of the significance of what he has done:

"You call me 'Teacher' and 'Lord,' and rightly so, for that is what I am. Now that I, your Lord and Teacher, have washed your feet, you also should wash one another's feet. I have set you an example that you should do as I have done for you. I tell you the truth, no servant is greater than his master, nor is a messenger greater than the one who sent him. Now that you know these things, you will be blessed if you do them." (John 13:12 – 17)

Motivation Through Affirmation, Involvement and Servant Leadership

All three of these core values become part of the spiritual power that God gives us when God delegates authority to us. We can witness the effect of affirmation, involvement and servant leadership in the joy, courage, commitment and determination of the men and women God chose as leaders throughout the record of biblical history. From this record we notice that in all relationships it is God's affirmation of God's people that provides the motivation to follow God's leading.

We may think of motivation as coming from within. We may also be critical of those who seem to lack it, as though motivation should indeed come from that place. Motivation, however, originates with God and flows through us to others by our living out these core values. Even the motivation we often feel from within is from God:

"Delight yourself in the Lord and he will give you the desires of your heart." *(Psalms 37:4)*

Adam was motivated by God's love for him. Created in God's image with God's own free will, he was empowered to be faithful in tending the garden. It was his free response to the bounties that God had given him.

All during his life, Joshua was motivated to serve the Lord thanks to the gifts God had given. With his death near, Joshua assembled the tribes of Israel at Shechem and recounted the acts of love that God had showed God's chosen people. Based on this love, Joshua motivated the people to follow his example:

"But as for me and my household, we will serve the Lord." *(Joshua 24:15)*

From the time the Great Commission was first given, Christians have also responded to the motivating power of the love of God. Peter and John were among the first Christians to share their source of motivation when the Jewish authorities ordered them to stop speaking in the name of Jesus. Peter and John replied:

"Judge for yourselves whether it is right in God's sight to obey you rather than God. For we cannot help speak about what we have seen and heard." *(Acts 4:18 – 20)*

Paul, too, shares with us what motivated him to preach the Good News in his second letter to the Christians in Corinth:

"If we are out of our mind, it is for the sake of God; if we are in our right mind, it is for you. For Christ's love compels us, because we are convinced that one died for all, and therefore all died." (2 Corinthians 5:13 – 14)

▶

Fear has no place in motivating people to fulfill their responsibilities

In a relationship-oriented organization, no other motivation other than the love of Christ is appropriate. Fear has no place in motivating people to fulfill their responsibilities:

"There is no fear in love. But perfect love drives out fear, because fear has to do with punishment. The one who fears is not made perfect in love. We love because he first loved us." (1 John 4:18 – 19)

Affirmation, involvement and servant leadership appear in healthy relationships throughout both testaments and in all the biblical cultures. In an organization of Christians we will want to follow God's example, acting on behalf of God who affirms, involves and supports us by repeating those values in our relationship with those who look to us for authority. It is this spiritual power that will enable us to be successful in our responsibilities.

Structures of Biblical Relationships

There are three major components in God's design of relationships. They are:

- authority (with limitations)
- responsibility (with expectations)
- accountability.

In the following pages we will explore the biblical bases of these components.

The Circle of Authority

The circle of authority that God gives us includes three elements:

- authorization
- resources
- competencies (gifts).

Authorization

God expresses His authorization in several ways. One of the ways is simply to claim God's authority by declaring who God is or what God has done. What better example of declaration than in God's response to Abraham's request for God's name:

"Moses said to God, 'Suppose I go to the Israelites and say to them, "The God of your fathers has sent me to you," and they ask me, "What is his name?" Then what shall I tell them?' God said to Moses, 'I AM WHO I AM. This is what you are to say to the Israelites: I AM has sent me to you.'" (Exodus 3:13 – 14)

More frequently God claims His authority on the basis of what God has done. Consider the first ten words of the Bible:

"In the beginning God created the heavens and the earth." (Genesis 1:1)

Another way in which God shows that God has the authority is by delegating his authority to another. God does this for Joshua:

"No one will be able to stand up against you all the days of your life. As I was with Moses, so I will be with you; I will never leave you nor forsake you." (Joshua 1:5)

The fact that authority is mentioned before responsibility in Joshua 1 should not go unnoticed. God affirms us by delegating to us God's own power and authority. Thus God equips us for the task before giving it to us. God wants us to begin with confidence instead of fear.

On the Mount of Transfiguration God used a unique way to delegate God's authority to the Son of Man:

"While he was still speaking, a bright cloud enveloped them, and a voice from the cloud said, 'This is my Son, whom I love; with him I am well pleased. Listen to him!'" (Matthew 17:5)

God empowers us when God assigns God's own authority to us in giving us the Great Commission:

"All authority in heaven and on earth has been given to me. Therefore..." (Matthew 28:18)

Resources

Authorization without resources can accomplish nothing. Therefore, resources must be provided in all relationships for authorization to be meaningful. The resources Christian organizations need for success include people, money, information and time. God shows us how this is to be done. In delegating authority to Adam, God tells him:

"I give you every seed-bearing plant on the face of the whole earth and every tree that has fruit with seed in it. They will be yours for food." (Genesis 1:29)

The resources that God gave to Joshua are described in Joshua 1:12 – 15. They consist of the help of the other tribes of Judah who will remain east of the Jordan.

Competencies

One of the most amazing realities about the six billion people who inhabit this planet is that no two people are alike. The closest we can come to being identical is in twins from a common fertilized ovum. Yet even in this example we see nuances of difference.

No one is exactly like you. Fingerprints and DNA set us apart from every other person. So do the combination of gifts that each of us possesses. Your set of gifts—abilities, interests, personality, potential to develop specialized skills—differentiates you. In this book we will refer to these gifts as competencies, a word that is explained in the next chapter. Here we simply want to affirm that the divine design includes giving you authorization, resources and special competencies that allow you to be a meaningful part of God's plan for humanity.

God gives to the Church all of the special gifts that are needed to carry out the Great Commission:

"It was He who gave some to be apostles, some to be prophets, some to be evangelists, and some to be pastors and teachers, to prepare God's people for works of service, so that the body of Christ may be built up..." (Ephesians 4:11)

Limitations to Authority

In all the relationships recorded in Scripture, every single one has limitations on the authority given. In the very first relationship God created, God gave Adam this command:

"You are free to eat from any tree in the garden; but you must not eat from the tree of the knowledge of good and evil, for when you eat of it you will surely die." *(Genesis 2:16)*

God limits Adam's authority and in so doing differentiates between God and human beings.

God also places a limitation upon Joshua's authority:

"Be strong and very courageous. Be careful to obey all the laws my servant Moses gave you; do not turn from it to the right or to the left, that you may be successful wherever you go. Do not let this Book of the Law depart from your mouth; meditate on it day and night, so that you may be careful to do everything written in it. Then you will be prosperous and successful." (Joshua 1:7 – 8)

Notice that this last line is an affirmation. The limitation is never intended to make Joshua's life miserable.

The Ten Commandments are probably the finest example of limitations to the authority that God gives to human beings. They go back to the time of Moses and are still relevant today.

In the Bible, one of the easiest ways of recognizing a limitation to authority is this—it is stated negatively. In Exodus 20, nine of the Ten Commandments are in the negative. It's quicker to give ten limitations than a thousand permissions.

Limitations to authority benefit us in two ways:

- They define the size of our circle of authority and thus our freedom to act.
- They balance our circle of authority with our circle of responsibility.

The Ten Commandments define our freedom to fulfill our purpose in life by setting clear limits.

Limitations: Our Circle of Responsibility and Freedom to Act

◀

It's quicker to give ten limitations than a thousand permissions.

It is very common for people to think of God as a micro-manager of all human life, that God has a plan for and controls every last detail. Certainly, all Christians want to echo Joshua's commitment "As for me and my house, we will serve the Lord." Thus, we often hear references to "surrendering to" and "obedience to" God's will. But how can we "know" that what we decide to do is in line with God's will? That thought troubles many people.

▶

God's will is not some tiny dot moving in the dark that we must hit blindfolded.

Remember this: we have an empowering God. God created us in God's own image. God wants each of us to enjoy what God Himself enjoys—perfect freedom and the absence of fear. God's will is not some tiny dot moving in the dark that we must hit blindfolded. In our organizations we have enormous freedom to decide what the values, vision, mission and priorities should be. We operate freely in the midst of a large circle defined by limits to our authority. This is the way God empowers people.

Limitations: Balancing Our Circle of Authority with Our Circle of Responsibility

Limitations to authority balance our circle of authority with our circle of responsibility. In any successful relationship these circles must be of equal size. The primary purpose of delegating authority (authorization, resources and competencies) is to achieve a result within the area of responsibility. The circle of authority must, therefore, be adequate to cover that circle of responsibility. To appreciate this, let's see what happens when they're out of balance.

The Circle of Authority Smaller Than the Circle of Responsibility

Several negative things may happen. The likelihood increases that the individual or group will not succeed in fulfilling their responsibilities. This is a situation Moses once found himself in when he came across two Hebrews fighting:

"He asked the one in the wrong, 'Why are you hitting your fellow Hebrew?' The man said, 'Who made you ruler and judge over us? Are you thinking of killing me as you killed the Egyptian?' Then Moses was afraid and thought, 'What I did must have become known.'" (Exodus 2:13 – 14)

Moses lost confidence. He thought he had lost the authority he needed to intervene in the conflict.

Having too little authority for the assigned responsibility is prevalent in many organizations. It is particularly common in tall hierarchical models where the source of authority is many levels distant from service delivery to the customer. Where this occurs we are likely to observe another result, poor morale.

People are designed to work and motivated to succeed. Not to have the authorization or resources to make success possible is frustrating and discouraging. This is what Elijah felt when the Lord found him taking refuge in a cave for the night:

"'What are you doing here, Elijah?' He replied, 'I have been very zealous for the Lord God Almighty. The Israelites have rejected your covenant, broken down your altars, and put your prophets to death with the sword. I am the only one left, and now they are trying to kill me too.'" (1 Kings 19:9 – 10)

Poor morale in an organization is an indication that people perceive themselves to be disempowered and that their circle of authority is smaller than their circle of responsibility.

Closely related to poor morale is fear of failure. It is natural to experience fear of failure if one is convinced that success in fulfilling one's responsibility is unlikely. Ultimately, if the authority is of inadequate size, then service delivery will not meet the expectations of customers who turn to us for the services we provide. The result? When the people in an organization do not have adequate authority, the whole organization fails in its responsibility.

Let's look now at the opposite imbalance.

The Circle of Authority Larger Than the Circle of Responsibility

The most common result of this imbalance is abuse of power. The Scriptures contain hundreds of examples. The saying "Absolute power corrupts absolutely," is seen all too frequently. Consider David's abuse of power when he took Bathsheba from Uriah. What David did was to write a letter to Joab and send it with Uriah. In it he wrote:

"'Put Uriah in the front line where the fighting is fiercest. Then withdraw from him so he will be struck down and die. So while Joab had the city under siege, he put Uriah at a place where he knew the strongest defenders were. When the men of the city came out and fought against Joab, some of the men in David's army fell; moreover, Uriah the Hittite died.'" (2 Samuel 11:14 – 17)

David exceeded the limits of his divine authority as king, taking more authority than he needed to succeed in his responsibility. Abuse of the extra power led directly to Uriah's death. Uriah, on the other hand, suddenly found himself in battle without the resources to succeed in his responsibility and failed immediately.

In the New Testament, the Pharisees continually took upon themselves more power than was rightfully theirs. Jesus criticized them for doing this. In this dynamic passage of teaching the crowds and the disciples, Jesus deals directly with the issue of creating a circle of authority that is larger than the circle of responsibility, thereby placing greater loads upon others than they have the resources to handle:

"The teachers of the law and the Pharisees sit in Moses' seat. So you must obey them and do everything they tell you. But do not do what they do, for they do not practice what they preach. They tie up heavy loads and put them on men's shoulders, but they themselves are not willing to lift a finger to move them…they love to be greeted in the marketplaces and to have men call them 'Rabbi.' But you are not to be called 'Rabbi,' for you have only one Master and you are all brothers. And do not call anyone on earth 'father,' for you have one Father, and he is in heaven. Nor are you to be called 'teacher,' for you have one Teacher, the Christ. The greatest among you will be your servant." (Matthew 23:1 – 11)

The Circle of Responsibility

The assignment of responsibility is both a gift of God and an act of affirmation by God. It is a profound privilege for us to be invited to participate in "tending the garden." From this loving decision comes our sense of calling. It is what prompted Joshua to respond to God's motivation by saying:

"But as for me and my household, we will serve the Lord." (Joshua 24:15)

Responsibilities in the relationships that God established are always clearly defined. Joshua was told:

"Be strong and courageous, because you will lead these people to inherit the land I swore to their forefathers to give them." (Joshua 1:6)

In Adam's case:

"The Lord God took the man and put him in the Garden of Eden to work it and take care of it." (Genesis 2:15)

In the Great Commission, the circle of responsibility is clearly defined for all of us:

"Therefore go and make disciples of all nations, baptizing them in the name of the Father and of the Son and of the Holy Spirit, and teaching them to obey everything I have commanded you." (Matthew 28:20)

In a relationship-oriented organization, it is important that we follow the biblical model of providing clear circles of responsibility to those to whom authority is being delegated:

- For the board of directors, responsibilities are stated in the bylaws.

- For individual board members and committees, responsibilities are set out in the governance manual.
- For each staff person, responsibilities should be documented in a clear relationship description.

As we shall see later, much confusion and conflict can arise out of unclear responsibilities.

Expectations of Responsibility

Expectations are to the circle of responsibility what limitations are to the circle of authority. Stated another way, expectations adjust and regulate the size of the circle of responsibility, just as limitations regulate the size of the circle of authority.

In the case of our relationship to God through the Laws of Moses and in Joshua's relationship to God, there is no question that authority is adequate for success. In the relationship between God and Joshua, God knows perfectly how to match authority with responsibility. For that reason, negotiation of expectations between God and people is rare. Yet there are strong references to God's sensitivity to that balance.

For example, Christ is portrayed as a shepherd caring for his sheep so that they are not put into a situation that would harm them:

"He tends his flock like a shepherd: He gathers the lambs in his arms and carries them close to his heart; he gently leads those that have young." (Isaiah 40:11)

Even in temptation the Lord is sensitive to our capabilities. He assures us that he will maintain a balance between the resources he provides and the loads we carry:

"No temptation has seized you except what is common to man. And God is faithful; he will not let you be tempted beyond what you can bear. But when you are tempted, he will also provide a way out so that you can stand up under it." (1 Corinthians 10:13)

Negotiating Expectations

Expectations should be matched with the abilities and resources each person possesses. In the following story, Jesus has an extraordinary knack of illustrating this concept:

"It will be like a man going on a journey, who called his servants and entrusted his property to them. To one he gave five talents of money, to another two talents, and to another one talent, each according to his ability. Then he went on his journey." (Matthew 25:14 – 15)

The departing master had expectations only in proportion to each servant's abilities and the number of talents he had been given. Accordingly, the amounts entrusted reflected the master's sensitivity to the differences in ability.

At the same time, the master had a range of expectations for each servant. The most he expected on his return was that the investment would double. At the very least, he assumed that the money would yield a return equal to the local bank interest. (The one who buried his talent and produced no result was told that he should have at least entrusted it to a banker and earned interest on the portion.)

Accountability

The examples of accountability are as numerous as the number of people and stories that make up the books of the Bible. Here are a few of those examples.

The first example is the accountability experienced by Adam and Eve. They were driven from the garden.

The next to experience accountability was Cain for killing his brother. He was cursed and told that he would spend his life a fugitive—and that the earth would never supply his needs.

Accountability has positive or negative consequences, depending on the results of being "weighed on the scales."

The Negative Side of Accountability

Daniel 5 and 6 contain the account of Belshazzar the king discovering the handwriting on the wall. Belshazzar was hosting a banquet when he looked up and saw a human hand write on the plaster. Pale with shock, he promised that anyone who could tell him what the words meant would be clothed in purple and have a gold chain placed around his neck. That would be their reward—a positive form of accountability.

The words were "Mene Mene Tekel Parsin." Daniel was able to read these words and explain their meaning to Belshazzar:

Mene: *God has numbered the days of your reign and brought it to an end.*
Tekel: *You have been weighed on the scales and found wanting.*
Peres: *Your kingdom is divided and given to the Medes and Persians. (Daniel 5:26 – 28)*

Daniel told Belshazzar that these words meant the king was being held accountable for worshipping gold and silver instead of the living God.

Daniel's success led to Belshazzar having him clothed in purple and gold and proclaimed the third highest ruler in the land. However, that very night Belshazzar was killed, called to account for failing to acknowledge God. Darius the Persian took over the kingship:

"It pleased Darius to appoint 120 satraps to rule throughout the kingdom with three administrators over them, one of whom was Daniel. The satraps were made accountable to them so that the king might not suffer loss."
(Daniel 6:1 – 2)

Many others throughout the biblical record were called to account. You'll recognize the following:

- God and Sodom and Gomorrah
- Moses and the Pharaoh
- God and the wandering Israelites
- Elijah and the prophets of Baal
- Nathan and David
- Jesus and the Pharisees
- Jesus and Simon Peter
- Peter and Ananias and Saphira

Judgment Day is the most obvious biblical example of being called to account. Traditionally, Judgment Day has inspired art throughout the ages of the terrors that are to come. Christ's death and resurrection have changed all that. Because of Christ, accountability is the final affirmation of God. It is the fulfillment of the plan God made before creating the world:

"For he chose us in him before the creation of the world to be holy and blameless in his sight...In him we have redemption through his blood, the forgiveness of sins.... And he made known to us the mystery of his will according to his good pleasure, which he purposed in Christ, to be put into effect when the times will have reached their fulfillment—to bring all things in heaven and on earth together under one head, even Christ." (Ephesians 1:4, 7, 9 – 10)

The Positive Side of Accountability

Christ did not shirk his responsibility but submitted to his Father's will. God also held him accountable in finding him faithful and raising him from the dead:

"Therefore God exalted him to the highest place and gave him the name that is above every name, that at the name of Jesus every knee should bow, in heaven and on earth and under the earth, and every tongue confess that Jesus Christ is Lord, to the glory of God the Father." (Philippians 2:6 – 11)

It is sad that the word "accountability" carries with it a connotation of fear and dread, of punishment and suffering. Accountability in the person and work of Christ is an eternal affirmation. Christ was given the responsibility of taking the sins of the world upon him, and he was given the authority (authorization, resources and competencies) to succeed. Now he sits at the right hand of the Father for all eternity. Should the relationship-oriented organization not pattern its accountability after the example of our heavenly Father for his Son?

The Role of Accountability in Conflict

Should we forgive and forget? No, forgive and reconcile.

Like almost every other Christian, you were probably taught to forgive and forget. In real life, however, this is easier said than done. Perhaps in a broken relationship you were able to manage the "forgive" part, but you haven't forgotten. The relationship is still broken.

Somehow your forgiveness set you free, but it didn't restore the brokenness. Why can't you forget? The truth is that Christians have adopted a process that isn't found in the Scriptures. You can't forget, because it really happened. And the idea that you should put it behind you refers to forgiveness, not to forgetting.

What the Lord actually teaches is "forgive and reconcile," and it's found in the well-known passage from Matthew 18.

◄

Perhaps in a broken relationship you were able to manage the "forgive" part, but you haven't forgotten.

"If your brother sins against you, go and show him his fault, just between the two of you. If he listens to you, you have won your brother over. But if he will not listen, take one or two others along, so that every matter may be established by the testimony of two or three witnesses. If he refuses to listen to them, tell it to the church." (Matthew 18:15)

The challenge of this familiar passage is to hold our brother or sister accountable with a forgiving heart. *Negotiation* is that first step, designed to reconcile, not to win.

If the private negotiation doesn't result in acknowledgement and reconciliation, the next step is *mediation*, but this time with two or three witnesses to assist you in your efforts. The final step is *arbitration*—standing together before a third party who will decide the matter between you.

►

The process of reconciliation requires a commitment to the person who caused the pain.

This is about as far from "forgive and forget" as you can get. And it's difficult. Leaving the relationship broken is easier and far more common. The process of reconciliation requires a commitment to the person who caused the pain.

Forgiveness was for *your* peace of mind. Holding the person accountable by negotiation, mediation and arbitration is for the *other person* and for reconciling the relationship.

The process of reconciliation requires tough love, and tough love is tough to find. Here's the pathway:

- Forgiveness leads to confrontation of the wrong.
- Confrontation leads to acknowledgment.
- Acknowledgment leads to making amends.
- Making amends produces justice.
- Forgiveness and justice produce reconciliation.

Why didn't God just forgive us? Why did God allow Jesus to be killed? Why didn't God say, "I made the rule that the soul that sins shall die. And I can change it!"

Why didn't God say, "I forgive you, but I'm sure not going to allow my Son to be killed over it." Because forgiveness alone would have helped only God, but justice satisfied by the death of Christ is what reconciled us to God. It's reconciliation that God was after, not just forgiveness.

God still doesn't forget. God confronts us with the Law, with the reality of our sin. God forgives us for what we cannot do. God also expects us to go forward with a faith that is translated into fulfilling God's expectations of us.

"Love God" and "love your neighbor" are God's two great expectations of us. Those expectations don't evaporate with God's forgiveness for our failing to do our job. "What shall we say then? Shall we sin that God's grace may abound?" Paul asks. "By no means" is his reply.

The primary lesson we can learn from the Bible is that forgiveness is a value and accountability is a process. They are not to be confused. Instead of replacing one with the other by pretending we can forgive and forget, we forgive and reconcile by including both of them in the process of resolving conflict.

Forgive and Reconcile

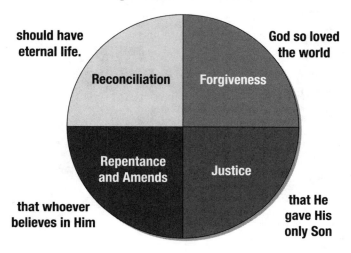

should have
eternal life.

God so loved
the world

Reconciliation   **Forgiveness**

**Repentance
and Amends**   **Justice**

that whoever
believes in Him

that He
gave His
only Son

Summary

In this chapter, we have observed that the Scriptures provide a wealth of teaching about relationships. We have seen that God's design of relationships is based on the core values of affirmation, involvement and servant leadership.

◄

The primary lesson we can learn from the Bible is that forgiveness is a value and accountability is a process.

The relationship itself has three major components:

- authority (with limitations)
- responsibility (with expectations)
- accountability.

We have also seen that the three core values have power to motivate us when the relationship is bathed in them.

In the next chapters, we will show how this design becomes the basis of a model of the relationship-oriented organization that can shape the way in which a board of directors and managers do their work.

An Organization
is Like a Tree

The Relationship Model Revealed

In the last chapter, we explored many of the relationships in the Old and New Testaments that were healthy if patterned after what we believe to be God's design. In this chapter we will begin to apply to our human organizations the principles behind that design. If we can achieve this in our organizations, we are likely to experience what God wants for all of us—productivity and personal fulfillment, in balance.

It begins, of course, with values. We have already seen that in terms of relationships, the most important and universal values are affirmation, involvement and servant leadership. Of these, servant leadership accords special significance to the tree as a symbol for healthy organizations.

The effect of servant leadership is being lifted up by our source of authority instead of being put down. We are empowered, given freedom to excel, and encouraged to take risks and learn from our mistakes. We speak of support instead of domination.

I was only 14 when I left home for boarding school. One of the first group activities I can remember was a wholesale cleaning of the dormitory we called home, starting with the basement. Believe me when I say that when you are only 14 and the lowest form of underclassman, you know you are going to get the dirtiest jobs.

I can remember clearly that room full of old chairs that had to be cleaned out to make room for a lounge for the residents of the dorm. What I remember most clearly, however, is not the chairs or the work of cleaning that day, but the presence of the president of the school in jeans helping us with that dirty work.

I didn't know anything about servant leadership at the time, but I did know what a powerful motivator it was to have Dr. Stuenkel working along side me. It gave an enormous sense of importance to the task and a sense that each of us doing the work was valued. He's in heaven now, but his spirit of servant leadership and the lesson I learned from him are still with me. "Prexy," as we called him, lifted more than chairs. He lifted each of us.

Think of Your Organization as a Tree

Somewhere long ago we adopted the "top-down" vocabulary of the world. We copied the Pharisees, instead of Jesus, in the way we think and speak of our organizations. Yet, wherever I introduce the tree as the symbol for how authority can and should flow within an organization, I find immediate understanding and acceptance. The "top-down" thinking to which we have become accustomed is not aligned with our true values.

By making a conscious effort to shift our paradigm from "top-down" thinking or lateral thinking to "roots-up" thinking, we will gain a far better understanding of the way in which God-designed relationships can work in our organizations.

Imagine then that an organization is like a tree. The greater the authority, the closer to the base you find it. The root structure that supports the tree is the membership along with seldom seen funders who supply the nutrients. Together they are the final source of authority and resources for the entire organization.

Imagine that a friend of yours described his experience of working in a Christian organization this way. This organization is *not* like a tree. Take a closer look at the language that we hear so frequently, even in Christian organizations.

"Ten years ago I was at the *bottom* of the organization, but I was determined to *climb the ladder* until I reached the *highest position* I could. I never expected that I would be the '*top dog*' in just ten years. Imagine that, me on the *top rung*. Now I have a dozen people working *directly under* me, and I have *control over* a budget of $20 million. Now I'm in a position to make changes from the *top down* to the *lowest employee*."

An organization is like a tree. Here's the same person stating his experience in a different way.

"Ten years ago I was at the leading edge of the organization, but I was determined to reach my full potential until I had the heaviest load I could possibly carry. I never expected that I would have this much responsibility in ten years. Imagine that. I feel like I'm part of the trunk of a tree. Now I have a dozen people looking directly to me for support, and together we share the responsibility of managing a budget of $20 million. Now I'm in a position to serve everyone in the entire organization from the base of the tree to the highest employee."

The *Laissez-Faire* Model
(Lateral Thinking)

The Authoritarian Model
(Top-down Thinking)

Above ground is a strong trunk that bears the weight of the tree, the board of directors. All nutrients pass upwards through this trunk to where the fruit grows. Connected to the trunk and looking like part of it, is the chief executive officer, the only person employed directly by the board.

At the cluster where the trunk branches out into the departments of the organization, we find the senior management team. Above them are the branches. In organizations they represent different branches or departments of the operation.

The leaves represent the staff. They reach the highest part of the tree and are supported and supplied by everything below them. Just as each leaf uses light to photosynthesize sugar from water and carbon dioxide to add value to the tree, so each staff member adds value to the organization through his/her own set of competencies.

▶

Making the shift from "top-down" thinking to servant leader-ship is never easy.

Making the shift from "top-down" thinking to servant leadership is never easy. Long after you've done it you'll hear "top-down" language still coming out of your mouth. It's important for others in the organization to transition to this supportive, "bottom-up" terminology. Even more important is that you "walk the talk" by ensuring that all your behaviours are consistent with servant leadership.

The Relationship Model™
(Roots-up Thinking)

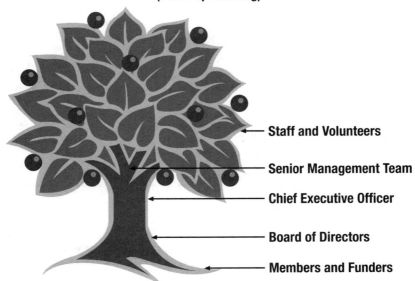

Staff and Volunteers

Senior Management Team

Chief Executive Officer

Board of Directors

Members and Funders

A Tree's Health

If a tree is healthy, it will bear healthy fruit. If a not-for-profit organization has healthy working relationships, it will deliver services of high quality. The opposite is also true.

Unhealthy Organizations

The tree is a living organism. If one part of the tree is diseased, it will affect other parts of the tree. If the values, structure or processes of the organization are flawed, neglected or abused, those flaws will eventually impact the quality of the organization's services. Just as tragic, the health (psychological, emotional and physical) of the individuals within the organization is at risk.

I have seen not-for-profit organizations where morale is very low, where organizations are deeply troubled or even completely dysfunctional. Amazingly, even in some of these, the fruit is still, by some miracle, of high quality. The staff members express a strong commitment to the mission of the organization even while suffering from poor governance, leadership or management. They continue to produce at their own expense, driven by personal values and beliefs, despite the pain they feel. Eventually, however, even these good people will burn out and leave.

The causes of unhealthy organizations are numerous, but they often stem from a common source—a board that is not holding itself and/or its chief executive officer accountable for what is happening within the organization.

I think of an organization that may not survive the abusive power it has suffered from within. In this case the board waited far too long before acting and now may be unwilling or unable to bring the dysfunction back from the brink.

An employee of an organization, made dysfunctional by a board failing to deal with its CEO's abusive behaviour, wrote recently to express just such a situation. "A board member called me looking for the addresses of staff that had left so that a card of thanks could be sent to each of them on behalf of the board of directors. I told this person, "'After all that had happened, it's just empty words on paper. The perpetrator is still at large. They're still protecting him and the deception to donors continues. It's too little, too late. And words on a card do not do justice to the wrongs that have been allowed to happen and continue to happen.'"

Too often, especially in abusive situations, productivity is given higher value than staff fulfillment, the health of relationships being regarded as a means to an end rather than a desirable objective. This condition is so prevalent —even in Christian organizations—that I am inclined to say, "Healthy relationships are more important than productivity." Of course, that goes too far the other way.

What produces a healthy tree? How do we balance the fulfillment of our staff with the fulfillment of our clients?

Healthy working relationships begin when the board, CEO and others in authority live out the core values of affirmation, involvement and servant leadership in their design of management structures and processes. In these organizations we find healthy people consistently producing healthy fruit.

Healthy Organizations

The structure of all working relationships in a healthy organization will include:

- *a statement of authority with clear parameters of the limits of that authority.* Ironically, the limitations of authority are the defining statements that describe the freedom that each person has.
- *a statement of responsibilities with expectations of those responsibilities that have been negotiated to balance with the available authorization and resources.*
- *the concept of mutual accountability between the source and recipients of authority.* The source of authority is accountable for maintaining the balance of authority and responsibility, a balance of resources and expectations. The recipient is responsible for delivering the expectations within the limits of resources. All are accountable for living the core values.

Processes

The core processes, which are basic to all other processes, and as we saw in Chapter 2, are:

- communication
- decision-making
- conflict resolution.

The next three core processes rest upon the first three:

- planning
- delegation of authority and responsibility
- accountability
  - monitoring performance
  - measuring results.

When these processes are driven by the same core values, people are affirmed, involved and supported as they find fulfillment in realizing the mission of the organization.

In this chapter our emphasis is on the structure. In it we will expand upon the points made in Chapter 2 and show in more detail the impact of the components that make up a healthy or unhealthy structure.

Structure and Values

If organizational values are the genetic code of the tree, giving it identity and determining what the tree will produce, structure is the shape that will carry the load and bear the fruit. There are many different relationships in organizations. Each one needs the structure that will enable it to fulfill its unique role. In this section, we want to examine that structure and understand what role each component fills.

There are many relationships in organizations. Each one, however, has the same design framework. As we saw in Chapter 3 there are three major components in a relationship:

- authority (with limitations)
- responsibility (with expectations)
- accountability.

Limitations (of authority) and expectations (of responsibility) are elements that enable us to design and maintain a dynamic balance in the relationship.

We think of these three components as circles. Limitations of authority and expectations of responsibility are lines that define the size of the respective circles.

Authority

Authority is the first main component of a relationship. It includes three elements within its circle:

1. authorization
2. resources
3. competencies (gifts)

The Circle of Authority

1. Authorization

In an organization, authorization is the formal or informal transfer of power from one level to another. Power, when used in a positive sense, is synonymous with authorization.

A job title is one way in which authorization is given to carry out a particular role in an organization. Although a job title gives some clarity, it is important to know who authorizes you to do what you do. Knowing the source of your authority provides a focal point to return to at any time, such as when resources or authorization are insufficient or responsibilities and expectations are excessive.

Authorization is like a vapour. The same day you leave a job, it's gone. Where once you had the keys to the building, you now have no access. Where you were expected to attend meetings, you are now a guest only by invitation. Where you once gave instructions and made requests, you now have no authority to delegate. The building and its people haven't changed. But overnight the authorization someone gave you, has gone. Vapourized. The working relationship is finished.

2. Resources

Authorization without resources cannot accomplish anything. Resources fall into four broad categories:

- financial
- human
- information
- time

All four are required in the right amounts.

Financial Resources

Financial resources take several forms:

- remuneration for doing the work, as in a salary and benefits package
- operating funds for equipment and supplies
- capital expenditures for buildings and major items of equipment
- endowment funds that bring long-term stability.

In all cases, the financial resources must be sufficient for the work to be done successfully.

Human Resources

These may be:

- people whom you hire to help you
- volunteers willing to assist without financial remuneration
- outside contractors and consultants.

Information Resources

Imagine the information that comes into the workplace through phones, fax machines, pagers, TV sets, the Internet, and other electronic devices. Think of the information exchanged or shared between individuals, in conferences, training sessions and meetings.

◀

Authorization is like a vapour. The same day you leave a job, it's gone.

We can't do our work without information. Cut any of it off—phone not working, power or network failures—and our productivity is jeopardized. It's worse if a co-worker, through insensitive oversight or a deliberate act, also cuts off our sources of information.

Time

Unlike the other resources, time is non-renewable and of extreme value. We never seem to have enough time to do all that we want or need to do. Time therefore requires careful management. We must:

- negotiate adequate time for the completion of a project
- prioritize time to use it efficiently and effectively.

Whatever the job, all these resources—financial, human, information and time—need to be appropriate and adequate. Only then can authorization be meaningful and the responsibilities of the job successfully accomplished.

3. Competencies

What an amazing design a tree is! The food that brings life and health for a tree to grow to maturity is taken from the earth through the roots. So, as water evaporates from the outer edges of the tree through the leaves, life-giving water and nutrients are drawn up from those roots. A transpiration stream is started. This "stream" ensures that food travels from cell to cell throughout the tree, no matter how high or wide the tree happens to be.

A tree isn't solely a "bottom-feeder" dependent on water and nutrients from below. Leaves are tree-manufacturing centres with every leaf playing its part in the tree's well being. As sunlight envelopes the tree, the green chlorophyll pigment in each leaf uses its built-in capacity to turn carbon dioxide from the air, and water from the soil, into carbohydrates. This activity, called photosynthesis, produces oxygen, essential to all life. It allows new plant tissue to be produced so that every cell receives the correct nutrients, letting the tree grow and develop.

This interdependence is essential to the growth of a healthy tree: the roots, trunk and branches provide the structure and conditions for growth; the leaves make their own unique contribution. Omit any of them and the tree would not flourish.

Now compare this amazing, interdependent tree to an organization. With its values, vision and mission, an organization provides the structure and conditions for its people to play their unique roles. When organization and staff are well-matched, staff members carry out the services the organization is designed to provide. Everyone, from the newest clerk "in the leaves" to the CEO at the base of the branches, makes a unique contribution. The organization and individuals work together, each delivering what the other cannot in order for the organization to fulfill its function.

Finding the Right Person For the Job

We've all seen people who are round pegs in square holes. There is a mismatch between their skills and those the job requires. That's like asking the roots of a tree to photosynthesize! It's a prescription for failure.

Everyone thrives—individual, organization, clients—when people do what they do best in the place where they can make their greatest contribution.

But how can we be sure about someone's real abilities or strengths? An interviewer might see a certificate stating completion of training and final test passed. That doesn't tell us about the attributes that make the difference between:

- doing a job successfully and the bare minimum
- a person committed to his/her work and one who couldn't care less
- someone you'd trust with your life and someone whose integrity you're never quite sure about.

A paper qualification also won't tell us whether the person:

- is open-minded and listens carefully to other people
- is able to handle ambiguity
- welcomes feedback so they learn as much as they can from others.

How can we assess people's attitudes towards work or the value system that guides their lives? If we have any responsibilities for assessing people and appointing them to positions in an organization, or deciding whom to promote, it's useful to understand competencies. The knowledge will help prevent mistakes that could damage both the person and the organization. Such "mistakes" are costly in financial terms, even more so in human terms.

The word "competencies" often gets confused with "competence!" This can cause all kinds of problems.

Competence

In countries where a system of national qualification operates, the stress is placed on the roles and tasks of an occupation or job. A person who is *competent* is expected to be able to perform to a minimum standard.

For example, a qualified teacher has met the minimum national standard for becoming a teacher; a pilot has passed the minimum standard to fly and is licensed for the particular plane we are on. (We hope that s/he has experience beyond the minimum!) *Competence*, therefore, is about meeting the minimum standard for a job. It is about *what* needs to be achieved.

Competencies

On the other hand, *competencies* are about the person and *how* they go about a task in order to complete it success-fully. They are the underlying characteristics of a person, intricately blended together, the gifts and talents they possess that make them successful at certain tasks.

One piano player slogs away at scales and eventually passes grade 8. That's *competence*. The concert pianist too has passed grade 8. That's also *competence*—but it's more than that. The concert pianist has a gift for it as well. We say that producing music is one of his/her *competencies*, like it was for Mozart, Chopin or Beethoven.

Two people learning to play the piano at the same time or tackling the same job may have very different levels of success. Their *competencies* are influenced by their values and beliefs, their motives, personality traits, self-image and attitudes. The successful person is said to have the right competencies for the job. The other person may have gifts or competencies that are better suited to an entirely different job – perhaps to carpentry.

A person's *competencies* are a window through which we can glimpse his/her strengths or aptitudes. Unlike traditional exams that tell us what the person can do—their competence—competencies tell us *how* they do their job – what the person is like.

Determining a Person's Competencies

We can determine what *competencies* people have by observing their behaviours. The more effectively and consistently we see them behaving in ways associated with particular *competencies*, the stronger the competency.

For example, we may look at a nurse and say s/he has all the right competencies to be an excellent nurse. S/he has the skills required by the job—competence. Plus s/he has the competencies required in terms of his/her behaviour: has empathy and initiative, endurance and self-esteem, is methodical, gives encouragement and is concerned with excellence.

We may say that the CEO of the organization has all the right *competencies* to be a successful CEO—life experience, logic, leadership, humility, delegation, effective judgment, communication skills, and so on. Or we may not, depending on our perspective!

Each job requires a specific set of *competencies*. So chief executive officers probably require a greater ability to think conceptually than individual board members. Organizational leaders need a greater degree of self-esteem and problem-solving ability than the person who makes the morning coffee. To understand *competencies* more fully, consider the following analogy.

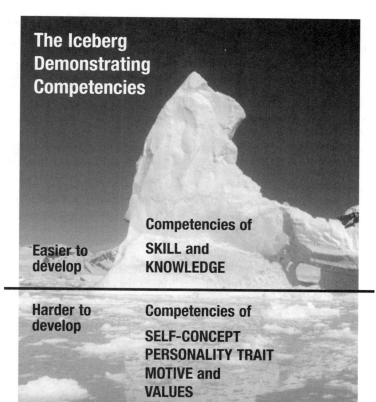

The Iceberg Demonstrating Competencies

Easier to develop — **Competencies of SKILL and KNOWLEDGE**

Water Line

Harder to develop — **Competencies of SELF-CONCEPT PERSONALITY TRAIT MOTIVE and VALUES**

A person's competencies are a window through which we can glimpse his/her strengths or aptitudes.

Competencies Are Like an Iceberg

Above the water-line are competencies more closely associated with knowledge and experience. They are easier to develop and can be improved by training and practice. They include communication, conflict resolution, process orientation and results orientation. A person who lacks the know-how to resolve conflict can improve by learning the process needed. S/he may learn of the need for objectivity, justice and impartiality and so improve the ability to resolve conflict.

Below the water line the competencies are harder to develop. Some may be almost impossible to change.

These include those associated with values, attitudes and self-perception, such as self-esteem, self-awareness, personal integrity and empathy.

If a CEO lacks personal integrity, self-esteem or a sense of justice, it will be very hard for him/her to develop such competencies at a later date.

Competencies – the Last Word

Competencies are the best way to predict success in the job. That is why they have, or should have, wide application in organizations. New staff can be assessed and selected, current staff promoted and succession planning accomplished. Used correctly and appropriately, they indicate what unique characteristics people can bring to a role to ensure success.

Competencies are also used to identify where development and training are needed, for performance management and appraisal.

Another illustration that helps to put the three components of authority into perspective is one of driving.

- Authorization is having the keys to the car.
- Resources are having fuel in the tank.
- Competencies are having the ability to drive!

Limitations of Authority

We saw in Chapter 3, that limitations of authority always exist in organizations. These limitations may be determined externally by God's laws and civil laws, or internally by the organization's strategic plans and policies. We're going to summarize the main points to reinforce their importance.

Limitations tell us where the boundaries of our authority lie. They define the freedom we have to fulfill our responsibilities. They are not there to make our lives miserable. Just as God gave limitations to Moses and Joshua, we have limitations to make our lives prosperous and successful.

Another benefit to limitations is that they balance our circle of authority with our circle of responsibility. In other words, we can increase our circle of authority by decreasing limitations to match a larger responsibility. Or we can decrease our circle of authority by increasing limitations.

If we imagine our authority as a circle, the line defining the circle is the limitations. Inside the circle, there is freedom—freedom to make decisions, to act, to be creative and to fulfill our responsibilities in the way we think best.

A *laissez-faire* value system usually won't define limitations because this value system misunderstands limitations as negative and oppressive. On the other hand, the *authoritarian* value system prefers not to set limitations, because it wants obedience from the employee, not his/her freedom.

The relationship values of affirmation, involvement and servant leadership are required to make this sense of freedom real.

Limitations of Authority

Responsibility

Responsibility, the second main component of a relationship, describes the purpose of a position within the organization.

Traditional terms of reference (board and committees) and job descriptions (staff) focus more on responsibility than on any other aspect of the working relationship. In the Relationship Model™, we think of the job description document as pertaining to the entire relationship, not simply the responsibilities of "the job." The tradition of writing job descriptions has, to some degree, prevented us from defining the other components of the relationship.

Our focus is on broad responsibilities, not specific tasks. In this way we emphasize the individual's freedom to be creative about handling responsibilities rather than supply a list of tasks that constricts them. Indications that a job description is too task-oriented are the words "the above is not necessarily a complete list of responsibilities" or "other responsibilities may be included from time to time."

A proper statement of a position's responsibilities likely includes from two to six broad areas. More than six may suggest that the position is either too demanding, or includes a list of tasks, not areas of responsibility.

Expectations Are Normally Expressed as Goals or Standards

Expectations of Responsibility

Responsibility is further defined by expectations. Expectations adjust the size of our circle of responsibility. They focus on our responsibilities, adding a distinct and personal touch to them.

Expectations and Goals

Expectations express what quantifiable goals we believe are appropriate. To be clear, goals should be S.M.A.R.T., that is:

- specific
- measurable
- achievable
- relevant to the mission
- time-limited.

Expectations and Standards

Our expectations may be further defined by standards. Minimum standards express the basic quality required by the organization. Staff members are expected to operate at or above this standard. A quality that we hope to work towards may be expressed as "standards to which we aspire."

Negotiating Expectations

In the Relationship Model™, expectations are normally negotiated by mutual agreement, not imposed. By negotiating, both recipient and source of authority can contribute essential information. Agreement can be reached on expectations that are:

- realistic and balanced with the authorization and resources available
- focused on achieving outcomes in line with organizational strategic goals.

If the source of authority cannot ensure the needed resources, then expectations must be reduced to restore the balance.

There may be times, however, when expectations are declared unilaterally, e.g., when deadlines negotiated with the client must be honoured by everyone on the staff. In

▶ *If the source of authority cannot ensure the needed resources, then expectations must be reduced to restore the balance.*

such cases, it is the authorization and resources that must be negotiated. Some adjustments to limitations may also be required. For example, extraordinary approval for deficit spending would be a relaxation of the normal limitations policy that prevents deficit spending.

When Relationships Unravel

In our experience, failure to negotiate mutual expectations is the most common component missing in a relationship. It is the point at which the relationship begins to unravel. When not explicitly stated, both the recipient and source of authority may be oblivious to the different expectations one has of the other. This usually happens in a *laissez-faire* value system. When a person doesn't know what volume or standard is expected, there is no way to:

- measure success
- make appropriate adjustments.

The authoritarian value system, on the other hand, is likely to impose expectations unilaterally, without negotiation. Since the focus is more on productivity than personal fulfillment, the recipient's personal fulfillment becomes less likely.

The Protestant Work Ethic

We are often our own worst enemy when it comes to fulfilling expectations of our responsibility. The reality may be that resources, such as time, finances, staff or information are insufficient. Under the good old Protestant work ethic, however, we often try to achieve far more than resources permit.

Lack of Competencies

Sometimes a person's competencies are lacking or insufficient to meet expectations. The gifts and talents an individual brings into the working relationship have a direct bearing on negotiating expectations. In the real world, the negotiating process may be unsuccessful when the recipient is unable to accept reasonable expectations because they know they don't have the "right stuff" for the position. This is the most difficult imbalance to deal with, even when relationship values are present. It reemphasizes the importance of getting round pegs in round holes in the first place.

In every case, it is the relationship values that build into the relationship both success and personal fulfillment. Affirmation, involvement and servant leadership will ensure that there is a balance between:

- productivity and personal fulfillment for the entire organization
- authority and responsibility for each individual.

Accountability

Accountability is the third and final component in a relationship. It is a neutral concept, although the word is often misunderstood to mean judgment, discipline or punishment.

Accountability has two chief purposes:

- It *monitors* whether the authority and responsibility delegated to a person or a group are in balance and, if necessary, makes a correction.
- It *measures* whether expectations of responsibility were achieved without overstepping the limitations of authority, i.e., it determines that goals have been achieved and standards kept within the available resources.

Balancing Authority and Responsibility

In any successful relationship, the circles of authority and responsibility must be of identical size. Let me remind you of what happens when they're not.

Circle of Authority Smaller Than Circle of Responsibility

To achieve successful results, sufficient authority and resources are needed to match responsibilities. When these are unclear or absent here's what happens:

- increased likelihood of failure to fulfill responsibilities
- missed goals
- poor service delivery
- poor morale and disempowerment.

Symptoms of Inadequate Authority

- **Low morale**
- **Missed goals**
- **Poor service delivery**
- **Fear of failure**
- **Discouragement**

Circle of Authority Larger Than Circle of Responsibility

When the circle of authority is larger than the circle of responsibility, abuse of power often results. It's very common, particularly in authoritarian organizations. Here are the defining elements of this category:

- abuse of power
- meddling
- waste of resources
- overconfidence.

Walter C Wright Jr. addresses this issue in his excellent book, *Relational Leadership*. He writes, "But power needs purpose. Power without purpose leaves a wake of debris, a trail of litter. Tornadoes have power, but look what they do. Power needs to be leashed to purpose." (page 16)

Symptoms of Too Much Authority

- **Misuse of power**
- **Meddling**
- **Overconfidence**
- **Waste of resources**
- **Arrogance**

Frequent violations of the limitations may indicate that:

- the limitations need adjustment to better reflect the freedom required to achieve the responsibilities
- the person has little respect for the limitations and couldn't care less about what s/he can or cannot do.

Either alternative requires corrective measures.

Annual Reviews and Accountability

The annual review of each working relationship is the primary opportunity for the measuring aspect of accountability. It is an opportunity to recognize achievements, to identify training needs as well as to make corrections and to give redirection.

Accountability Flows Back to Authority

Accountability always flows back in the opposite direction as authority. In other words, we are always accountable to the person or group from whom our authority comes. We can delegate authority and we can delegate responsibility, but we can't delegate accountability. Thus, if a CEO delegates significant management authority to a senior manager and that manager fails to perform, the CEO remains accountable to the board for the manager's performance.

Accountability – The Gift We Fail to Give

We usually think of accountability in negative terms. We don't like being negative, so we avoid it.

Accountability is no more than monitoring performance and measuring results. Being neutral, it is neither positive nor negative. It is the balance arm in the old-fashioned balance scale. Accountability is often the gift we fail to give one another.

Accountability is also a gift to people who have flaws they aren't aware of. Our humourist (Richard in the example in Chapter 2) changed his behaviour dramatically when an employee with less authority in the office, risked telling him the truth about his bad habit. She gave him a gift.

Accountability and the Relationship Model™

In our model, accountability is the process that maintains that delicate balance between authorization and resources available on one side and the expectations of our responsibility on the other.

(Remember that resources also include the competencies that people bring to the workplace with them.)

The CEO and founder of the not-so-small mission in the Southwest had never had a performance review. The board didn't think she needed one. Everything was going pretty well. Most importantly, the board members knew that the visionary they followed was impeccably honest and had such a high degree of personal integrity, that they were never concerned about her performance or her behaviour. She was so demanding of herself, they knew they didn't have to worry. "If it isn't broken, why fix it?" was their position, although it was always a position by default, not a policy.

They knew there was some dissent within the staff, but they figured it was professional jealousy and an unwillingness of some professional staff to measure results. Some staff figured God should measure what goes on inside the human heart. Whatever strategic outcomes there were couldn't be measured in spiritual matters. It was an ongoing debate that was never resolved.

When the staff staged a coup to oust the founder who insisted on measuring results, the board members didn't know what to do. Because of years of neglect in giving their CEO a meaningful performance review, confirming her strengths and developing her weaknesses, they had no real understanding of the dynamics. They loved the founder but didn't want to alienate the entire professional staff either. They tried in vain to find a compromise that wouldn't require taking a position. They couldn't find one.

The sad ending was the departure of the CEO and the gradual disintegration of the organization. The board never was able to manage the fallout and the disunity of the staff members who gradually left the organization themselves. Most importantly, the board never did see its own role in failing to exercise accountability in its relationship with its founder. The board decided it was a personality conflict. Within two years all the board members were gone too.

The Affirming Nature of Accountability

Accountability enables us to affirm people when they deliver what we expect of them. An annual review is a gift to people whom you might think of as being so dependable that you don't want to waste time giving them one. There's nothing to criticize, you say. If it's not broken, don't fix it. But there might be something to commend, to reward or to make even stronger. Ironically, sometimes the best employees are the least likely to receive the gift of accountability.

Accountability and the Abuse of Power

To remove destructive and dysfunctional behaviour, even when it leads to the termination of employment, is a gift to everyone, the abuser and the abused. That piercing look that Jesus gave to Peter in the courtyard was a gift that changed Peter's life for the better.

We cheat people when we simply forgive people instead of holding them accountable when wrong has been done. We also cheat ourselves when we hold them accountable without a forgiving heart.

Accountability Builds Trust

I have often said to people who are struggling with trust issues that forgiveness is free, but trust is expensive. Trust is a misunderstood value among Christians. It certainly isn't a value that we can turn on like a faucet just because someone with more authority demands it. That's because trust is the result of our behaviour first and the cause of more good behaviour second, not the other way around.

People who want to be trusted will want to be found trustworthy. As much as I want to be trusted, I would rather be called to account for my decisions and actions and found *worthy of trust*. Trust, therefore, is the result of a successful accountability process. It does not replace accountability.

Building a Trust Account

Whenever we enter into a new relationship, our co-workers give us a "bank account" of trust. We want to believe the best about each other, so we take the risk of trusting a new associate or employee.

Having a good experience with a new co-worker is a return on our investment. As a result, we deposit more trust into that account. Trustworthiness results in more trust.

By the same token, a bad experience means that we have withdrawn from that account, leaving less trust than before.

There may come a time in that relationship when the account goes into deficit, when trust is not being deposited by trustworthy behaviour. A deficit trust account is a broken relationship. Rebuilding it requires behaviour worthy of trust before more trust will be deposited.

▶

For some reason Christians sometimes substitute trust for good business practice.

Steven Covey puts it this way, "Just as you cannot fake world-class culture, so also is it impossible to fake high trust. It has to come out of trustworthiness." ("Three Roles of the Leader in the New Paradigm," an article in *The Leader of the Future*, p.150)

In the relationship-oriented workplace, the best way to build trust is to design an accountability system into the structure and processes at every level of the organization:

- Strategic and tactical goals should be negotiated between the source and recipient of authority.
- Regular relationship reviews should be a fundamental part of every direct working relationship.

◀

Forgiveness is free, but trust is expensive.

- Important communications should be made in writing.
- Assumptions should be replaced by agreements.

For some reason Christians sometimes substitute trust for good business practice. "I trust you" is a common phrase, and a lovely one to hear. Yet when we make assumptions instead of documenting understandings or rely on memory instead of keeping records, we set ourselves up for misunderstandings and disappointments. Trust begins to erode between us. *Accountability establishes trustworthiness.* Trustworthiness gives trust its foundation.

Summary

Healthy relationships are based on the core values found in all productive and fulfilling relationships—affirmation, involvement and servant leadership.

The structure of a healthy relationship involves defining authority with its limitations and responsibility with its expectations.

The final component of structure is accountability, the neutral and mutual process that maintains a balance between authority and responsibility. This balance is kept by adjusting limitations of authority and/or negotiating expectations of responsibility.

Accountability also allows us to measure results by confirming that expectations have been realized without exceeding the limitations of authority.

In the next two chapters, we shall turn these "circles" into "cycles" by exploring the six core processes of a healthy organization. We will put the structure to work.

The Relationship Model™
Principles of Governance, Leadership and Management

1   The organization seeks a balance between the fulfillment of the needs of the clients and the personal fulfillment of the staff and volunteers.

2   The affirmation, involvement and servant leadership of every individual and group at every level in the organization are vital to the success of the organization.

3   Authority, responsibility and accountability are the primary components of all relationships. Limitations of authority and expectations of responsibility are the secondary components.

4   Circles of authority and responsibility are defined clearly and are maintained equal in size by placing limits on authority or by negotiating expectations of responsibility.

5   The board of directors, acting on information from all stakeholders, is responsible for governance: defining target groups, services/needs, vision, mission and priorities, monitoring performance and measuring results.

6   The CEO is responsible for managing the delivery of services to the clients in accord with board-stated priorities and for achieving the strategic goals within the limitations of the authorization and resources available.

7   Each individual has a share in responsibility for creating, owning, understanding and implementing the mission of the organization.

8   Decision-making proceeds from shared values, vision and mission, not unilaterally from the board or the CEO. Decisions are made as close as possible to where they are implemented.

9   The organization is results-oriented. Indicators of results are identified. Strategic and tactical goals are set in balance with available resources. Results are measured.

10 Accountability is mutual. The source of authority is accountable to the recipient for providing adequate authorization and resources. The recipient is accountable to the source for achieving results.

Communication, Decision-making, Conflict Resolution

Circles and Cycles

Process is the structure in motion. In the Relationship Model™ we speak of a "circle of authority" and a "circle of responsibility." Correctly designed, these two circles overlap perfectly to form a "circle of freedom."

When this static circle of structure goes to work, it becomes a dynamic cycle of process. Thus, we can speak of a communication cycle, a decision-making cycle, a conflict resolution cycle, a planning cycle, a delegation cycle, or an accountability cycle. Knowing and following the components of each cycle will ensure a high quality process that produces what we all want at work:

- productivity for the organization (fulfillment for clients)
- fulfillment for staff and volunteers.

If we consider every possible process that takes place in our organization, there is no end of little wheels spinning in our workplace. There is the purchasing process, the recruiting process, the hiring process, the payroll process, the emergency response process and so on. In fact, hundreds of processes all linked together. In this book we deal with the six core processes to which all other processes are linked. We also deal with the relationship values of affirmation, involvement and servant leadership as they relate to each process.

In the following diagram, we show you once again how these six core processes "stack up." Communication, decision-making and conflict resolution are fundamental to the processes of planning, delegation, and monitoring/measuring.

Here's how the six core processes of an organization stack up.

The Communication Process

In Chapter 2 we stated that communication is the first of six core processes, perhaps the core process, since communication is also an inseparable part of every other process. Thus, the quality of communication will affect every other process for good or ill.

Communication is the transfer of information through the spoken, written or visual presentation of thoughts and feelings. We have already spoken of information as part of the circle of authority. Along with the resources of people, money and time, information fuels success at work. When information is available as required, it will add power to the other three resources.

When information is guarded, manipulated, twisted or withheld, it will put the brakes on what the other resources can produce.

From Chapter 2 we saw the effect of the *laissez-faire* and authoritarian value systems on the communication process. In this chapter we position the process on the relationship-oriented value system.

Affirmation

We can all tell when a person is communicating with affirmation, involvement and servant leadership. We see it in the eyes. We hear it in the tone of voice. We sense it in the time taken to help us understand. We know whether our opinion has value and when our information seems important. Values are often communicated in "body language."

We give away so many non-verbal signals in the communication process that it's important to consider our values before we begin to exchange our thoughts and feelings. The values that underpin our communication will have as much effect on the listener as the information itself—sometimes more.

A simple test to check your own values is to ask these three simple questions:

- Am I affirming this person?
- Am I involving this person?
- Am I supportive of this person?

The person or group will easily be able to tell if you are authentic. Your affirmation will be obvious in the way you listen, your eye contact, the time you take and the fact that you focus on the person and the issue at hand, instead of your watch, the background activity, your next meeting or yourself.

Involvement

Your involvement is obvious by your concern for the thoughts and feelings of the other person and in your questions to clarify what you are hearing. How much you share your own feelings is another indicator. Somewhere between "the great stone face" and "wearing your heart on your sleeve" is the real you, the "you" who comes to this interaction with aspirations and pressures of your own.

Servant Leadership

Your support is obvious in your intent to make the person's life and work easier, your offer of help and encouragement, and your sensitivity to their feelings and their workload.

Confidentiality and Secrecy

Confidentiality and secrecy may reveal the difference between a communication process that is open and one that is closed. The following scenario points out the dangers to an organization of such practices.

Were you ever present when someone was embarrassed suddenly in front of your fellow board members because it came out that s/he shared something from a previous board meeting with another person? You didn't think s/he was doing anything wrong at the time. You still don't think of it as being confidential. Still, it feels very awkward when it is suggested in front of the board that a member broke confidence.

In many Christian organizations there is an overuse of confidentiality. Whenever I see that, I begin to wonder if it really is confidentiality. It might be secrecy in sheep's clothing.

The easiest way to describe the difference between confidentiality and secrecy is to identify the motivation. Of course, it isn't easy to know the motivation of others, but you can certainly identify it in yourself. If you are justifiably trying to protect someone by withholding information, *that's confidentiality*. If you are withholding information, trying to hurt someone or to gain the upper hand in a group decision, *that's secrecy*.

Confidentiality is important in board governance. Many items of information might hurt people in an organization if disseminated prematurely or without thought about its impact on them. Can you imagine what would happen if someone released information that the CEO was going to be dismissed before the CEO was informed?

That information is confidential, not secret. What would happen if information were released prematurely to the local newspaper that an entire school was going to be shut down before the board could first explain the reasons to those people directly affected? Releasing that information prematurely hurts people. Keeping it confidential until it can be shared appropriately is an act of caring.

Secrecy, on the other hand, is the withholding of information to gain an advantage over people or to deliberately hurt them. It happens often, sometimes routinely, in some organizations. Imagine a CEO who is accused wrongly of an inappropriate act. The accusation and the evidence, and perhaps even the source of information are kept "confidential" until after the board has rendered a decision. The CEO has no opportunity to face his/her accusers or to defend him/herself. That's secrecy. In one recent example, a CEO was not invited to "tell his side of the story" because some board members feared that would change the board's decision to terminate the CEO's employment!

Information is power. There can be just as much effect in withholding information as in sharing it. When information is withheld to gain advantage or to hurt people, it is secret information. When information is withheld to heal or to protect, it is confidential information.

Responsible governing boards use confidentiality judiciously, not routinely. It is important for the board to be in agreement that withholding information in a particular situation is for a good cause, and that releasing it would cause unnecessary harm and perhaps even result in a liability to the organization. The same board must be sure that information is not being withheld because one or more board members are trying to "do someone else in," or simply to gain an advantage in a conflict of interest situation.

Imagine a board member not disclosing her knowledge that the recipient of a contract is a close relative. To disclose it would mean that she shouldn't be speaking in

▶

Information is power. There can be just as much effect in withholding information as in sharing it.

◀

It might be secrecy in sheep's clothing.

favour of tendering a contract to that company. Withholding the information is an example of secrecy to gain unfair advantage. Even kind and caring people can confuse confidentiality with secrecy. It can happen when you:

- participate in a group action that you haven't thought through
- aren't taking the time to identify your own values
- align your own decision with those of the other decision-makers even though your motive is not aligned.

Aligning motives means that when you know someone is withholding information inappropriately, you have the obligation to share it with the board. Withholding that information is keeping it secret, not confidential. Your values make all the difference.

The Decision-making Process

Decision-making, like every other process, is built on values. In the case of group decision-making, the values of the board chair or team leader are especially critical. We will explore that aspect of group decision-making when we discuss the role of the board chair.

The values important for all others in the group to bring to the process have already been discussed. Affirmation, involvement and servant leadership are demonstrated in:

- the listening that goes on within the group
- the issue-oriented discussion and debate
- the time the group is willing to take to allow all members to express their opinions.

What's the Issue

What's the agenda item? It may seem too obvious to say, but sometimes a discussion will begin with the assumption that everyone is on the same page on a particular issue. That assumption may be invalid. Let me give you an example:

- The CEO thinks that the board is making a decision about whether the CEO had a conflict of interest on a decision s/he made recently.
- The board thinks it is making a decision about whether the CEO should be disciplined.

You can appreciate that the process is going to be confusing at best.

Another example:

- Some think it's a decision on whether to build, or buy an existing building.
- Others assume that decision has already been made and that this decision is whether to employ an outside contractor or to act as the general contractor themselves.

Defining the Issue

Obviously, the issue requiring a decision must be clearly defined. The individuals in the group must be focused on the same issue for the process to produce a satisfactory result. This is not to say that the decision may not change during the process. For example, the decision to engage an outside contractor may indeed shift to a discussion about the relative merits of building or buying. The transition from one decision to the other, however, must be acknowledged by all members of the group for the agenda item to change.

Information Gathering

The quality of the decision that results from the process will be equal to the quality of the information available to the group at the time. The complexity of the decision will determine the degree of effort, time and research required. For example, in order to set a date for the next meeting, the group only needs information from members' schedules. On the other hand, to decide whether the organization should be registered in another country requires information that will take much more time and effort to obtain.

One important decision a group needs to make is whether it has the expertise to make a given decision. It may be unaware of the complexity of a decision and reach a flawed conclusion due to lack of information the group didn't realize was important. "I had no idea there was that much to it," one might hear later. Regardless of how obvious it seems, if the decision has any significant implications, the group should ask itself if outside consultation or support is needed.

The time and expense of gathering information are other factors. Saving money on information may cost more later. It can be more expensive to fix something than to do it right the first time. "Haste makes waste," the saying goes. Taking the time to gather the information necessary will have the same positive effect on the outcome as spending the money to obtain it.

Discussion and Debate

The difference between discussion and debate is the presence of conflict. When parties agree on the statements that each other makes, the discussion adds value because of the additional insights that each contributes.

Debate occurs when there is a difference of opinion, and it can have a positive or negative effect. Debate that is issue-oriented is healthy and should be encouraged. Debate, however, may seem like a damaged word. It is often associated with a clash of values that harms relationships. When values clash in a discussion, it helps if we recognize what is happening. In itself, the clash can be a positive learning experience. However, it should take place as a separate discussion. When opposing values become confused with the issue, the result is more likely to be a "win-lose" decision.

Outcomes of the decision-making process are determined by the group's assessments of facts, thoughts and feelings. So it should be, but it's important to know the degree to which the decision is being shaped by each factor.

Discussion should be issue-oriented. Clear thinking about the facts is vital to a quality decision. That does not mean, however, that feelings are of no account.

Where feelings can't be identified, it is especially important to probe the values behind the feelings. For example, if the decision to build a new office makes sense, but some members are opposed to the decision because of values related to indebtedness, the decision could have been made not to build because of feelings instead of facts.

In our example, the group realized that it was a value related to indebtedness that prevented some participants from supporting the decision to build. It was able to separate that value from the issues related to the building. As a result, the project went forward without anyone having to violate personal values. It was a "win-win" decision.

To build or not to build. Is that the question?

The organization had rented office space for years, but the building was being sold, and the new owners were going to move in and use it for their own work. The board now had to decide whether to rent other facilities, purchase an existing building, or build a new one.

A lot of time and money went into this decision. A consulting firm was engaged to gather data about available space to rent or purchase compared with the cost of building a new structure.

There didn't seem to be much debate about the matter. Everyone agreed that in the long term, building new would result in the best value for money. Renting amounted to buying a building for a landlord, while the organization was committed to its ministry in this small city. Buying an existing building was out of the question, because the only two available were either too old or didn't provide convenient access or parking. Building new meant that the office could be designed to enhance service delivery in addition to providing office space.

But two members of the board opposed the proposal to build. They were both highly respected for their long, committed service and their integrity. "I don't have the right feeling about this move," one said, "but I don't know why." "Well, I know why I don't like it," said the other, "I don't believe in debt. I don't think it's right for us to borrow money to build. If we can't pay for it up front, we shouldn't do it. I'm not opposed to building, but doing it this way just isn't right."

The chair suggested that the decision to build be set aside in order to focus on the issue of funding and financing. After a lot more discussion the board decided to design an interest-free financing and fundraising campaign and to build only after the campaign was successful.

The decision to build a new facility was approved unanimously.

Making the Decision

Boards, management teams and other groups making decisions have two choices in how to approach the making of decisions—*consensus or majority vote*. That assumes, of course, that the leader of the group (or a small faction within the group) doesn't force a personal agenda, pretending that the group has made a decision freely.

This subject is dealt with in more detail in Chapter 15, since consensus is an important part of senior management team decision-making, but we will also highlight it here.

Consensus occurs when the majority agrees on a certain course of action and everyone else in the group is willing to proceed for the sake of the group, even though some may not have chosen that course of action and would prefer another.

Consensus and Involvement

Boards often use consensus to encourage involvement and ownership. The Relationship Model™ leans towards this form of decision-making. The difference between management teams and boards is that if the board cannot reach consensus, the decision cannot default to a stronger authority. In this case, the board has no alternative but to revert to a vote where the majority determines the outcome.

Normally, board members are expected to support the decisions of the board, but the sense of ownership may be lost in the process. For this reason, my suggestion is that boards make an effort to make decisions by consensus and move to voting only when the board cannot reach consensus. The minutes may refer to the decision as, "It was agreed by consensus…"

Was it consensus or a majority vote? You decide.

The discussion on a motion to change the bylaw had finished and the board chair called the question. "All in favour?" Some hands go up, some don't. Some seem to mumble assent. The new board members aren't sure if this is a vote or if it's an expression of consensus. It appears to be somewhere in between, but no one seems to have objected so they assume it passed. People did seem to agree with the motion during the discussion. Anyway, the chair has moved on to the next item. The experienced board members understand what it all means. The new ones assume that they will catch on to the system with time.

The Conflict Resolution Process

◀

Boards often use consensus to encourage involvement and ownership.

Some types of conflict are healthy for an organization. Others are not. Discussion and debate on an issue often highlight the conflicting ideas and opinions on:

- what things should be done
- how things should be done.

Healthy Conflict

Sharing divergent perspectives and enabling them to converge into a group decision is one of the main strengths of a group. The synergy of a group can often produce a more effective and efficient solution than an individual acting alone. That's because of the various ideas a group can generate, some of which may be in conflict with another. This kind of conflict is usually healthy and should be encouraged.

Warren Bennis writes in *An Invented Life*, "Today the laurel will go to the leader who encourages healthy dissent and values those followers brave enough to say no. The successful leader will have not the loudest voice, but the readiest ear. His or her real genius may well lie not in personal achievements, but in unleashing other people's talent." (p.107)

In fact, sometimes the conflict should be allowed to continue so as to produce a dynamic tension within the organization. For example, the continual struggle between risk and caution, effectiveness and efficiency, the tension between remedial or preventive efforts, and the conflict between small and intimate or large and less personal, are some of many issues that remain in tension and can benefit the organization's service delivery. Such types of conflict can not only build relationships but the respect people have for each other's perspective and contribution.

Unhealthy Conflict

Unhealthy conflict occurs when values are at stake and people hurt one another. Relationships become strained and sometimes break. It requires effort to reconcile the relationships after this type of conflict in order that they can once again function effectively within the organization.

As we saw in Chapter 3, there are three pathways to reconciliation:

- *Negotiation* – between the individuals and/or groups experiencing conflict
- *Mediation* – the addition of "two or three persons" to facilitate the resolution of the conflict
- *Arbitration* – a third party is asked to hear both parties and make a decision in the hope that the parties can be reconciled.

The Role of Values

Reconciliation requires both forgiveness and justice. Neither forgiveness nor justice, acting alone, will result in reconciliation. That's because successful reconciliation, like all other processes, begins with values. So when the relationship is in negative territory, forgiveness is an expression of *affirmation*.

Involvement brings the conflict into the open. It results in transparency instead of secret meetings to decide the fate of someone who cannot defend him/herself.

Servant leadership looks to the resolution of the conflict and the reconciliation of the relationship. It seeks to support, rather than win.

The five-step justice process that now follows is based upon forgiveness.

The Justice Process

The justice process that we know from our understanding of Matthew 18 appears in the documented literature of many cultures. The sequence includes:

- making an accusation
- giving evidence
- allowing for a defense
- reaching a decision
- compensation.

The words we use in our organizational context are different from those of the civil court, but the concept is the same. The difference? Forgiveness and reconciliation, the first and the last steps of the process, are not normally a part of the civil or criminal justice process.

Justice in Organizations	Justice in Litigation
allegation	charges
documentation	evidence
defense	defense
deliberation	jury deliberation
decision	verdict
recompense	sentence
repentance	appeals
amends	fine, incarceration

◄

Neither forgiveness nor justice, acting alone, will result in reconciliation.

Making allegations about the performance, integrity or behaviour of another person is very serious. Without evidence that can pass the test of scrutiny and defense, it is called slander or libel. This kind of behaviour is outside the limitations of the Ten Commandments and civil law. Unfortunately, many innocent people have been hurt, their lives put on hold, their reputations irreparably damaged and their careers destroyed due to this form of injustice. Even in Christian organizations the damage from innuendo and rumor is appalling.

There is a better way to achieve reconciliation from brokenness. Here are four important steps:

1. Allegations must be clearly framed in writing so that they are understood in the same way by all parties. This also records the allegations in a manner that can be referred to later. There will be no doubt what was said. "I never said that," is not an option when the matter is documented in writing.

2. The source of the allegations should be identified. Is it an individual? Is it a group? Is it the official record of the group, or is it an individual using the name of a group?

3. The person or group who is the object of the allegation must be identified. This prevents an accuser from covering tracks by saying later, "I didn't mean you personally. I was talking about the organization."

4. The person to whom the allegation is addressed should have access to this information so that s/he can have the information and the time required to prepare a defense.

The basic justice process is documented throughout history in some of the most well-known and respected records of various cultures. Here are some of them.

Code of Hammurabi (1795 – 1750 BC)

1. If any one ensnare another, putting a ban upon him, but he can not prove it, then he that ensnared him shall be put to death.

2. If anyone bring an accusation against a man, and the accused go to the river and leap into the river, if he sink in the river his accuser shall take possession of his house. But if the river prove that the accused is not guilty, and he escape unhurt, then he who had brought the accusation shall be put to death, while he who leaped into the river shall take possession of the house that had belonged to his accuser.

3. If any one bring an accusation of any crime before the elders, and does not prove what he has charged, he shall, if it be a capital offense charged, be put to death.

Acts 25:16 (Festus to Agrippa circa 60 AD)
Roman Law

I told them that it is not the Roman custom to hand over any man before he has faced his accusers and has had an opportunity to defend himself against their charges.

Magna Carta (King John 1215 AD)

38. No bailiff for the future shall, upon his own unsupported complaint, put anyone to his "law," without credible witnesses brought for this purposes.

39. No freemen shall be taken or imprisoned or disseised or exiled or in any way destroyed, nor will we go upon him nor send upon him, except by the lawful judgment of his peers or by the law of the land.

40. To no one will we sell, to no one will we refuse or delay, right or justice.

U.S. Bill of Rights, Amendment VI

In all criminal prosecutions, the accused shall enjoy the right to a speedy and public trial, by an impartial jury of the State and district wherein the crime shall have been committed, which district shall have been previously ascertained by law, and to be informed of the nature and cause of the accusation; to be confronted with the witnesses against him; to have compulsory process for obtaining witnesses in his favor, and to have the assistance of counsel for his defense.

Canadian Charter of Rights and Freedoms (1981)

11. Any person charged with an offense has the right a) to be informed without unreasonable delay of the specific offense; b) to be tried within a reasonable time; c) not to be compelled to be a witness in proceedings against that person in respect of the offense; d) to be presumed innocent until proven guilty according to law in a fair and public hearing by an independent and impartial tribunal.

United Nations General Assembly (December 10, 1948) Universal Declaration of Human Rights

Article 11.(1) Everyone charged with a penal offense has the right to be presumed innocent until proved guilty according to law in a public trial at which he has had all the guarantees necessary for his defense.

Towards Reconciliation

It seems obvious that people in not-for-profit organizations should have the same right to defend themselves in the conflict resolution process. Closed-door sessions and secret backroom decisions should never take the place of this vital process.

For both parties, reconciliation is the reward of a successful process. Of course, the process is rarely this simple. Sometimes both parties share in the responsibility for brokenness. Most significantly, perhaps, reality hits home when conflict goes to the third stage, arbitration by a third party, and the likelihood of reconciliation diminishes. Some of the reasons that may account for a failure to reconcile include:

- a lack of forgiveness
- a flawed justice process
- no admission of guilt or acceptance of the board/arbiter's decision
- a refusal to make amends.

The Conflict Resolution Cycle

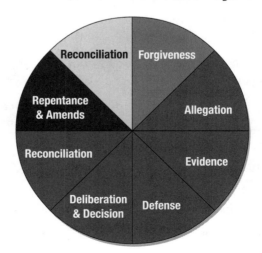

Each step of the conflict resolution process must take place successfully to proceed from forgiveness to reconciliation. The process may break down at any stage. It is possible to have:

- forgiveness without reconciliation
- justice without reconciliation.

Reconciliation of both parties will result only from:

- forgiveness that is responded to with repentance
- justice that is perceived to be fair.

Summary

The six core processes of an organization are:

- communication
- decision-making
- conflict resolution
- planning
- delegating
- accountability – monitoring and measuring

Processes are the structure in motion. The first three processes, which are discussed in this chapter, are the foundation for the other three in the sense that communication, decision-making and often conflict resolution are a vital part of the other three processes.

Communication is the transfer of information through the spoken, written or visual presentation of thoughts and feelings.

Decision-making may be done by consensus or majority vote. The involvement in building consensus results in greater ownership of the decision.

The conflict resolution cycle involves the four steps of:

- forgiveness
- justice
- repentance
- reconciliation.

All four stops are necessary to achieve reconciliation.

In the next chapter we discuss the other three core processes that build on these three.

Notes

Planning, Delegating, Monitoring and Measuring

PART ONE
CHAPTER
6

The Planning Process

The planning process consists of an organization's strategic and tactical planning. The two types of planning are quite different and done by different groups. The principles, however, are the same. In this section we deal with the elements common to both. We will deal with applications in Part 2 of this book.

Values

The values of affirmation, involvement and servant leadership will be apparent in each step of the planning cycle. It will be evident in:

- the sensitivity towards the target groups whose needs the organization seeks to meet
- the quality and scope of involvement of all stakeholders, including staff and volunteers
- the realism and negotiation in setting goals
- the degree of preparation and resources made available
- the quality of management in the implementation and evaluation of the plan.

To be reminded how values can also have a negative effect on planning, review Chapter 2 on this topic.

The Planning Cycle

Needs Analysis

All planning is an effort to meet the need of some individuals or group. It is common for organizations to make assumptions about what the needs are. Needs change. If the assumptions that underlie the services and programs don't change with those needs, ineffectiveness or inefficiency or both will result. Tradition is a powerful factor in keeping plans from changing. "We've always done it this way," describes an unwillingness to look afresh at how needs move on from past rationales.

It is crucial to understand the need for change that is expressed by the beneficiaries of the organization.

Divergence and Convergence

Divergence

Divergence is brainstorming. (*Thought shower* is the politically correct replacement suggested in the UK.) It is a creative process that produces a flood of ideas without any discussion or debate. In a wonderful and stimulating way a group can generate a large number of ideas in a remarkably short time, ideas worthy of closer consideration. The premise is that people who have a stake in the finished plan have valuable thoughts and insights to offer, so let's involve them in the process.

Responding to Change

One excellent indicator for a needs analysis is shrinking demand for a given service or program. One of the Roman Catholic Sisters' Orders is an excellent example of how an organization can respond to changing needs. With the aging and death of an increasing number of nuns, more and more capacity became available in their residence. Rather than close the residence, this Order discovered an entirely new need. It made the extra space available to not-for-profit organizations and companies looking for retreat venues, while still retaining part of the facility for its original use.

Divergence works best when completely separated from convergence—that is, the analysis of the ideas, ranking them, or discussing whether they will work or not. All you want at this stage are the ideas.

Prepare a group for the exercise in this way:

◀

It is crucial to understand the need for change that is expressed by the benefici- aries of the organization.

- Invite them to think of any idea that might even come close to reality. Humour adds to the dynamic.
- Set a time limit of five or ten minutes. If necessary, you can always extend the time.
- Ask someone who can write both fast and legibly to keep up with the flow of ideas. A flip chart is very useful for this. So is the use of "stickies" on a wall or other surface.
- Advise the group that there will be no discussion or requests for clarification during the brainstorming.

Convergence

Only when the brainstorming is complete can convergence begin. This is the slow, careful process of testing the ideas that emerge to meet the identified needs. In this way the plan begins to take shape. This stage may also require:

- research
- use of accumulated data
- discussion
- outside expertise
- more time.

Risk Analysis

Luke 14:28 – 33 gives some biblical examples of risk analysis. In counting the cost of discipleship, we are invited to ponder the cost of building a tower, lest we are unable to finish what we started and are ridiculed for our lack of planning. Or consider the king who considers the risk of facing an opposing force of 20,000 men with his own army of 10,000.

The easiest and probably the most widely used model for analyzing the risks associated with new plans is called a SWOT analysis. SWOT stands for:

- strengths
- weaknesses
- opportunities
- threats.

Strengths and weaknesses are the internal factors that help and hinder. Opportunities and threats are the external factors that can make or break your plans.

A SWOT analysis allows an examination of the internal and external factors that will either help or hinder the plans being considered. This model also deals with the cost/benefit ratio of any given plan, since costs and benefits fall into one or more of the four categories. Brainstorming may be used as well to generate the wide range of possible factors that may fall into one of the categories.

In working through each factor that may help or hinder your plans, remember the limitations placed on your organization by its regulatory authority. These external factors may threaten the development of your plans. For example, a medical service organization may find that regulatory requirements raise costs beyond sustainable service delivery. Those same regulations may also provide an opportunity, e.g., to meet the needs of other beneficiaries who can benefit from your services.

Goal-setting

▶

You can't measure progress towards a goal that doesn't exist.

Deciding how much your organization or department can "bite off" is a very significant part of the planning process. You can't measure progress towards a goal that doesn't exist.

The key to setting goals lies first in identifying indicators of results. Anything worth doing can be measured in some way. Furthermore, every organization has an obligation to assure its stakeholders of the return on their investment.

Out of the Mouths of Babes

I shall always remember the words of the five-year-old girl seated next to me at the Sunday school opening. As I waited for my introduction to speak to her class, she was swinging her legs under the chair and warming up the quarter in her hand, preparing it for the offering. Obviously deep in thought, she paused, looked up at me and asked, "How does God get the money?" How could such a little girl ask such a difficult question? Don't ask me to remember my answer. What I remember is the importance of her question. I remember thinking how valuable it would be for adults to ask organizations that question before and after they make their contributions.

Benchmarks

The next step is to establish meaningful benchmarks. This comes from the experience of others with some history of past achievements within your own organization. This information may be difficult to obtain. As an alternative it may be necessary to establish a base for a year or more so that meaningful goal-setting can follow.

S.M.A.R.T. Goals

The acronym S.M.A.R.T. stands for goals that are:

- specific
- measurable
- achievable
- relevant to the mission
- time-limited.

Overall Goal

"We shall increase our enrollment in Choral Music 101 by ten percent to 50 students by the beginning of the next school term."

Specific

"We shall increase our enrollment in Choral Music 101..."

Measurable

"...to 50 students..."

Achievable

"...by ten percent..."

Relevant to the mission

"The mission of Zippity Do Dah School is to train young musicians in choral and instrumental music."

Time-limited

"...by the beginning of the next school term."

God's Will

"As much as God allows" is not a S.M.A.R.T. goal. It's D.U.M.B. (Deifying Underachievement, Mediocrity and Bungling). Oddly, this vital element is missed by some organizations, sometimes for theological reasons: "You can't measure what goes on in the heart," is an all-too-frequent lament of Christians in organizations. Ah, but the person whose heart has changed can measure it. Base the measurements on information the beneficiaries can give.

Some Christians excuse themselves from striving for excellence and from monitoring and measuring accountability by explaining that God will decide the success of any human effort. If it doesn't succeed, it probably wasn't God's will in the first place. That "model" of goal-setting relies on the truism that if you don't have a target, you can't miss it.

This leads to another important element of setting goals. The best and sometimes the only way to measure results is to ask:

- specific stakeholders
- the beneficiaries of the services
- the staff and volunteers for whom you wish to offer personal fulfillment.

▶

It is not an easy thing to measure strategic results.

It is not an easy thing to measure strategic results. In fact, its difficulty is what inspires some to avoid it or spiritualize it so as to excuse themselves from doing the work.

A staff/volunteer fulfillment survey, for example, can ask specific questions inviting reviewers to rate their level of fulfillment in particular areas, using a numeric scale. The scores can be compared with those recorded in the following year's survey. In this way, S.M.A.R.T. goals can be established for growth in staff/volunteer fulfillment.

Preparation/Resourcing

Before any plan can be implemented, the resources must be in place. In an earlier chapter, we presented resources as part of the circle of authority. To remind you, resources consist of four elements—human resources, financial resources, information and time. The first three must be in place before implementation can begin:

- human resources – with the appropriate competencies
- financial resources – for capital and operating costs. Endowment funds may also be required.
- information – to match services with needs and a host of other kinds of information.

These items can form a useful checklist for the preparation of the authorization and the resources required for implementation.

Implementation

> *"The proof of the pudding is in the eating."*
>
> *"Well, here goes nothing," we say.*
>
> *"Let's jump into the deep end. It's sink or swim."*

A new fiscal year begins. Usually, all the planning isn't done yet. Not all the resources are assembled, but the time has come. Our purpose here is not to deal with the complexities of management. Even in Part 2 of this book we condense the variations and complexities of diverse not-for-profit organizations into the relationship between the CEO and the senior management team.

Our purpose is simply to highlight the reality that the actual operation of the plan is an important component to the next planning cycle. We learn from doing. We accumulate wisdom and incorporate what we learn into a better future.

Evaluation

Monitoring and measuring are the two components of the accountability process. Evaluation of our plans utilizes this final core process of an organization. Evaluation has two separate elements:

- monitoring performance
- measuring results.

Monitoring Performance

Monitoring is the ongoing checking of progress, performance and behaviour that takes place during the operational phase. We will explain this in detail when we deal with specific relationships in governance, leadership and management in Part 2. We monitor compliance with limitations of authority and expectations of responsibility. Monitoring allows us to make minor changes and improvements while the implantation is proceeding.

◄

Monitoring and measuring are the two components of the accountability process.

Measuring Results

We compare our actual results with the goals we set. We learn what we did well, what we did poorly, what worked and what didn't work. This gives us valuable information for better planning in the next cycle. It also enables us to set S.M.A.R.T. goals to build a stronger, service future on the foundation of the past. The cycle repeats itself annually.

The Process of Delegating Authority and Responsibility

In the relationship-oriented organization virtually every direct working relationship will have a current relationship description. This process documents that relationship.

Definitions

►

In any direct working relationship there should be no more than one source of authority.

A *direct working relationship* is one in which authority and responsibility are delegated from one person or group to another. In any direct working relationship there should be no more than one source of authority. (No person can serve two masters.)

An *indirect working relationship* is one in which:

- peers share authority
- services are provided to an individual or group that is not the source of authority for the person providing the services.

The board chair and the CEO or two members of a senior management team would be examples of indirect working relationships. So would a mail room clerk who delivers mail directly to the CEO.

Indirect working relationships are not normally documented because authority does not flow from one to the other.

"Who is your source of authority?"

Knowing how authority flows in an organization is one of the most basic aspects of organizational life. I am constantly amazed to discover how many people in the workplace have no idea how authority flows in their organization. When I ask the question I get a number of reactions:

- a blank stare
- "I wish I knew."
- "You must be kidding. I don't have any authority."
- "I have two or three people who think I work only for them."

The fact is, we all have some authority. The problem is that too often we don't know:

- where it comes from
- how much we have
- what to do with it.

Writing Relationship Descriptions

Delegating authority and responsibility should answer all the questions we have ever had about how authority flows and what our role is in the big picture. This cycle has six components:

1. delegating authority
2. setting limitations of authority
3. delegating responsibility
4. negotiating expectations
5. monitoring performance
6. reviewing the relationship

1. Delegating Authority

Delegating authority clearly defines the source of operational authority and adds a broad statement of what that authority covers. It is a far more powerful and effective statement than we might consider.

We understand the power of having authority delegated to us if we can recall an experience of having lost it. Losing authority is much more dramatic than receiving it. Ask anyone who has just:

- received an unexpected notice of termination, or
- learned that s/he has not passed the probation period successfully, or worst of all
- discovered that his/her employment has been terminated for cause.

◄

Knowing how authority flows in an organization is one of the most basic aspects of organizational life.

Being asked for the office keys, being observed while packing personal items and then being ushered to the door are pretty dramatic ways to feel the vapour-like characteristic of authorization dissipating rapidly into the air.

A key part of the delegation of authority is assurance that you will receive the resources needed to be successful. Getting the keys to the car without fuel for the tank is empty authority.

The relationship description should contain a statement recognizing the source or sources of regulatory authority. That may include:

- government departments
- a professional association or union
- the national body of which your organization is a member.

2. Setting Limitations of Authority

Empowerment and freedom to use the delegated authority are given boundaries by limitations to authority. It is like drawing the line that forms the outer parameter of the circle of authority. In the relationship description, these limitations may be:

- imposed upon the entire organization
- shared with your source of authority
- imposed by the regulatory authority
- negotiated in balance with expectations.

These sources of regulatory authority may have limitations affecting your operational authority and should be acknowledged in this section.

In the next chapters, we will give examples of relationship descriptions incorporating these limitations.

Limitations are stated in negative language, simply because it is more efficient to give ten limitations than to document a thousand permissions.

3. Delegating Responsibility

The traditional job description (which the relationship description replaces) contains this element of the relationship more than any other. It is often expressed as a list of tasks. Task orientation may be fitting within an authoritarian value system. Here we focus on broad areas of responsibility, emphasizing the freedom of the recipient of authority to develop those tasks, programs and activities that best deliver what is expected from the areas of responsibility. In making the paradigm shift from tasks to broad areas of responsibility, we have found it helpful to write the relationship description "starting from scratch."

Normally, as we mentioned in an earlier chapter, there should be no more than six broad areas of responsibility. If there are more, they may either need restatement or document the need for another position!

Because responsibilities evolve, we have also found it helpful to seek out the experience of job holders in preparing the first draft of the relationship description. The recipient of authority often knows more about his/her area of responsibility than the source of authority.

4. Negotiating Expectations

In this section of the relationship description, we generally make a simple reference to the tactical goals that have been negotiated between the source and recipient of authority. Normally the goals themselves are contained in another document along with those of other staff members.

The number of employees in not-for-profit organizations who do not know what is expected of them is so great that the problem qualifies as one of the seven deadly sins of organizations.

This section also contains an expectation that the recipient of authority will behave in a manner that is consistent with the relationship values of affirmation, involvement and servant leadership.

5. Monitoring Performance

6. Reviewing the Relationship

◀

It is more efficient to give ten limitations than to document a thousand permissions.

Both of these elements are part of the last section of the relationship description: accountability. Because accountability is the sixth core process—which we will discuss next—we will mention only what the content of this section of the relationship should cover.

The accountability section of the relationship description includes a basic four-point outline:

- a review of the source of authority's expression of values and provision of authorization and resources
- a review of the recipient of authority's performance towards goals negotiated at the beginning of the year
- goal-setting for the next planning period. This process may be implemented at another time when the staff is preparing the tactical plan for the next fiscal year
- a review of professional development needs and opportunities that may make the relationship more productive and fulfilling.

The Accountability Process – Monitoring and Measuring

As you read this book, I invite you to understand the word "accountability" in its neutral sense. The reason I ask you to do this is because accountability is a vital component of maintaining healthy relationships. To repeat what I've already said several times:

"Accountability is the gift we too often fail to give one another."

Unfortunately, accountability is a "damaged" word. Even though it names a neutral process, it is often taken to mean punishment or discipline. For example, the famous handwriting on Belshazzar's wall, "You are weighed on the scales and found wanting," was a judgment that resulted in the death of that Babylonian king on the very same night that Daniel interpreted the handwriting. It is sometimes overlooked that Belshazzar's gift of a robe of royal purple to Daniel was also an example of accountability. Daniel, too, was "weighed on the scales" and found faithful.

I have been encouraged to use a different word to name this important process, but I have chosen to reclaim the word instead. Being "weighed on the scales" is a neutral process, even if the news is sometimes negative. When you step on the scale to see how effective your diet has been, the news might be good. The fact that sometimes it isn't is no reason to blame the scale for being the bearer of bad tidings.

Not a day goes by that newspaper headlines don't deal with the need for accountability from some corporate executive or abuser of women or children. Since accountability is always mentioned in a negative context, it's a challenge to think of it as being neutral or ever resulting in a commendation, promotion or a raise.

What Can Accountability Bring to Relationships Within Organizations?

In the first paragraph of this book, we mentioned that the most important balance to maintain in an organization is that between the fulfillment of client needs and staff needs. The process of accountability—monitoring and measuring—provides and maintains that balance.

The Accountability Cycle

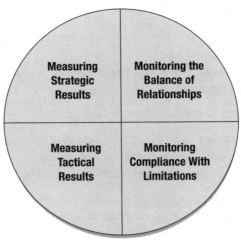

| Measuring Strategic Results | Monitoring the Balance of Relationships |
| Measuring Tactical Results | Monitoring Compliance With Limitations |

The Four Roles of Accountability – Monitoring and Measuring

1. Monitoring the Balance of Authority and Responsibility

At every organizational level it is important to maintain a balance between authority and responsibility, i.e., between what is invested in an individual or group and what is expected in return. The only way that staff and clients can experience fulfillment is to ensure that this balance is maintained in every relationship where authority is delegated to another. Nothing is more important in an organization than balancing staff fulfillment with client fulfillment (personal fulfillment with organizational productivity).

This is the first and most important role of the accountability process.

Accountability is mutual. Everyone has a role in maintaining this balance—the source and the recipient of delegated authority and responsibility. We speak of the annual relationship review, not the annual performance review. Thus, the first section of that review concerns the source of authority's performance in:

- demonstrating affirmation, involvement and servant leadership in the relationship
- providing adequate authorization and resources for the job holder to meet his/her responsibilities.

The failure to meet goals may be due to:

- the shortage of resources (it may not necessarily be the failure of the job holder to use those resources effectively.)
- unrealistic goals negotiated in the planning process.

The whole purpose of this process is to restore or maintain this balance. It is not to find fault or blame, but to affirm, involve and serve one another in the pursuit of productivity and fulfillment. Needless to say, this process should not be limited to the formal annual review of the relationship. Either party should be free to approach the other whenever an imbalance exists. Goals, human and financial resources, information and time may be adjusted at any stage of the year in order to ensure the success of the relationship.

2. Monitoring Compliance with Limitations and Expectations

This is another component of the relationship review. Like the first, it takes place annually, but may also occur during the year on a formal or informal basis.

In the relationship between the board and the CEO, this is the most significant way in which the board can monitor the CEO's management without becoming involved in management itself. The limitations of authority and expectations of responsibility are entrenched in the board's policies and are monitored on a predetermined schedule.

Limitations of authority are also a part of every working relationship within the management of the organization. When these limitations are specific, they clearly define the freedom of the recipient of authority. It is important to monitor compliance with these limitations to ensure that the relationship remains in balance. Exceeding the limitations of authority may be an abuse of power. It may also indicate that the limits are unrealistic for the expectations and need to be adjusted.

3. Measuring Tactical Results

This form of measurement requires identifying indicators of results. In this case, the indicators are related to the programs that deliver the services, not to the services themselves. This process is the responsibility of the CEO and staff. It indicates the effectiveness and efficiency of the programs in delivering the strategic results of the services offered by the organization.

4. Measuring Strategic Results

Measuring strategic results means measuring the extent to which the organization is realizing its mission. It is a measure of productivity—the degree to which the needs of clients are being met. This process is primarily a board responsibility, although it cannot be done without the involvement of the CEO and the management team.

▶

Usually organizations rely on anecdotes— stories and letters from satisfied clients.

It is surprising how few organizations measure strategic results. Usually, organizations rely on anecdotes—stories and letters from satisfied clients. Sometimes tactical results are confused with strategic results measuring, e.g., how many people come to the shelter for the homeless instead of measuring what happens in the lives of the people who come.

Measuring the degree to which we are meeting the needs of clients cannot be done without asking those clients to measure the effects of our work. Even before that we must identify the indicators that tell us what to measure. Once that is done we can design a questionnaire based on the services we offer, asking clients to reflect on how well these services met their needs.

All four of the monitoring and measuring processes we have just covered have a role in insuring that the balance between staff fulfillment and client needs is maintained or restored.

Summary

The other three core processes of an organization are:

- planning
- delegating
- monitoring and measuring (accountability).

Processes are the structure in motion. These three processes rest on the foundation of the other three in the sense that communication, decision-making and often conflict resolution are a vital part of planning, delegating and monitoring and measuring.

All six processes have an important role in ensuring that we achieve the balance between productivity and the fulfillment of staff and volunteers.

The values that support the processes are the most important single component in determining our success in achieving that balance.

From the Roots Up

Governance, Leadership and Management

PART 2

Governance
Context

Introduction

Not-for-profit organizations are made up of people who share values, a vision for the future and a sense of purpose. Each organization is a complex network of relationships. It is in understanding and defining these relationships, using the Relationship Model™, that we discover how to build organizations that are productive and fulfilling.

The primary relationship within the organization is that between the members and the board. At the beginning of an organization's life, there may be no difference between these two groups. The founding board members are possibly the organization's only members. As the organization grows, however, more people who share the values and vision become involved. This group meets annually (minimum requirement) to elect the board and to handle the organization's basic business transactions.

In some cases, the board fails or chooses not to develop a membership base.

We shall see later that, in some cases, the board fails or chooses not to develop a membership base. This results in the board having more authority and responsibility with less accountability. It often leads to serious problems, such as limited growth or abuse of power.

Constitution/Regulatory Authority

The relationship between the members and the civil government with whom the organization is registered as a charity is described in its *constitution*. In the UK this document is called the Memorandum of Association, the first of two documents, commonly referred to as "Mems and Arts."

This document lists the founding members, states the purpose of the organization and its "place of business." In this relationship, the civil government, or as it's better known, the *regulatory authority*, isn't concerned whether the organization feeds the homeless, supports the disabled, or seeks a cure for disease.

What it is concerned about is that the organization does what it says it does and works within the applicable laws and regulations.

Bylaws/Operational Authority

Operational authority is different. Its authority comes from the membership of the organization. People become members, because they care very much about what the organization does. They may not, however, be interested in regulating how that work is accomplished.

The most important thing that members do is elect a board of directors. They delegate to the directors the detail on how to accomplish the vision and mission. This relationship is described in the organization's *bylaws*. In the UK this document is called the Articles of Association, the second of two documents popularly known as "Mems and Arts."

The bylaws give the board its authority to govern the organization as well as control its operations. Bylaws contain statements of authority and limitations to that authority. For example, the members authorize the board to transact its business but then require the board to meet not less than four times per year. They don't want too much time to pass between board meetings—simply because they have delegated so much authority to the board.

Members have the right to limit the board's authority, regardless of whether the board would limit itself in those same ways.

Bylaws also cover some board responsibilities and expectations as well as accountability to the members. These include, for example:

- publishing the financial statements
- having statements audited by an external auditor
- calling a meeting of members following the end of the fiscal year.

The bylaws are intended to describe the relationship between the members of the organization and the board. The confusion comes when the bylaws also try to describe the working relationships within the board. Because the initial set of bylaws is almost always drawn up before the board has met to develop governance policies, much bylaw material often deals with internal board relationships.

Bylaws should be limited to the relationship between the members and the board. However, it usually doesn't work out that way. Some bylaws define who its officers should be and what committees the board should have. That's more than the sole relationship the bylaws are supposed to handle and makes for a cumbersome relationship within the board. We see members making policies that prevent the board from developing and changing the very policies that allow them to govern with excellence.

These internal board relationships should be described in a third document, the board's *governance manual*. They include the:

- board/board chair relationship
- board/board member relationship
- board/committee relationship
- board/committee chair relationship.

The distinction—and it is an important distinction—between the bylaws and a governance manual, lies in the different working relationship that each is designed to describe.

◀

Members have the right to limit the board's authority, regardless of whether the board would limit itself in those same ways.

It becomes even more confusing when the bylaws attempt to deal with yet a third level, the board/CEO relationship. This important relationship should also be described in the governance manual.

Focusing on the working relationships within an organization is the key to understanding what should be in the bylaws and what should be in the governance manual, not in the bylaws.

The Board Is the Trunk of the Tree

The one thing all not-for-profit organizations have in common is a board of directors. It may not always be called that, but in all jurisdictions a not-for-profit organization is required to have a group ultimately accountable for allocating the funding it receives.

Various names are given to boards. These names emphasize aspects of their work:

Board of Directors emphasizes the strategic direction that the board gives to the organization.

Board of Governors places the emphasis on the broad responsibility of setting governing policies to guide all aspects of the organization.

Board of Managers emphasizes the hands-on management role of some boards.

Board of Control emphasizes the ultimate authority that the board has over the entire organization.

Board of Regents emphasizes the status of the board within the community.

Sometimes the board is called a *council*, a term that focuses on the process of deliberation that takes place.

These terms tend to stress one aspect of board work over another. Whatever name your board or council uses will identify only one perspective of your group. It may not be the best name to select. In this book, we default to the term "Board of Directors" because of the strategic emphasis it contains. It is also the most common term used in North America and Europe.

Boards Come in All Shapes and Sizes

There are working boards, advisory boards, managing boards and governing boards. To some extent, the order reflects the age, size and complexity and its position in the life cycle of the organization.

In practice, boards are usually a combination of the types mentioned above, with one type more dominant.

When organizations begin, the workers are often volunteers as the new organization doesn't have sufficient funds to hire staff. Some volunteers also serve on the board. Board members are expected to be directly involved in the work. As the organization matures, board members may still volunteer for fundraising, manage- ment or service delivery, but their volunteer work is no longer a requirement of board membership. Paid staff members carry most of the professional service delivery as board members take on more of an advisory role.

Some of the operational work may continue, particularly in the area of fundraising. This activity is also associated with younger organizations that don't yet have a fund development department. Fundraising, however, unlike the client-focused operations of the organization, can occupy the time and attention of even a more mature board.

The Charismatic Founder

Very frequently, organizations are "founded" by a gifted, experienced and charismatic individual. S/he recruited the first board among like-minded friends and associates. This is usually done for regulatory reasons and because the founder wants and needs support and advice.

Few founders recruit board members for the purpose of governing. Founding board members know this intuitively. They are willing to become board members largely because of their confidence in the founder and the values they share. They are fully aware that they are in no position to "direct" the founder, whose experience and charismatic presence they admire.

Enter the Cheerleading Board

Confessions of a Founder

I knew that the idea I had been developing for years would meet a great need among people. I believed that the hard work of founding a new organization would pay rich dividends in the lives of people. So I founded one.

The first thing I did was recruit my board of directors. Looking back now, I realize I didn't know what a board was supposed to do, but I did know that you can't start a not-for-profit without one. Besides, I had some close friends whom I knew I could count on for support. We started with a board of seven people.

They were wonderful. They were there for me to bounce off my ideas, and they really believed in the vision that I shared with them. They were everything I needed at the time to bring my ideas into reality.

Now 20 years have gone by. My personal vision has been realized. The organization is successful and still growing. But there is a gnawing problem.

Everything still depends on me! And I'm thinking about moving on. I want to make a major change in my life. Besides—and this is most important—I want the organization to survive my departure. Well, not just survive. I mean flourish.

My board—all different people now—is no less supportive than they have always been. Unfortunately for me, however, they are in no better position to take the organization forward without me. I was hoping that the board, like a flywheel, would be able to carry the momentum of change. I thought they would be able to take on the load of strategic planning, of searching for and selecting the perfect successor and to take the organization into the future without me.

But they are still cheerleaders. They are definitely not a mature, governing board. Where did I go wrong? What should I have done? What can I do now in order to position the organization for my departure?

The "confession" on the previous page describes a scenario that is far more common than we might imagine. Most organizations were started by an individual with a good idea. In this oft-repeated example, the board never did make the transition from being an advisory board to a governing board. What goes wrong? What is the right way?

Sadly, many boards that do make a transition make the wrong one. They go from advice to management. This usually happens when the organization meets a crisis that the founder can't handle alone. It may be anything from a financial crisis to the sudden loss or departure of the founder.

Managing or Governing. What's the Difference?

▶

A governing board is a board that controls the organization by policies rather than a steady stream of management decisions.

A *governing board* is a board that controls the organization by policies rather than a steady stream of management decisions. Governance involves:

• designing board structure and process
• directing strategic priorities
• delegating authority and responsibility
• monitoring performance and measuring results.

Compare the following boards for a restaurant.

A *managing board* would:
• spend most of the time in the kitchen stirring the stew and discussing ways to make it taste better
• have a host of great ideas for the cook.

A *governing board* would:
• hire a chef to do the cooking
• spend most of its time:
  - talking to customers about their needs and wants
  - planning the future of its restaurant
  - giving direction about its clientele and their needs (but not management advice) to the chef
• improve its service by talking to the customers, not by board members tasting the stew themselves.

Governance Is Like Parenting

As I said in the very first chapter, governance is more like parenting than managing. Good parents who give as much freedom to their children as they can handle, but always with clear limits, and always with expectations, will see them thrive.

Parents who "manage" their children's activity will have children who under-perform without ever learning and growing from their mistakes.

Governance is a more effective method of control than management for larger and more complex organizations. A governing board delegates as much authority to the CEO as possible. That authority, with limitations, is directed to specific strategic goals and thus, accompanied by specific expectations. Where the board is more involved in day-to-day management issues, I suggest that such organizations cannot grow beyond their present size. That's because volunteer board members can no longer manage the operation as a group.

It's normal for newer, smaller organizations to have managing boards, particularly before they are large enough to hire a chief executive officer. However, every managing board should seek to move towards governance as the organization grows and becomes more complex.

Sadly, the managing board remains the most common type of board today. Even boards that have adopted a governance model complete with manual, often drift back into managing. Becoming an effective governing board requires a paradigm shift. The best way I know to describe that shift is *"Think parenting, not managing."*

Governance Has Advantages

Change can be painful. The gain *from* change must be greater than the pain *of* change, or there will be insufficient motivation to make the transition from managing to governing.

Here are some of the advantages of governance:

1. The board is able to measure the past, monitor the present and focus on the future.

2. The board leaves day-to-day tactical (hands-on) issues to the CEO and can focus on strategic direction for tomorrow. (A managing board spends most of its time on financial and operational management issues, evaluating the tactical decisions of the CEO and staff and making decisions where necessary.)

3. Governance empowers the CEO to:

   • plan the tactical programs to deliver the strategic services
   • create the management structure
   • hire and develop staff
   • manage the finances and operations, etc.

4. Governance allows a board to accumulate wisdom. It records and refines the policies that result in sound decisions. In this way, every board can build upon and enhance the past instead of reinventing the wheel in the present.

5. Governance allows board members greater personal fulfillment knowing that governance isn't merely duplicating what would be done anyway. Rather, the board is providing a dimension to the organization only a board can add.

Let's Do It

Installing the Relationship Model™ in your organization means establishing the relationship that should exist between the board and the CEO. It also means defining the relationships that should exist within the board.

These are the very relationships that usually go undefined in organizations. Boards and CEOs make assumptions about what these relationships should be. Seldom do their assumptions meet the present needs of governance, let alone the future of the organization.

The Relationship Model™ defines and establishes these relationships in such a way that the authority of each position and the expectations of responsibility are clear and agreed upon by all parties. This provides the structure for the relationships.

In other policies, the key processes must also be defined and used within these relationships:

- strategic and tactical planning
- delegating authority and responsibility
- monitoring and measuring (accountability).

Summary

All not-for-profit organizations have a board of some type and description. Those boards have a variety of primary functions, including working, advising, managing and governing.

As an organization matures, it become increasingly important to focus on governance as a means of controlling the entire organization by policy, instead of managing or shadow-managing the organization.

The Relationship Model™ provides a systematic way of defining the internal board relationships and the key relationship between the board and the CEO.

In the next chapter, we shall explore the competencies that members of a governing board require for successful governance.

Notes

Competencies
of Board Members

Who Will Serve On Your Board?

The processes of nominating, electing, orienting, training and evaluating board members are often the processes least likely to get quality attention.

Commonly, boards rush, and sometimes panic to find nominees to fill vacancies on the board. Members are asked to continue, not necessarily because of their effectiveness, but as an act of courtesy or simply to save time finding a replacement.

Nominees are elected because of their availability rather than their competencies.

Orientation may be limited to telling the new board member, "Don't worry, you'll get the hang of it after a few meetings."

Evaluation is often non-existent. Sometimes when a board member or chair behaves or performs poorly, a policy will be adopted to limit terms of office to coincide with the time he or she has already served. If that person is replaced by another who is successful, the policy no longer fits. No one wants a successful person to leave because the policy says it's time. So the policy gets changed once again.

Who Makes the Best Board Member?

In our research, we have identified 20 strengths demonstrated by successful board members in their performance and behaviour. We have sorted these strengths into four clusters:

- achieving competencies
- thinking competencies
- leadership competencies
- personal competencies.

The strengths we discuss "cross over" from one cluster to another because of their interconnectedness. However, it's useful to place them into specific groups.

Achieving Competencies

These generally lie above the water line in our iceberg analogy and are, therefore, possible to improve by training. They are:

- commitment to the organization
- communication
- conflict resolution
- initiative
- objectivity
- process orientation.

Commitment to the Organization

The attachment a person has to the organization when its values, vision and mission are aligned with his/her own

Commitment to the organization is essential in board members. It comes from a clear understanding of the values, vision and mission of the organization. When these are aligned with the beliefs and values of the individual, commitment is at its strongest.

Commitment is expressed in a variety of ways. Personally, an individual may authenticate his/her beliefs and values by consistently living them out. At work, commitment ranges from conscientiously fulfilling board responsibilities to making an all-out effort, even sacrifices when necessary, on behalf of the organization.

No abundance of other competencies will compensate for an individual's lack of commitment to the organization. It is a prerequisite for election to a board.

Communication

Gives and receives information with clarity, attentiveness, understanding and perception

As we have seen throughout this book, communication is a core process, and is a part of every other process. It is not surprising, therefore, that communication is perhaps the key strength required by successful board members.

Communication in its widest sense includes speaking, listening, reading and writing. All are used regularly in the course of board work.

Effective communication is helped or hindered by the atmosphere created between board members. A sense of openness in which people know their opinions are valued, encouraging them to speak out, provides a context for good debate and decision-making and the potential to bring out the best in ideas and creativity.

One of the most important aspects of communication is listening. To listen attentively and without inappropriate interruption is a large part of successful communication. For example, in setting the organization's strategic directions, board members need to understand how others are thinking and feeling in order to set a strategic direction that all stakeholders can own. This requires careful listening, paying attention and asking relevant questions.

A person who cannot listen attentively or interrupts inappropriately, shows not only a lack of empathy but a disinterest in what the speaker has to say and consequently in the speaker personally.

Members need to write and speak with clarity and control, concisely conveying the meaning in a way that captures and holds the recipient's attention and interest.

◄

Commitment to the organization is essential in board members. It comes from a clear understanding of the values, vision and mission of the organization.

Board members who consistently fail to understand the true meaning of a message, either written or spoken, or fail to accurately disseminate information, cannot successfully fulfill their obligations.

It is always helpful if members have an intelligent knowledge of another field, possibly allied to the business.

Conflict Resolution

Ensures conflict is resolved with justice and fairness in order to restore healthy relationships

It is essential to deal with conflict in any relationship—particularly conflict that involves board members, the board chair or the CEO.

Restoring working relationships can only happen when conflict is honestly and openly addressed. Too often conflict is "swept under the carpet," because of lack of know-how about how to resolve it or the mistaken idea that forgiveness is all that is required to mend broken relationships.

For Christians, the biblical teaching of Matthew 18:15 – 17 addresses the process of restoring wholeness to a broken relationship. One way of interpreting this passage is to see it as a three-stage process.

Stage 1: There is a desire to win over the other person through a personal and private *negotiation*. The conflict is successfully resolved when a conclusion is reached that has been agreed to by both parties.

Stage 2: If a successful resolution of the conflict is not reached, *mediation* becomes necessary. An objective third party is drawn in to mediate the dispute. Ideally, the aim is to reach a conclusion that has been agreed to by both parties. The mediator must have no affiliation with either party and must be free to offer support to both.

Stage 3: *Arbitration* follows if mediation is not effective. Arbitration is the least likely to bring about a successful healing of relationships since the "resolution" is a decision made by the arbiter and not by the parties directly involved in the conflict.

In order for reconciliation to occur in the boardroom or elsewhere in the work context, a number of attributes and skills are needed:

- values of honesty, openness, justice and fair play
- a commitment to follow process
- a persistence in seeking resolution without being distracted or deflected

- impartiality and objectivity
- an understanding of the difference between accountability and forgiveness and the importance of both
- listening skills and patience.

To be successful in resolving conflict, the board needs a measure of all these attributes. Resolution, within the context of forgiveness, ensures that hurts and injustices do not fester or lie dormant until a future time. Trust and respect can be rebuilt.

Initiative

Proactively grasps opportunities and ensures that neither issues nor people are forgotten or overlooked

◄

Too often conflict is "swept under the carpet," because of lack of know-how about how to resolve it or the mistaken idea that forgiveness is all that is required to mend broken relationships.

A board member who uses his/her initiative can be an invaluable asset in bringing forward forgotten issues or drawing attention to new ones and ensuring that they are placed on the agenda. This keeps the board focused and alert.

Individuals or splinter groups are prevented from using board meetings to manipulate information or events. A proactive board member can help the board consider new initiatives and ideas originating outside the boardroom, rather than adopting a reactive stance towards them.

Initiative is needed in many other situations, e.g., to challenge any tendency to bypass process or ignore individual contributions. In the "busyness" of fulfilling board responsibilities, particularly when meetings are spaced apart, items that need attention are often overlooked. Issues that arise only once a year are all too easily forgotten.

Initiative is also needed outside board meetings. Board members alert to the mood of others, whether on the board, staff, or the wider group of stakeholders, can confidently use their initiative to speak or act on their behalf when required.

In addition, from time to time, personal (but not confidential) news about individual board members needs to be communicated to the board as a whole. To take the initiative and disseminate such information with sensitivity, takes little effort but can mean a lot to the individual member, especially if participation in the board meeting has been costly for that individual.

Taking the initiative, however, does not mean rushing in before anyone else with an answer for everything. This simply discourages the involvement of others, stifling creativity and motivation. A board member who uses his/her initiative must be sensitive, allowing others the freedom to speak or act first when appropriate.

Taking initiatives and grasping opportunities does not necessarily guarantee success, particularly if motivated by a desire for achievement or independence. However, a board member who uses his/her initiative, particularly when balanced by sensitivity to others and to the working environment, will help the board as a group to grasp opportunities appropriately.

Objectivity

Draws conclusions by impartial evaluation of other perspectives and views without prejudice or bias

The correct way for decisions to be made is to share the best of ideas, debating them and drawing conclusions together. Objectivity allows individuals to be influenced by the quality of new concepts, perspectives and views. Objectivity comes from an ability to assess, analyze and apply information to the issue under discussion, clearly understanding and using one's values and beliefs as a guide. When board members feel they have contributed freely to making an objective decision, they are more likely to own the decision.

It is important for a board member to maintain a healthy balance between coming to the decision-making table with a mind already made up, and being tossed in different directions because of the influence of others. This lack of objectivity can emanate from a desperate desire to be right or from a blindness caused by personal prejudice or bias. It can happen when members want to be popular and find it easier to make the decision along the lines of least resistance. It can also happen by default when an opinion, made by another member, is presented as though it is factual and therefore goes unchallenged.

If board members cannot apply objective reasoning to an issue, there is a danger of either abdicating responsibility or alternatively, demanding obedience to a course of action or policy that may be flawed.

◄

A board member who uses his/her initiative must be sensitive, allowing others the freedom to speak or act first when appropriate.

Whenever objectivity is abandoned in the boardroom, individually or corporately, it is likely to lead to faulty decision-making. The consequences can be significant.

Process Orientation

Makes decisions and seeks outcomes by consistent application of a logical sequence of agreed steps

As "objectivity" (above) says, the best decisions come from a consensus based on information, discussion and debate. This is achieved by following a process incorporating an agreed, logical sequence of steps.

Involvement of all members takes time. Problems can arise when a proactive or achievement-oriented chair finds it difficult to stick to the process. Beware the board whose decisions are made by a few members in the car on the way to the board meeting! A predetermined decision only requiring a "rubber stamp" is likely to overlook important information, leading to frustration and a devaluation of other board members.

◄

When board members feel they have contributed freely to making an objective decision, they are more likely to own the decision.

A commitment to "doing the right thing" through careful process rather than pushing through the ideas of a few or seeking quick solutions, prevents mistakes and thoughtlessly hurting others. Following all the agreed decision-making steps takes longer initially but ensures an outcome in which everyone has participated. Decisions are more likely to be consistent, fair and transparent with full ownership and commitment from board members.

Ideally, the wisdom that an organization accumulates through the years is captured in written policies and processes. Then decisions are not dependent on the whim of a few individual board members who happen to be present on a particular day. Commitment to written process ensures that decisions are based on the wisdom gained through the years and avoids having the board reinvent the wheel.

Board processes that require consistent and logical attention include strategic planning, delegation, decision-making, monitoring, measuring results and conflict resolution.

A successful board chair will be particularly strong in this competency. Indeed, as we shall discuss in the next chapter, the chair will demonstrate a commitment to process, not merely an orientation to process.

Thinking Competencies

Often below the surface, there is a limit to how much thinking competencies can be changed by training. They reflect a person's cognitive ability. They include:

- conceptual thinking
- effective judgment
- independent thinking
- logical thinking.

Conceptual Thinking

Makes connections between apparently separate issues, seeing patterns, trends or relationships and developing mental frameworks to explain and interpret information

Strategic thinking is conceptual thinking applied to the future. Because they set the strategic plans of the organization, board members must have the ability to think conceptually. They need to see the work of the organization as a whole, building mental jigsaws with pieces of information, which develop into a larger picture. Equally, they need the ability to take that larger picture and break it down into its components.

Up-to-date information, provided by stakeholders, has to be interpreted so that the organization can be seen in a wider setting. Trends and patterns that affect the work must be understood in order to draw a mental image of the organization in a future context. From this image, realistic long-term organizational strategies can be developed.

As with all board processes, listening to the contributions of stakeholders is led by the board chair. However, board members also need to be alert to other, widely-held views and to the potential consequences of a range of options. Individual perspectives of board members and stakeholders can then be integrated and drawn into a cohesive picture.

The resultant strategy can then be communicated through the organization in order to provide a clear sense of direction and help staff focus on where the organization is going.

Effective Judgment

Applies common sense, measured reasoning, knowledge and experience to come to a conclusion

Effective judgment is an amalgamation of a number of abilities. In the course of board duties, members are required to accurately weigh a range of information and to make choices between a number of options.

The choice may be simply rejecting the bad and choosing the good. It may also involve making a judgment between options that either all possess some merit or options that all possess some flaws. This ability to judge between the good and the best, or between the lesser of a number of flawed options, is what characterizes effective judgment. This differs from ambiguity tolerance, where no choice has to be made or conclusion reached.

◄

Strategic thinking is conceptual thinking applied to the future.

Effective judgment requires an ability to gather and analyze information and apply reasoning and experience. Effective judgment recognizes facts that are inconsistent with the values or policies of the organization.

Staff and other stakeholders want a board they can rely on —one that consistently makes trustworthy, sensible decisions. Trust in the judgment of the board grows as the track record of effective decision-making increases.

Independent Thinking

Maintains own convictions despite undue influence, opposition or threat

It is important that board members be free of the constraints and influence of others, able to exercise sufficient authority to carry out the responsibilities of board membership.

Board members should not be susceptible to undue influence or lobbying, either inside or outside the boardroom. There should be no sense of obligation to represent the views of another individual or subgroup, or a need to return to a person or group for instruction or permission to speak or act in a particular way.

A board member should be free to think, act and vote according to his/her conviction, based on a clear understanding of the information presented at the board discussion. The ability to think independently is essential in resisting power plays by individuals or subgroups. Independent thinking will help stop those who seek to wield power and influence by coercing individual members too weak to resist either real or imagined threats.

Board members sometimes agree with previous board speakers simply because they have either not understood, not listened attentively to the debate or do not want to appear ignorant of previously discussed issues. A multilingual board, where first languages differ between members, is particularly susceptible to this problem. Rather than simply voting with the majority, an independent thinker will not be afraid to ask for a point to be repeated in order to get clarification.

A board of independent thinkers is able to take a stand on critical issues and is willing to bring difficulties to the surface rather than covering them up. The independent thinker sees the benefit of putting issues on the table for open debate, even if other board members would rather ignore the issue.

There is a fine line between independent thinking and stubbornness. When a person is able to explain the reasoning and logic behind a particular point of view, s/he has probably come to a conclusion independently. Inability to explain the reason or the logic behind a conclusion is likely to be the result of stubbornness.

Logical Thinking

Breaks issues down into their constituent parts and predicts cause and effect in a sequence of steps

Logical thinking stands alone, but it also plays a part in some other competencies, such as conceptual thinking. Board members who lack the ability to think logically can take board discussion down irrelevant paths that have little bearing on the subject under discussion. Such "red herrings" prevent outcomes from being reached, create frustration in other members and waste time and other resources.

Logical thought, on the other hand, enables a person to follow a step-by-step discussion where one thought leads inevitably to another in a natural sequence. Every fact, or cause, leads naturally to an effect. This enables boards to reach conclusions and make decisions.

Logical thinking is associated with the ability to think independently rather than being distracted by the inputs of others. It enables a board member to assimilate relevant information and, through a logical sequence of steps, reach his/her own conclusions.

◄
Board members should not be susceptible to undue influence or lobbying, either inside or outside the boardroom.

Leadership Competencies

Often below the surface, these may be improved through increased knowledge and experience. These competencies influence others. They are affected by a person's attitudes and self-image. They are:

- accountability
- interdependence
- stewardship.

Accountability

Welcomes giving and receiving objective evaluation of working relationships and performance of self and others

The board is the source of authority for the CEO. Authority flows through him/her throughout the organization to all staff members.

Lack of accountability is arguably the most significant problem in Christian organizations. It is present in many, if not all, problems. An accountability mechanism is required in every interface between source and recipient of authority, in order to review the working relationship and the consequent performance. Yet, despite the board's responsibility in governing the whole organization, accountability of board members themselves is rare.

Accountability is frequently misunderstood and interpreted in a negative way conveying the idea of punishment and discipline. When a person hasn't 'come up to scratch,' aren't Christians taught to forgive? Where then is the place for accountability?" It is this kind of thinking that causes Christians to shy away from accountability.

Sometimes board members mistakenly assume that as the group with the greatest authority and control, the board has no need to be held accountable. The board, it may be thought, is answerable to no one. The reality is, that the greater the authority, the greater the opportunity for abuse of power and, therefore, the greater the need for accountability. With little training available for board membership or board office, the importance of giving and receiving feedback on performance becomes even more important.

Informal interaction between board members occurs regularly at board meetings, giving some opportunity for issues to be addressed. However, despite any practical difficulties, a formal mechanism of accountability should also be in place. This provides opportunity for excellence to be commended, problems to be addressed and working relationships clarified and strengthened. Such a regular, formal accountability review, particularly for those holding board office, is essential and should occur at least once during each term. Board members with the relevant competencies need to be appointed to conduct such reviews.

Accountability is not simply an opportunity to be nice to each other. It is an inherent requirement in confronting difficult issues. When fulfilled in a spirit of affirmation, accountability is a gift, returning the individual to balance, preventing conflicts and misunderstandings, and building positive relationships.

A sense of accountability is essential in order to sensitively and appropriately accept feedback, as well as to hold others accountable.

Interdependence

Works effectively with others, demonstrating commitment to the group decision or activity

In conducting its business, a board needs to work in harmony, collaborating and cooperating as a united whole. Interdependence enables a board to act as one, overcoming any tendency to follow a subgroup or the personal agenda of a dominating individual.

Interdependence does not smother independent thinking or imply a mindless following of the crowd. It means being committed to finding a decision that the whole group produces and owns. Genuine disagreements may still occur even when a board works together in a spirit of interdependence. It does however foster the objective of reaching consensus.

Interdependence builds group identity, commitment and trust among board members who cooperate and participate in reaching outcomes together. They are not motivated by self-interest but share power in order to reach common goals.

Boards with members who are interdependent develop a bond, guarding and promoting their reputation. Interdependence usually increases harmony in the boardroom. Members show greater support for each other and are better able to handle any conflicts that arise.

Stewardship

Makes the best use of resources while striving for high standards and a balance between effectiveness and efficiency

This competency enables a board to balance effectiveness with efficiency, quality with quantity, thereby making the best use of available resources.

The board of a not-for-profit organization is accountable to the relevant regulatory body and to the organizational membership for the way resources are used. When income is limited, particular wisdom is needed to decide which resources can be used with the greatest efficiency and effectiveness.

Upbringing and family circumstances contribute significantly to a board member's attitude towards the use of resources. Board members who are perceived as wasting resources, particularly financial ones, need to be reminded and challenged by other members to exercise stewardship.

Waste at board level sets a pattern that staff may find easy to copy. A board that promotes a healthy regard for efficiency and effectiveness while supporting the highest standards of operation, encourages stewardship throughout the organization.

Personal Competencies

These mostly lie well below the surface and are therefore hard to change by training. Although all competencies are personal, these particularly reflect individual attitudes, traits, motives and self-image. They are:

- ambiguity tolerance
- empathy
- open-mindedness
- personal integrity
- self-awareness
- self-esteem
- transparency.

Ambiguity Tolerance

Operates effectively when issues are unresolved or inconclusive and is willing to take a measured risk even when the outcomes are uncertain

The ability to accept opposing views and conflicting variables allows a person to live comfortably with ambiguity and avoid taking a black and white position in a complex, decision-making situation.

Lack of tolerance to ambiguity can be both unnecessary and disruptive since group thinking almost always includes a range of varying conclusions reflecting a number of different perspectives. A conclusion cannot reflect the perspective of every member of the board. Even with the best information, outcomes cannot be assumed.

A board member needs to maintain a balance between two extremes—over-caution and recklessness—being willing to listen to all views and then to make a considered decision despite any uncertainty or gaps in knowledge.

Empathy

Shows awareness and appreciation of the feelings, concerns and needs of others

This competency is like an emotional radar—sensing and responding to what others feel—without them having to say so. There is inherent understanding, though not necessarily agreement, with the issues or concerns that lie behind the feelings.

▶

Therefore to show empathy, a board member must first recognize and manage his/her own emotions.

Empathy builds on a foundation of self-awareness and self-control. Therefore, to show empathy, a board member must first recognize and manage his/her own emotions.

Empathy towards others picks up signals through tones of voice, facial expressions and other body language. There are some people who appear emotionally "brain dead," socially gauche and hopelessly out of touch with the moods of those around them. They are always misinterpreting or misunderstanding the feelings of other people, appearing insensitive, blunt or indifferent.

Experiments show that psychological "mirroring" happens between individuals, particularly observable in facial expressions. Board members, who continually see a smiling chair with a positive attitude, are likely to mirror what they see. Conversely, a dour, unresponsive and preoccupied chair is likely to evoke a similar response in members.

In hierarchical organizations, power and empathy often appear in inverse proportion. Empathy is likely to decrease as power increases. In organizations that are flatter and where power is more evenly distributed, this is not such a problem.

As those with the largest circle of authority, boards are particularly vulnerable to showing poor empathy. Wherever power is concentrated, especially an imbalance in the distribution of that power, abuse can result. The inequality between those with power and those without can sometimes be used as a form of direct or indirect manipulation.

Empathy towards others recognizes and appreciates diversity. It shows appreciation for differing value systems, experiences, gender, status, and backgrounds.

Board members who demonstrate empathy are sensitive to the thoughts, concerns and feelings of those both in the boardroom and outside it. In acknowledging the validity and worth of the contribution of others, they are more likely to generate fulfillment and productivity in the organization.

Open-mindedness

Maintains an open and flexible mind towards new information, thoughts and ideas, welcoming the opportunity to grow in knowledge and understanding

At a time when the world's knowledge doubles in months, a board that stops learning is very quickly left behind, especially when it operates at a distance from the everyday business of the organization.

Board members may be highly skilled in their own areas of excellence, but need humility and realism about the limits of their knowledge and experience in other areas of the business. Acknowledging and being willing to learn from the skills of others is important in order to better understand the full dimensions of the business.

Board members need to understand and appreciate change, both that generated from within the organization and/or that imposed from outside. This allows them to evaluate the strategic impact of such change and avoid switching erratically from one direction to another.

An open mind has to be anchored in effective judgment in order to distinguish between information that is relevant to the issue under discussion, and that which is not. Open-mindedness, therefore, does not imply constant change from one point of view to another.

Open-mindedness leads to personal growth through an increase in knowledge and sets an example to the rest of the organization. Open-mindedness in a board, particularly when accompanied by humility, creates a culture ripe for the birth of new ideas and concepts. People are not afraid to share thoughts and insights. This leads to a creative and flexible organization that continually grows through increased understanding and knowledge.

Personal Integrity

Is trustworthy and conscientious and can be relied on to act and speak with consistency and honesty

Board members need to be seen as truthful, consistent, honest and reliable and fulfilling their board duties ethically. Such behaviour comes from a clear understanding of personal beliefs, values and principles. Actions are consistent with what the board believes and thinks so members can afford to be open.

Integrity leads to credibility. Board members are "real," credible and authentic rather than appearing distant and unapproachable. Mixed with a sense of confidence, there is an ability to admit to being "human" and to having faults and failings. Rather than undermining credibility, this vulnerability adds to it.

▶

Integrity leads to credibility.

Individuals with high levels of personal integrity are likely to be conscientious and disciplined. They want meetings to start on time, have the relevant documents beforehand and be well prepared. Potential conflicts of interest are declared so that relevant board members forgo the opportunity to participate in certain discussions. Declaration of expenses is consistently accurate and fair.

◀

Open-minded-ness in a board, particularly when accompa-nied by humility, creates a culture ripe for the birth of new ideas and concepts.

It is important that integrity be balanced with empathy; otherwise, board members are likely to demand too high a price from others. If the standard they require of themselves is not reached by others, they can become judgmental and critical.

There is an increasing erosion of personal integrity and ethical behaviour in public and corporate life as well as in the boardroom. Such levels of integrity and behaviour can no longer be assumed in organizations, even Christian ones. "Everyone" appears "to be doing it" and the line between right and wrong is increasingly blurred.

Great trust is placed in board members and the highest expectations are demanded. As a result, stakeholders and the public at large are increasingly unwilling to tolerate what they perceive as a lack of personal integrity or unethical actions. Holding a position of status and power in an organization is no longer a protection against unethical practice. Being well-known no longer prevents the organization being dragged down or an issue becoming public knowledge.

Self-awareness

Accurately assesses own strengths and weaknesses and can manage them successfully

Increasing self-awareness is characteristic of increased maturity. The more self-aware a board member, the more accurately he/she assesses personal capabilities and inner resources, e.g., values, faith, personality traits, gifts, motives and emotional responses.

Knowing one's strengths also gives valuable insight into one's weaknesses. Board members who are self-aware, know their personal value system and the feelings, thoughts and actions that arise as a result. They learn to recognize which emotions they are feeling and why. They manage their negative emotions rather than expressing them destructively. This provides a personal "shock absorber," allowing members to remain composed and balanced in a crisis while keeping emotions in check.

Board members with good self-awareness know when they have reached the limits of their knowledge, strength or abilities. Those who recognize the strengths of others while acknowledging their own inadequacy, create learning opportunities for the whole board. They also increase motivation by giving a gift of affirmation to the member whose knowledge or ability has been recognized.

Self-awareness, especially when enhanced by a positive self-image, enables a person to celebrate his/her strengths and to depend on others without being threatened by their strengths.

Self-esteem

Respects and likes him/herself, confident in his/her self-worth and capabilities

Self-esteem is foundational to healthy relationships. When God commands us to love others as we love ourselves, it really does mean to love ourselves.

Either a lack of self-esteem or an overwhelming abundance of it can cripple an otherwise capable board member. There is little point in possessing talents if he/she doesn't believe it! On the other hand, self-esteem can be ruined by having too much self-confidence not matched by the level of talent! The person simply appears arrogant.

The right amount of self-esteem is attractive. Believing in yourself somehow encourages others to believe in you too. Board members with self-esteem tend not to take themselves too seriously and usually have a good sense of humour.

There is a close link between self-awareness and self-esteem, although people may not possess them in equal amounts. People with good self-esteem often have good self-awareness, knowing and accepting their abilities and limitations. However, a person may be self-aware with an accurate understanding of his/her strengths and weaknesses and yet not possess good self-esteem.

▶

Board members who believe in themselves are more likely to grasp opportunities and be motivated to succeed.

Board members who believe in themselves are more likely to grasp opportunities and be motivated to succeed. Conversely, a lack of self-esteem may cause members to hold back, fail to express good thoughts and ideas, shy away from tasks and suffer from chronic indecision.

Poor self-esteem can hide in many guises, such as an apparent overconfidence or inability to accept any form of criticism. It can be at its most destructive when associated with a desire to control or wield power. Since a board has the greatest circle of authority in the organization, it is particularly vulnerable to this kind of abuse.

It is unlikely that a person will be appointed to a board position if he/she is significantly lacking in self-esteem.

Transparency

Has no hidden agendas but is open with information while respecting the privacy of individuals

Concern for transparency rests on a foundation of personal integrity. The one is unlikely to exist without the other. Confidentiality must not be confused with secrecy. These were discussed previously in Chapter 5. Because of their importance, we repeat the main points here.

For some reason, Christian organizations are particularly prone to getting transparency wrong. There is either an overuse of confidentiality verging on secrecy or, alternatively, personal information that should be kept confidential, is shared around freely under the guise of prayer information!

Boards are party to much information that may be confidential. Generally, information that is about or affects the organization (not an individual) is information that someone requires and needs to be passed on. However, it is the timing of the dissemination of the information that is often critical. It may be entirely appropriate for information to remain confidential until some time in the future.

There is an ordered sequence that must be followed in disseminating information outside the boardroom so that communication happens at the appropriate time and in the appropriate way. Consideration must always be given to the impact the information might have on others. Much information discussed at board meetings could hurt or confuse others unless the information is supported by additional facts.

Motivation is probably the key to distinguishing between confidentiality and secrecy. Withholding information, motivated by a desire to protect another person, is keeping information confidential. Deliberately withholding information, motivated by a desire to keep someone "in the dark" in order to gain an advantage or to achieve a particular outcome, is secrecy. Although making a judgment about another person's motive is almost impossible, assessing one's own personal motive is certainly worthy of consideration.

Information is power and the effects of withholding it can be as significant as releasing it. Individual board members who handle quantities of information need to develop a sense of transparency and openness about the information they hold and question their motives in order to be sure they are not withholding anything for false reasons either of confidentiality or secrecy.

Should Board Members Have Professional Skills?

One of the common beliefs about selecting board members is that particular knowledge should be represented, usually by specific professions. Often a person with financial acumen in accounting, banking or investment is sought. Another profession sought after by some boards is law. Depending on the specific nature of the organization, boards may also seek other professionals, e.g., physician, educator, social worker, administrator, clergy or other.

◄

Motivation is probably the key to distinguishing between confidentiality and secrecy.

How important are these skills to building a healthy board? Our research tells us that the competencies listed distinguish successful board members. Each one should consistently, or at least frequently, demonstrate the competency.

You will notice that neither financial acumen nor law is on the list. Does this mean that boards don't need members who understand finance or law? By no means! Clearly, every board must have the ability to govern the financial health of the organization with complete reliability and credibility. This means that someone must be able to read income and expense statements and balance sheets in order to monitor the organization's financial condition. Someone must also know when organizational law is contravened. Someone must be able to ask the right questions. But financial acumen or legal knowledge are generally skills, acquired and practiced within a profession. They show a level of competence, not an inherent competency.

►

Financial or legal understanding is a skill required on the board, but not necessarily by every member.

So, unlike "personal integrity," a competency required by every board member for successful governance, financial or legal understanding is a skill required on the board, but not necessarily by every member.

Of course, the more members with such understanding, the better. Although organizations are required by law to have their financial statements audited by an accounting firm or a financially trained professional, this should not excuse a board from undertaking its own transparent financial health check.

The same may also be true of other professions listed above or others not mentioned.

Having certain professionally trained disciplines, such as finance, represented on the board, has its own inherent problem. The entire board might defer to the judgment of the professional, whether he or she is a physician, member of the clergy or lawyer. Yet that is only one judgment and may not reflect the values of other board members.

One person's values on matters, such as medical ethics, theology or legal issues, could determine the position or action of an entire organization. It would be wiser to ask the specialist to give the board an opinion as to when the board should seek outside advice on those matters. For example, the lawyer may be able to advise the board when it should seek legal advice from a specialist in the area of law under discussion. However, the lawyer, who is also a board member, should never be asked or allowed to act as the board's attorney in any matter.

Having a professional on a board should never be simply to save money. It should be done to increase the quality of governance.

Summary

There are many competencies that enhance a board member's ability to govern with success. This chapter lists 20 strengths under the headings of achieving, thinking, leadership and personal competencies. Every board member should be able to demonstrate these competencies at least frequently, if not consistently.

There are specific skills, e.g., law, medicine, theology, related to the organization's services that need not be represented in every board member. Even when a board member does agree to serve because of a specialized skill, that contribution should not be automatically taken as either a board position or board decision. Rather, the specialist can advise the board when it should be seeking expert input from outside the organization.

In the next chapter, we will begin to explore the structure of the board generally and the internal board relationships specifically.

Notes

Designing
the Tree Trunk
(Governance Structure)

In this chapter we will examine the structure of the governing board using the Relationship Model™. Our focus will be on the relationships involved in a governing board including those between:

- the board and the members of the organization
- the board chair and the board
- the committees and the board
- the individual board member and the board.

We will discuss structure in terms of authority, responsibility and accountability as they apply to each relationship. And we will emphasize the importance of supporting the structure with the core values evident in healthy relationships.

In almost all not-for-profit organizations, the board receives its authority to govern from the members of the organization.

The Board/Members Relationship

In almost all not-for-profit organizations, the board receives its authority to govern from the members of the organization. This theoretical principle may be expressed in different ways.

Where Board Members Are the Only Members

Since most organizations start small, the board members may be the only members of the organization. You may perhaps have attended an annual general meeting (AGM) where the only members present were board members. The AGM is a brief perfunctory meeting in which board members re-elect themselves by acclamation.

Unfortunately, in some organizations this structure perpetuates itself for years. There are several reasons for this.

- Board members won't risk building up membership, because they might lose control of how board members are chosen and, therefore, who will represent them.
- No attention is given to the need for a larger membership.
- Little connection is made between support from donors and the control or the organization those same donors should have. The board of a growing organization simply doesn't see the value of having a membership beyond the symbolic one required by law.

Where Staff Members Are the Only Members

In a number of large, successful organizations, one must be personally involved in the international work or management of the organization in order to be a voting member. When international staff persons complete their service, they automatically cease to be members of the organization, unless they become part of management at the headquarters.

This arrangement, though probably unintentional, places international staff at a higher level of authority and importance than those who provide them with financial support. This denies donors the opportunity to practice good stewardship by ensuring the best use of those resources.

To make matters worse, it becomes difficult or impossible for voting members to attend board meetings. They are obliged to elect non-members to the board, since they do not have the time, expertise, experience or physical proximity to participate themselves.

The CEO of one such organization labels it a "two-headed monster." That's because an unhealthy tension can develop between the international staff, who are the only voting members, and the board they had to elect in order to govern the services the organization provides—services the very international staff must carry out.

Where All Persons Who Are Committed to the Mission Are Members

A healthy organization will actively seek to increase its membership rather than regard members as simply a legal requirement. The prospective membership list should include donors and other stakeholders. It might also include beneficiaries of the organization's services, such as the parents of children in a not-for-profit daycare facility, or adult children of aging parents in not-for-profit retirement facility.

Good stewardship means that donors:

- should follow their giving to ensure that it achieves the intended results
- must delegate authority and responsibility to a board to use their investment wisely
- should not and can not delegate their accountability to be good stewards.

One major donor once told me that when he gave the money to his chosen organization, he no longer felt responsible for what happened to it. It's great to trust the organization you support. It's far better to have a process in place to ensure that organization's trustworthiness.

The members are the true owners of the not-for-profit organization. They choose a board because logistics make it impossible for them to govern the organization directly. They elect to the board men and women who appear to have the abilities and time to govern the organization on their behalf.

- Members delegate their authority and responsibility through the election process.
- Members do not and can not delegate their accountability.

These family beneficiaries may also have a prime interest in and motivation to serve as board members. Of course, some beneficiaries will be unable to serve on the board due to factors, such as age, mental capacity or distance. Donors, too, may be prime candidates for board membership.

> ▶
> *A healthy organization will actively seek to increase its membership rather than regard members as simply a legal requirement.*

Designing Board Structure

The membership should give the board as much freedom as possible to develop its structure, only including in the bylaws those "rules" that members consider essential. My experience is that the bylaws go into more detail than required, probably because no board governance manual existed when they were written.

For example, including a list of officers in the bylaws and then requiring that each position be filled by election at the annual general meeting, forces the board to:

- adopt a structure that may not be appropriate for its governance
- fill the positions with people who may not have the competencies required.

The bylaws of the organization (or Articles of Association in the UK, the second part of the "Mems and Arts") contain the basic components of the relationship between the membership and the board. The board/membership relationship description that follows forms part of the governance manual, not because its contents don't appear in the bylaws, but because most bylaws include this material in a somewhat random order. Some even miss components, such as limitations of authority and expectations of responsibility.

There is an additional need for this relationship to be formally presented. I refer to the weak accountability process in the relationship between the membership and the board. The only real means of dealing with a board's failure to govern the organization is to elect other members to the board at the next AGM. In the real world, however, the members are not likely to have the information they need to hold a board accountable.

For this reason, the board itself must develop the relationship between the membership and the board by putting in place accountability processes that will ensure the trustworthiness of its governance, regardless of whether or not members themselves require it.

Role of the Board

The role of the board of directors is to direct and control the entire organization through the process of governance. Four types of activity enable the board to accomplish its responsibilities. They are:

The board itself
must develop
the relationship
between the
membership and
the board by
putting in place
accountability
processes that
will ensure the
trustworthiness
of its
governance.

- to design the board's structure and gove processes
- to provide strategic leadership by determining organization's values, services, target groups, vision, mission and priorities as well as other components of the strategic plan
- to delegate management authority and responsibility to the CEO
- to be accountable for strategic results and to ensure that the organization and each individual in it act within the limitations of delegated authority.

The main focus of the board is on strategic planning, the basic question being, "What services shall we deliver to which people in which places and in what order of priority?"

Careful delegation of management authority and responsibility to the CEO allows the board to monitor management rather than manage itself. The board can then spend more time considering the needs of its clients and providing strategic direction to the CEO to meet those needs.

The main focus
of the board is
on strategic
planning, the
basic question
being, "What
services shall
we deliver to
which people in
which places
and in what
order of
priority?"

The following page has an example of the relationship between the board and its sources of authority.

The Board Chair/Board Relationship

The board chair leads the processes of governance:

- to design the structure and the processes
- to plan for the future
- to delegate management to the CEO
- to monitor performance and measure results.

Leadership of the process is essential to the success of the board chair/board relationship. This crucial element of the chair's responsibilities is not commonly practiced.

The ideal relationship between the board chair and the board is like that of an orchestra conductor and the musicians. Each member of the orchestra specializes in

The Board of Directors/Stakeholders Relationship

1. Authority

The ultimate source of all the board's authority is the body of stakeholders. Those stakeholders include primarily the members, donors, clients and strategic partners of the organization and the civil authority, which grants the organization its legal and charitable status.

The board's sources of moral authority are the stakeholders and the appropriate government agencies and departments.

The board's sources of strategic/operational authority are the stakeholders—the members, donors, the strategic partners and the clients.

The board's sources of legal/regulatory authority are the governmental authorities where the organization is registered and where its services are delivered.

2. Limitations of Authority

In exercising its moral authority and its legal and regulatory authority, the board may not violate the civil laws in the countries where it is registered and operates.

In exercising its strategic/operational authority, the board may not violate the bylaws of the organization.

3. Responsibilities

The responsibilities of governance of the board are to:

- design the board's structure and governance processes
- provide strategic leadership by determining the organizations' values, services, target groups, vision, mission and priorities and the other components of the strategic plan
- delegate management authority and responsibility to the CEO
- be accountable for strategic results and to ensure that the organization and each individual in it act within all the limitations of delegated authority.

4. Expectations

The expectations of the board are described in its governance manual, strategic plans, the annual strategic goals of the organization and the annual tactical goals of the board.

In fulfilling its strategic and operational responsibility, the board shall seek and follow the counsel of its stakeholders in its strategic planning process and in its governance of the strategic mission and priorities.

5. Accountabilities

The board is accountable to the stakeholders of the organization and to the civil authorities where it is registered and where it delivers its services.

The board's accountability will be exercised by the submission of required documentation to civil authorities and by clear and true reporting to all of its stakeholders—members, employees and volunteers, donors, strategic partners and clients.

producing a certain sound. The conductor's role is to lead a process of blending those sounds, without personally producing any of the sounds. Together, conductor and musicians bring a beautiful symphony to life.

How can it happen that a group makes a decision that does not reflect the thoughts and opinions of the individuals within it? Here are some common reasons why:

1. One or more members of the board dominate the discussion. They speak more with emotion than reason. People feel intimidated and belittled. The chair either willingly allows it to happen or can't control it.

2. A small group has already made a decision prior to the meeting. They manipulate information in such a way that the board doesn't have the full picture. Pressure is applied to trust those who have already looked into the matter.

> Think back to a board meeting where the discussion of an issue went badly. After the meeting, a typical conversation between you and another board member might follow this format... You mentioned to someone that you didn't agree with the board's decision. Your fellow board member said that she didn't either. She only voted for the motion because there was so much pressure. You agreed with her that it would have taken forever to overcome the passionate arguments in favour of the decision, so you both just gave up. In talking to other members, you realize that the majority of directors disagreed, but the motion passed anyway.

3. The chair has a personal agenda. Instead of relinquishing the chair at the beginning of the specific item, s/he uses his/her position to jockey the decision around to his/her way of thinking. Some board members agree with the chair's position. No one calls the chair on the inappropriate behaviour.

4. The material has been sent out beforehand. However, preparation by board members is so poor that many are embarrassed to speak to the matter, even though they aren't comfortable with the discussion or the decision. They believe that their lack of preparation disqualifies them.

5. The CEO has surprised the board with a new recommendation. Instead of providing alternatives and highlighting their strengths and weaknesses so the board can make an informed choice, the CEO makes a single recommendation. Not having the recommendation ahead of time, the board rubber-stamps the CEO's idea.

6. The shy board member who has deep insights and is always prepared, does not speak up. The chair fails to ensure that all board members contribute to the discussion. The quiet member's insights are never heard.

Process that results in quality decisions is the responsibility of the chair. Almost every time a board makes a decision that most of its members don't personally support, I would say that the chair has failed in his/her responsibility to lead the process effectively.

In my experience it makes little difference whether the chair abuses his/her position or simply lacks the competencies required to be a good chair. I have observed chairs working from an authoritarian value system, abusing the authority of the chair, and from a *laissez-faire* value system, unwilling to use the chair's authority. The result is the same: poor process and flawed decisions.

Choosing the Chair

Not every board member can be an effective chair. Although the competencies required of a board chair are the same as for board members, it is the strength of certain competencies that makes the difference, e.g., a real commitment to process, not just an orientation to it. These two competencies set the chair apart from other board members:

- Process Orientation
- Objectivity

◄
The ideal relationship between the board chair and the board is like that of an orchestra conductor and the musicians.

Although we have just discussed all twenty in the previous chapter, we present these two again here. This time, however, they are addressed specifically to board chairs.

Process Orientation

Boards make the best decisions from a consensus position based on information, discussion and debate. This is achieved only when the chair follows a process of an agreed, logical sequence of steps, taking into consideration the thoughts and perspectives of all board members.

Involving all board members takes time. A proactive or achievement-oriented chair usually finds it difficult to stick faithfully to process. Beware the board whose decisions are made by a few members in the car on the way to the meeting! Coming to the table with a predetermined decision to be rubber-stamped is likely to overlook important information, leading to frustration and the devaluing of other board members.

A board chair needs to be committed to "doing the right thing" rather than pushing through the ideas of a few or seeking quick solutions. In this way, s/he will prevent mistakes and people from being hurt. Following the agreed decision-making steps takes longer initially but ensures the best outcome. Decisions are more likely to be consistent, fair and transparent with ownership and commitment from all board members.

The wisdom that an organization accumulates through the years is captured through a careful process of committing policies and processes to writing. This provides assurance that board decisions are not dependent on the whim of a few members on any particular day. A chair who makes certain that board decision-making is based on a commitment to follow written process, ensures that decisions are based on accumulated wisdom, not by reinventing the wheel.

Objectivity

It is surprisingly easy for a chair, even one with honourable intentions, to influence the outcome of a decision by expressing his/her personal views. The chair is often in closer contact with the CEO than anyone else. S/he may also be perceived to have more information. Because they respect the chair (they were the ones who elected him/her) board members uncertain about the issue, may be influenced by the chair and agree to the position s/he takes.

The chair is the chief servant of the board, not the individual with the most power. In my view, it is unwise for a board chair to cast a vote at all, and very unwise to cast a deciding vote in any but exceptional circumstances. Such a circumstance may be when the board has no choice but to make a decision, even when that decision emanates from a divided board. Normally, it is wiser to let a matter die and to reformulate the motion for later consideration. Groups that proceed on strategic issues with divided commitment are far less likely to succeed. Chairs who "push things through" are weak leaders, not strong servants.

How does a board chair deal with strong personal convictions in a matter of importance to him/her? And how does a chair bring to the table information crucial to a quality decision—information that perhaps only the chair may have?

A board chair may certainly speak for or against an issue. The proper way to do that is to relinquish the chair to the vice-chair or another board member who can lead an objective process. The chair should give up the chair before the agenda item is brought to the table and return only after a decision has been made.

Here is a checklist that a board chair can use to assure good board process:

1. Ensure that the item has been included on the agenda and supported by information in the board preparation materials. Provide these materials to members at least a week before the meeting.

2. Ensure that all board decisions, wherever possible, are based on choices, not recommendations. Governance should be proactive, not reactive.

3. Avoid taking a position on the issue without relinquishing the chair before the agenda item begins. Return to the chair only after the matter is decided.

4. Ensure that the motion is clearly presented in writing and understood by the entire board. Handle any amendments or substitutions in the same manner.

5. Ensure that no individual or group dominates the discussion and that every member is heard.

6. Encourage issue-oriented debate and disallow personal attacks. If necessary, call a recess to cool things down or delay the matter till the next meeting.

7. Attempt to achieve consensus through discussion rather than settle for a simple majority.

Process, Process, Process. It's a beautiful thing when it happens, but it doesn't happen automatically.

Following is the board chair/board relationship description. The vice-chair and committee chairs follow these same principles of leadership.

Board Chair/Board Relationship Description

1. Authority

The board chair receives his/her authority by the election of the board of directors.

The board chair is authorized by the board to provide the leadership of the process of governance

The board shall provide the board chair with the material resources required for that process.

2. Limitations of Authority

In the fulfillment of the responsibilities of this position the board chair may not:

- take any action not authorized by the board of directors
- direct the decision-making process towards any specific outcome
- give management direction to the CEO or his/her staff
- cause the board of directors to be in violation of the limitations of its authority
- prevent any proposal from any director from being considered at the next meeting.

3. Responsibility

The responsibilities of the board chair are to:

- lead the governance process, including the preparation of the agenda, ensuring the flow of relevant governance information to the board of directors and chairing the meetings of the board
- lead the process of designing and maintaining board structure and process
- ensure that the process of strategic leadership is initiated and continued

- lead the process of delegating authority and responsibility to the CEO
- lead the process of board accountability, including an evaluation of the strategic results, the annual review of the performance of the board, the individual directors, the CEO, and a process of evaluation of the board chair
- ensure that all decisions are documented accurately in minutes, policies and other documents
- ensure that the requirements of the board's accountability to civil government and the stakeholders are met
- act as the official spokesperson of the organization to the stakeholders and the public.

4. Expectations

The expectations of this position shall be negotiated in the annual review of the board chair and shall include:

- preparing for and attending every meeting of the board of directors
- flow of all relevant governance information to the directors
- conduct that is consistent with the core values of affirmation, involvement and servant leadership.

5. Accountabilities

Accountability in this relationship is mutual.

The board of directors is accountable to the board chair for:

- providing all the authorization and resources required for the responsibilities
- providing an annual review of the board chair's performance
- negotiating reasonable expectations of the board chair's responsibility
- expressing affirmation, involvement and servant leadership in its relationship with the board chair.

The board chair is accountable to the board of directors for:

- performance with respect to the negotiated expectations
- compliance with the limitations of authority of the position.

Scheduled at predetermined annual intervals, the relationship review shall be lead by two members of the board appointed by the board and may include one additional person who is not a member of the board.

It shall include:

- a review of the authorization and resources provided and values expressed to the board chair
- a review of the board chair's performance towards expectations of the responsibilities of the relationship
- a negotiation of expectations for the next planning period
- a review of the authorization and resources required for the next period, including plans for personal development.

Another very significant feature of the board chair's responsibility is the relationship between the chair and the CEO. This issue is mentioned in the limitations of authority section in the relationship description above. We will deal with CEO/board chair relationship more fully in Chapter 12 in the context of the CEO's authority.

The Committee/Board Relationship

When a board forms a committee, it delegates some of its authority and responsibility to a smaller group. Committees can both help and hinder the governance process. The important issue to understand is just how much authority the board is delegating and for what purpose.

Specialized Committees

The committee structure may be used when the board requires particular skills for policy development or for specialized monitoring or measuring. Specialized committees may include a finance and audit committee, a safety committee and other regulatory committees. We will deal with one example here.

The Finance and Audit Committee

The finance and audit committee is a prime example of a standing committee set up to take on a specialized form of governance on the board's behalf.

The board has an important, even vital role in monitoring the financial planning and financial condition of the organization. This responsibility requires skills that many board members lack. Only a few board members of not-for-profit organizations are able to understand sophisticated financial statements. In some cases there may not even be enough to form a committee. Those who make up the finance and audit committee—from within or outside the board—can provide the vital function of monitoring the finance-related limitations and expectations policies on behalf of the board. While the board is still accountable for the financial health of the organization, it may not be able to exercise that accountability without delegating some of its authority to specialists.

We would suggest that every governing board establish a properly functioning finance and audit committee. Doing so will empower a board to devote more time to governance and will be less likely to be drawn into management.

Here is a relationship description for the finance and audit committee. Appendix B also includes this sample relationship description for the finance and audit committee/board relationship.

Finance and Audit Committee/Board Relationship Description

1. Authority

The finance and audit committee shall be appointed annually by the board of directors and shall function with the authority of the board within its relationship description.

Membership shall consist of not less than three (3) and not more than four (4) of the directors. The committee chair and at least one other member of the committee shall be members of the board of directors.

A quorum shall be three (3) members.

2. Limitations of Authority

Advising the board on matters of finance, the committee may not, without additional authorization by the board:

- manage the day-to-day operations of the organization
- give management direction to the CEO or his/her staff
- monitor management performance not covered in financial limitations policies
- request reports not required for the monitoring of financial limitations policies.

3. Responsibilities

As a committee supporting the board in financial matters, the committee shall:

- review CEO financial limitations and expectations policies and recommend changes to the board of directors
- monitor financial empowerment policies in accordance with the monitoring schedule
- receive action plans from the CEO when financial limitations and expectations policies are violated and report significant violations to the board
- advise the board on matters of financial audit and internal controls
- consider and recommend to the board the appointment of external auditors and their remuneration
- review the external auditors' management letter and management's response.

4. Expectations

The committee shall meet not less than four (4) times per year, not later than sixty (60) days following the end of any quarter of the fiscal year.

Members of the committee are expected to attend all meetings of the committee.

The committee shall provide copies of the financial limitations policy monitoring reports to each director in a timely manner.

5. Accountabilities

The committee shall report the following to the board of directors in writing at the first board meeting of the year:

- dates of meetings and committee member attendance
- summary of financial policy recommendations for the year
- summary of monitoring of financial limitations policies.

The board of directors and the committee shall confirm or renegotiate the committee/board relationship annually.

The Nominating Committee

The nominating committee is another example of a committee with a specialized function, one that also requires more time than any governing board could give to the task.

An important feature of this committee is this: a mature, governing board would have one or two of its members participate on a committee that nominates individuals for election to the board. The committee itself, however, would be a committee of members, not of the board. This gives members some control over who will represent them on the board—a very important point. It prevents a board from becoming self-perpetuating and from straying too far from the will of members. On the other hand, board participation ensures that the committee deals realistically with the competencies required for board membership.

Ad Hoc Committees

Unlike a specialized committee which is likely to be a standing committee, an ad hoc committee will exist only while the specialized function is needed. An ad hoc committee, e.g., a building committee, may support the decision-making process and add quality when it does pre-work in bringing *options* for the board to consider. Such options invite more thought and discussion, allowing the board to be proactive instead of reactive, thus increasing the quality, sense of involvement and ownership by board members.

Extraordinary Management

A committee may also be formed to handle a specialized management function that the board decides not to delegate to the CEO, such as managing investments or a major building project.

It is a misunderstanding to think that a governing board will absent itself entirely from management issues. It should decide, however, which issues it will retain and which it will delegate to the CEO. This does not mean that the board has a license to surprise the CEO by taking over an area that has previously been the CEO's responsibility.

Misuse of the Committee Structure

More often than not, committees are established to perform functions that the full board is capable of doing more effectively. Reasons given are "to save time" or "to avoid extra meetings." There are several risks to good governance from this practice. They include:

- disempowering board members not on the committee
- reducing the quality of the final board action
- reducing the sense of board ownership of that action
- abuse of power by a small group within the board.

Executive Committee

The executive committee is probably the most common example of a committee that should not be formed. Such a committee is usually given the board's authority between meetings. This means that the board delegates most of its authority and responsibility to a small group 99% of the time. The board is only a board when in session. Between meetings it relies on an executive committee to convene and make decisions on its behalf.

A board that allows an executive committee to make crucial management decisions between meetings is very likely a board that still controls the organization through management, not governance. A true governing board has policies that allow the CEO to manage between meetings within clearly defined limits of authority, without the need for an executive committee.

When I examine the minutes of executive committees, I usually make the same two observations.

First, *most executive committee actions are management decisions that should be made by the CEO within clear policies.*

◄

It is a misunder-standing to think that a governing board will absent itself entirely from management issues.

Some executive committee decisions are management decisions, made only because no governing policy exists. If the CEO has no policy to guide him/her, the committee has to make a one-time decision.

Management decisions should be left to the CEO. The reason they aren't, is because the board/CEO relationship hasn't been completely developed. In the absence of clear limitations of authority and expectations of responsibility, the executive committee participates in shadow management or "advising" management.

Second, *some of the things that executive committees do should be done by the board as a whole.*

A common responsibility for an executive committee is to do some pre-work in preparation for a board meeting. This function can help or hinder the process. It hinders when it brings in a *recommendation* to which the board is invited to react. Reactive decision-making is likely to reduce the quality of the decision, decreasing the sense of ownership in that decision. Board members, trusting their committee, don't have to think through the pros and cons of various options. They may not contribute their own depth of experience to the process. The result is that they may feel disempowered or even disinterested in the process.

You will find no sample of an executive committee/board relationship in the governance manual attached in the appendix. We recommend against the establishing such a committee and discontinuing executive committees that already exist.

Walter J. Salmon puts it this way in "Crisis Prevention," an article in *Harvard Business Review on Corporate Governance*, "*…executive committees with too much muscle, by encouraging the emergence of two-tier boards, are obstacles rather than aids to better corporate governance. In essence, directors on the executive committee become the 'first tier,' dominating decision-making, while the role of the 'second tier' directors is, like that of the House of Lords, reduced to giving advice and consent.*'"

Many boards of large, complex and widely dispersed organizations function effectively without an executive committee. I think of the executive committee as a vestigial remain of a managing board that thinks, erroneously, that it has made the transition to a governing board.

Advisory Committees

Sometimes committees are formed to mirror the work of the organization. They are designed to monitor management decisions and to maintain a familiarity with the daily issues the organization faces. Such committees are helpful in keeping board members more closely informed on the changing environment in which the organization operates. They may also give the board good information on what factors are critical to the success of the mission and monitor how those are being addressed by management.

Sometimes, however, these committees are given an actual advisory role. Advice from a board member or board committee is as likely to be problematic as helpful for both board and management.

On the one hand, advice from a board source tends to carry more weight, with the implied obligation that the advice be accepted. There may even be recrimination, if the advice is not heeded and something adverse happens.

On the other hand, if the advice is taken, even though management would prefer to ignore it, it is more difficult for a board to exercise objective and fair accountability with management. After all, it was a board committee that advised the action in the first place.

Deciding Which Committees are Appropriate

Here are some questions to guide a board in deciding which committees to establish. If the answers are "yes," the committee will likely be a positive element to the governance process. If "no," the board should not establish the committee.

- Does the committee add value by performing a specialized function that the board cannot fulfill itself?
- Does the committee add value by researching specific issues and bringing options to the board instead of recommendations?
- Does the committee avoid managing, shadow-managing, or pressuring management with "advice"?
- Does the committee add value to the governance process without disempowering non-committee board members or distancing them from the issues?

The best quality of governance normally results from full board involvement! The extra time it takes adds value.

The Committee Chair/Committee Relationship

This relationship is essentially the same as the board chair/board relationship. The chair has the same responsibilities for process and the same or similar limitations of authority. Thus, the primary responsibility is to deliver process of high quality. To ensure that, however, the chair may need the same specialized skills as other committee members. This is particularly true for finance and investment committees, as well as for those involving social services and health care.

The Board Member/Board Relationship Description

1. Authority

The board member is authorized by the members by virtue of his/her election to the board of directors. Once elected the source of authority is the board of directors.

The board of directors shall provide costs of board meetings, including travel and accommodation, directors' liability insurance, board materials and resources for orientation and training.

2. Limitations of Authority

Without specific authority from the board, an individual director may not:

- speak officially on behalf of the board or organization
- enter into any legal or financial agreement on behalf of the organization
- give direction to the CEO or the management of the organization.

3. Responsibility

The responsibility of each director is to:

- participate in the governance process of the board
- share in the responsibilities of the board of directors as defined in its board/membership relationship description
- represent accurately and support the official positions and decisions of the board when interacting with the stakeholders and the public.

4. Expectations

Each director is expected to:

- participate in an orientation program in the Relationship Model™ and the bylaws, governance manual and strategic plan of the organization
- read reports and study materials provided for preparation of board meetings

- attend all board meetings and meeting of committees of which he/she is a member or to indicate to the board or committee chair the reason for his/her inability to attend
- participate actively in discussion and the decision-making process
- display personal conduct that reflects the values of the organization.

5. Accountabilities

Accountability in this relationship is mutual.

The board is accountable to the director for providing the authorization, resources, affirmation, involvement and servant leadership required for the successful realization of the responsibilities of the position.

Each director shares in the board's accountability to the stakeholders for achieving strategic results, and in governing the organization with due diligence and integrity and in its accountability to civil governments for compliance with all relevant laws and regulations.

Each director is accountable to the board and to the civil government's regulatory body under whose laws the organization is registered, for handling the finances of the organization with integrity.

The director is accountable to the board for performance with respect to the negotiated expectations and for compliance with the limitations of authority of the position.

The components of this working relationship shall be reviewed at predetermined intervals at the initiation of the board and shall include:

- a review of the authorization and resources provided and values expressed to the director
- a review of the director's performance towards expectations of the responsibilities of the relationship
- a negotiation of expectations for the next planning period
- a review of the authorization and resources required for the next period, including plans for personal development.

The Board Member/Board Relationship

The primary role of the individual board member is to participate in the process of governance. Members study information and decision-making materials, are involved in discussion and debate, and share in the decision-making process of consensus building and voting.

Individual board members have no authority or responsibility to act on behalf of the organization as individuals except by specific delegation from the board. Yet, as a member of the board, each shares to a major degree the authority and responsibility for the health of the relationships within the organization, its members, clients and other stakeholders.

Because of the importance of developing a strong board, we devoted all of Chapter 8 to the competencies required by successful board members. Based on these competencies we have included a sample relationship description for the board member/board relationship on the previous two pages.

Did We Forget the Treasurer?

No, we didn't overlook this traditional board position.

The planning and management of financial resources are management processes. Mature governing boards realize that a volunteer treasurer cannot be held accountable for the management of millions of dollars actually managed by others. The position is symbolic. The treasurer may submit a report or a budget, but the presentation is only a polite gesture to an obsolete position. Why does the position continue? Because the bylaws would have to be changed in order to eliminate it.

Perhaps in new, small organizations without paid staff, a treasurer can manage the finances on behalf of the board. Once that board hires its first employee, the treasurer should consider him/herself a volunteer staff person in addition to being a member of the governing board.

This is not to say that the board should not be involved in the finances of the organization. By no means. Planning and monitoring of the organization's financial condition is a matter for the entire board to deal with through governance.

If the entire board does not fulfill this role, it will delegate it to a finance and audit committee of specialists, not to an individual treasurer.

Summary

In this chapter we identified and defined the four primary relationships within the board:

- the board and the members of the organization
- the board chair and the board
- the committees and the board
- the individual board member and the board.

The other very important relationship involving the board is the one with the CEO. The board/CEO relationship is discussed in Chapter 12.

By defining the five components for each of these relationships, the board can design a structure for its governance in which the entire board, the board chair, the committees and individual board members will know the limitations of their authority and the expectations of their responsibility.

With this structure in place, we move to the four processes of board responsibility in the next four chapters.

Designing
Governance
Processes

Chapters 10 – 13 deal with the responsibilities of the board. As you will see from the following graphic, four quadrants make up the circle of responsibility of every governing board. For each quadrant a governing board needs to formulate policies to:

- design the structure and process of governance
- define the elements of the strategic plan: values, services, target groups, places, vision, mission, priorities, strategic goals and critical success factors
- delegate authority and responsibility to the CEO
- deal with monitoring of board and CEO processes and measuring the strategic results.

We will devote an entire chapter to each of these four processes. The basic principle of governance is that structures and processes are documented in the form of governance policies so that everyone in the organization will be able to work within a predetermined framework.

Circle of Responsibility
The governing board has FOUR responsibilities

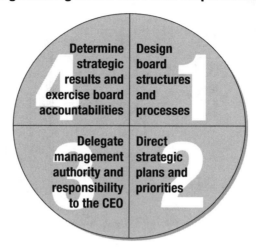

Determine strategic results and exercise board accountabilities	Design board structures and processes
Delegate management authority and responsibility to the CEO	Direct strategic plans and priorities

Designing Board Processes

In Chapter 9 we mentioned that some of the board's structures and processes are determined by the members and documented in the bylaws (Articles of Association in the UK).

The bylaws may limit the board's authority to design structure and processes whether those limitations are appropriate or not. When formalizing a new governance manual, a wise board will review the bylaws. It will then make any changes necessary for the bylaws and governance manual to complement each other through consistent description of the relationships required by the organization. This step may require careful education of the membership, bringing about change as it does. Otherwise, members may feel manipulated and disempowered by the board members they elected to serve them.

Here is a list of the primary board governance policies that would appear in this section of a governance manual. Some of these policies may be included in the bylaws and repeated in the governance manual for easy reference.

- Election of Directors, Chair, Vice-chair, Secretary
- Election of Committee Chairs
- Removal of Elected Officers
- Board Meetings
- Board Meeting Preparation
- Quorum
- Meeting Procedures
- In Camera Sessions
- Confidentiality
- Extraordinary Board Meetings
- Voting
- Conflict of Interest
- Governance Manual Reviews
- Expenses
- Minutes, Recording, Distribution
- Staff and Guest Attendance
- Communication with Staff
- Conflict Resolution

See Part 3, Appendix B for a sample governance manual, including these policies, written in the Relationship Model™.

Governance in Real Life

More often than not, the governance process is a pleasant experience for individual board members. In real life, however, some weaknesses tend to show up in various board rooms. Here are some things to watch for, and some advice that may help you deal with them.

▶

More often than not, the governance process is a pleasant experience for individual board members.

Governing policies add value to the work of boards in several important ways.

1. Current policies are a storehouse of wisdom, enhanced by the experience of past boards. They allow the present board to benefit from the wisdom of its predecessors in addition to its own. In addition, proven board policies are passed on to those who follow.

2. Policies bring stability to the planning and decision-making of the board. They prevent sudden reversals from:

    • not remembering precedents
    • lacking the wisdom present in a previous board.

3. Policies give future direction to the chief executive officer. The limitations they provide to the CEO's authority give him/her a much larger and clearer circle of freedom in which to manage the organization's operations.

4. Policies assure the staff and other stakeholders that the board is mature and wise…that it is in control in an ever-changing environment and in any crises that arise.

5. Policies help to ensure the efficient and effective management of the organization by having specific means of monitoring performance and measuring results.

6. Policies provide a "firewall" against the abuse of power from a board chair or from a small group within the board, as well as a buffer against the incompetence of weak board members.

What Board Minutes Should Include

Board minutes "speak volumes" about the culture of the board that produces them. Some boards have long, detailed minutes. Others have minutes so sparse that you wonder if anything happened at the last meeting.

Some boards have minutes so accurate that their approval at the next meeting takes only a few minutes. Others produce minutes that don't read anything like what happened at the meeting.

1. Record the names of all board members, indicating who was present and who was absent. Record the names of staff and guests present. Avoid repeating those names in the recording of discussion, moving and seconding resolutions. Indicate names only when requested or when the name is material to the subject being recorded.

2. Record only the factual information that was available to the board during the discussion that produced the action. Avoid recording perceptions, conjecture, opinions and any other non-factual information that was shared during the discussion.

3. Record the action in the actual words that were agreed by the mover and seconder. Avoid paraphrasing the motion and approving it, only to realize at the next meeting that it says something different from what the mover and seconder actually said. It is vital that the minutes record the actual words of the motion read by the secretary just before the vote was taken.

4. Attach to the official copy of the minutes the copies of information tabled to support the discussion. Avoid making vague references to documentation or no reference at all. Identify the documentation clearly (e.g., date, author, source) in the minutes in addition to attaching a copy to those minutes.

5. Draft a carefully designed policy to guide successive board secretaries and recording secretaries in the taking of minutes. Avoid changing styles of minutes with each succeeding secretary.

There is a wide range of practice in writing minutes. Is there a "best way"?

On the previous page are a few principles to guide you in preparing minutes that document the decisions, as well as the discussions that produced them.

Remember, the board's minutes are the only official record of what the board has decided. Any action not recorded in the official minutes is not a legal action of the board. The board speaks with one "voice." The minutes are the only record of that voice.

In Camera Board Meetings

In camera refers to a closed session of the board. Used properly, and no more often than absolutely necessary, the closed session is necessary and useful. Unfortunately, closed sessions are sometimes misunderstood and misused.

An *in camera* session is simply a session of the board where only board members are present, and possibly others are specifically invited. All other staff and guests are excused. For example, when the board discusses changes to the CEO's salary, the CEO may be excused. In some cases of conflict of interest, a board member may ask (or be asked) to be excused so that no possible perception of impropriety will result.

Except for the absence of an individual or several individuals, there is no difference between an *in camera* session and an open session. There is an agenda. The same decision-making process takes place. Decisions are made and recorded in the minutes. The board has the same fiduciary responsibility as at any other time. Its liability for acting responsibly is the same.

In my experience, a board that gets itself into trouble with poor process will most likely do so in an *in camera* session. There is a lot of misunderstanding about what such a session is and how it is to be used. In my opinion, every board should have a policy to define a closed session and to determine when and how one should be conducted.

The worst abuse of the *in camera* session is that the very people who should be in the discussion are asked to be excused, since the discussion is about a concern or an allegation that relates to them. This type of discussion may indeed be required, but only after the issue is raised in that person's presence, giving him/her the opportunity to respond with either an explanation, more information or a defense.

In the final analysis, any board should ask the following basic question in order to determine whether a CEO or other persons, who are normally a part of the board process, should be excluded:

"Is our decision to excuse this person in the best interest of a quality decision and fair to the person(s) being excused?"

Discussion, Debate and Decision-making

Honest, issue-oriented debate is the key to quality decisions. Sometimes, however, the debate becomes personal and the quality of the process begins to suffer. Each board member is responsible for maintaining an issue-orientation during board decision-making. Here's a simple checklist to monitor the quality of your participation:

1. Am I taking the position I have because of my commitment to the organization and its well-being?

2. Am I affirming the person or persons whose point of view I am questioning?

3. Is it the issue that I am challenging (as opposed to the person)?

4. Am I asking questions to clarify the issue, rather than making an uninformed judgment?

5. Am I able to accept the board's decision, having had my opportunity to speak?

◄

A board that gets itself into trouble with poor process will most likely do so in an in camera session.

If your answer is "yes" to all these questions, then you are very likely taking a responsible part in the debate of the issue. If, on the other hand, your answer to one or more of these questions is "no," then it may help to re-evaluate your motivation. Consider discussing your participation and any feelings of being misunderstood with one or more board members.

What should board members or the chair do when the quality of decision-making is impaired by personal attacks instead of issue-oriented discussion and debate?

In my work with boards, I have come to the conclusion that board members are often too courteous to one another. Sometimes I hear conversations after the meeting that express someone's dissatisfaction with the behaviour of a board member. Very seldom, however, do I hear a board member's behaviour challenged during the meeting itself.

Generally, we shy away from confrontation. We often think accountability is negative, perhaps unforgiving. We consciously allow incidents with which we disapprove to pass without challenging words and actions. Consequently, problems continue unresolved.

On the other hand, confrontation must be done appropriately in order for it to be effective. Sometimes the manner of the confrontation cancels the benefit it should have had in the decision-making process.

We do everyone a favour when we apply the core values of healthy relationships to inappropriate behaviour. Our affirmation, involvement of the other person, and our servant leadership make our motivation obvious. More often than not, our gift of accountability will create a win-win outcome.

Board Confidentiality

Decisions of the board are usually, but not always, matters that can be made known outside the boardroom. That is particularly true of strategic decisions, as well as actions that affect staff or people outside of the organization. These decisions should be announced in a process chosen by the board. It may be a memo from the CEO, a press release, perhaps an official verbal announcement by the board chair or CEO. Decisions made in these ways are transparent. No one needs to wonder about the status of such news.

The board speaks with one voice. Board members are obligated to support the decisions of the board, unless the member's conscience prevents him or her from doing so. It is not appropriate for an individual board member to gainsay a decision outside the boardroom just because the decision didn't go his or her way.

In order to preserve an open process, one in which each person on the board is free to mention information relevant to the debate, there should be an understanding that details of the discussion will not be spoken of outside the boardroom. Breaking this confidentiality should not be tolerated. It breaches trust and adversely affects the quality of discussion and debate. Any dissent should be voiced openly in the meeting during the debate, never outside.

There may be a time when a board member cannot, for reasons of conscience or personal convictions, vote with other board members on a given matter. It is appropriate for that individual member to register a negative vote on a motion, particularly if he or she thinks that there is a risk of personal liability in the matter. That negative vote should be recorded in the minutes with the person's name. The other board members should respect this personal privilege. However, the dissenting member should still not gainsay the board's decision in public.

"Whistle Blowing" and Resigning in Protest

In extreme cases, it may be necessary for a board member to be a "whistle blower." This could occur in the case of serious abuse of power or irresponsible governance. When this happens, the individual needs to decide, first of all, whether s/he can, in good conscience, remain on the board. If the individual decides to go to a higher authority, such as a regulatory body or the membership at an AGM, s/he should realize that, depending on the outcome of the matter, it may result in his/her removal from the board of directors.

This is not to say that a board member should not take extreme action when conscience dictates. However, it may result in a decision that will dramatically affect the organization or his/her future role in it. It takes a lot of courage to be the voice in the wilderness. It also takes careful judgment to discern the difference between responsible "whistle blowing" on one hand, and pride and stubbornness on the other.

Finally, every board member must decide how important the organization is to him/her. Some board members resign their positions too easily, rather than taking a stand on an issue. Sadly, too many good board members leave at the very point when their expertise is needed most.

The other extreme is also tragic, where an individual stays too long and attempts to force the organization into following a personal agenda not supported by the majority.

The best approach to dissent of any kind is to be transparent within the meeting itself and to rely on the confidentiality and good judgment of other board members. Trustworthy members will see the most difficult issues through to a conclusion, enabling the organization to realize its mission within its moral and legal limitations.

Summary

In this chapter we have reviewed the board's responsibilities. We observed that all of a governing board's responsibilities are included in four quadrants of its circle of responsibility. The quadrants are:

- design board structure and processes
- direct strategic plans and priorities
- delegate management authority and responsibility to the CEO
- determine strategic results and exercise board accountabilities.

We included the first of these responsibilities in this chapter. We also gave specific attention to some of the more common and urgent issues that boards encounter including:

- what board minutes should include
- how to ensure quality discussion, debate and decision-making
- the appropriate uses and the dangers of *in camera* sessions
- distinguishing confidentiality from secrecy in the governance process
- dealing with extreme conflict—"whistle blowing" and resigning.

In the next chapter we will discuss strategic planning, the second area of the board's responsibility.

Notes

Strategic
Planning

Strategic or Tactical – What's the Difference?

Strategic Planning

Strategic planning is the responsibility of the board. In an ever-changing environment, the question the board must continually ask and answer is:

"What services shall we offer to which people in which places and in what order of priority?"

The answer becomes the core of the strategic plan of the organization.

The board cannot answer this question without being in regular touch with key stakeholders. In my view, a board should spend at least 50% of its time listening to and learning from a parade of stakeholders entering its boardroom. That parade should include clients and customers, donors and funding sources, representatives of the regulatory bodies—government, church leaders and specialists in the fields in which the organization works, partners and "competitors."

The one who can properly introduce these stakeholders is the one who likely knows them best—the CEO. The CEO should involve other senior members of the management team to suggest names of people who can help the board stay in touch. And, of course, senior managers are themselves important stakeholders.

Tactical Planning

Tactical, or operational planning, is the responsibility of the CEO and his/her management team. This is a much more detailed document, one that forms the basis of all expectations of responsibilities from the management group and the individuals in it. The tactical question is:

"How shall we achieve our mission within the limits of our resources?"

We will deal with this type of planning in Chapter 15. We mention it here to differentiate tactical from strategic planning. If your organization has a "long-range" or "strategic" plan that is more than ten pages long—sometimes they are more than 100 pages—you can assume that it incorporates both strategic and tactical plans.

The difficulty with this practice of combining the two plans is that it creates confusion about what the governance and management components are in the planning process. Boards often drift into management, leaving senior staff to take up the governance responsibility for making strategic decisions.

Strategic Planning Simplified

Strategic planning should be simple, straightforward and brief, enabling the board to give clear direction to the CEO without becoming entangled in tactical planning. In the Relationship Model™, a strategic plan for a multimillion dollar, multinational organization or a small private school will be the same length—six to ten pages. The strategic plan will be kept current by board interaction with stakeholders, as well as by annual review and revision of the plan.

In the Relationship Model™ the strategic plan is an official governance policy. You will find the actual strategic plan of Hope Seeds Inc. in Part 3, Appendix C so that you can see how this concept appears in actual practice.

The ten components of a strategic plan include:

1. Historical Context

A one-page history of the organization and its development places the strategic plan into the historical context of the organization's life cycle. One-line highlights of the major events that have brought the organization to its present status provide a context for the strategic direction that follows.

2. Values

Values may be expressed in at least three categories:

- personal (e.g., integrity, openness, truthfulness)
- relationship-oriented (e.g., affirmation, involvement, servant leadership)
- organizational (e.g., music, health care, emergency shelter)

▶

Every organization bases its mission more on organizational values than it does on the needs of people around them!

In this section we want to identify the organizational values—those special interests important enough for an organization to be created around them. Every organization bases its mission more on organizational values than it does on the needs of people around them! This is normal and healthy. For example, an organization that provides emergency shelter for battered women is unlikely to be interested in providing special education to gifted children, even if there is a dramatic need for that service.

Even the people who work in the organization's infrastructure—finance, administration, maintenance—will normally prefer working in an organization whose corporate values match their own personal interests. An accountant may choose an educational institution over a hospital, even though it is farther to drive and the benefits are less attractive.

These values may reach another level of detail that will further define its mission. For example, an organization's people may prefer to focus on prevention rather than research or treatment of a given disease, even though the other needs are compelling. We choose to meet the needs that interest us, not necessarily those that are most urgently needed, closest to home or the most cost-effective.

It is important that the organization identify its organizational values. Failure to do so may lead to attempts to meet needs that are compelling or more cost effective, but not in the area of interest or expertise of the organization's people.

3. Target Groups

This component and the next are so closely related that it doesn't matter which is taken first. They are inseparable.

Target groups are the individuals and groups who are the focus of the organizational values. They may be expressed in national, ethnic or religious groups, as gender or age groups, in terms of physical or emotional or economic wellness, or any other designation that enables the organization to identify individuals or groups in mutually exclusive terms. To begin to identify the target groups, the organization must consider the needs for which it wants to provide services and/or products.

The easiest target group to miss are the people within the organization. Some leaders argue that the staff—even the board—are a means to the end of providing services to the target groups, not target groups themselves.

In the Relationship Model™ we take the view that client satisfaction (productivity) and staff fulfillment must be in balance for an organization to be successful. For this reason we suggest that the staff is always one of the target groups to benefit from the organization's mission. The people in the organization are not merely a means to another end.

4. Services/Needs

Services deliver the benefits (strategic results) to the target groups. Services are different from programs in that services are strategic ("what" the organization does) while programs are tactical ("how" the organization delivers the services). For example, feeding the hungry is a service. Preparing Christmas dinners is a program that delivers that service.

Strange as it may seem, some organizations may not be able to list the services they offer. That is because there is so much focus on the programs delivering the services that the services themselves remain undefined. Ask your board or management team to take five minutes to list the services the organization offers on paper and another five minutes to compare the lists. You are likely to find some interesting variations.

A helpful exercise is to list all the programs your organization has operated in the past and present, including those contemplated in the future. Then begin to group those programs by the services they deliver. This same exercise will pay additional dividends when we get to priorities, because we shall see how our resources are divided among the programs and services.

Some programs may deliver more than one service simultaneously. For example, an educational institution may provide practical training for future teachers, at the same time providing education for students. It is important to identify what needs the organization wants to meet with its services and which needs might be "means to the end" of its mission.

5. Places

This is a geographical reference to where the services are delivered. It may be expressed in terms of countries, states, provinces or counties, cities and towns, or locations in a city, depending on the scope of the organization.

◀

Strange as it may seem, some organizations may not be able to list the services they offer.

This component is also a priority of the mission, because locations change with increases or decreases of need, plans for expansion, political and economic factors. Accordingly, boards will want to review this component annually.

Only when target groups, services and places have been accurately identified has the board answered the strategic question, *"What services shall we provide to which people in which places and in what order of priority?"* Then we can complete the last five components of the strategic plan.

6. Vision

This is a statement of the difference you believe the organization will make in the community 20 years hence, beyond the planning horizon. The vision is challenging, drawing the members of the organization into the future, motivating them to achieve more than they imagine possible. Vision determines mission, not the other way around.

A vision is not organizational navel-gazing. "ABCDE Elementary School will be the largest school in the city," is not a vision statement. "The vision of ABCDE Elementary School is that no child in our city will be denied an elementary education and that every student who attends will graduate to high school, university and a meaningful career." Now that's a vision.

7. Mission

The mission is a statement of purpose, what the organization exists to accomplish. It is the organization's expression of how it intends to realize the vision. Some organizations call this the purpose statement. It should be built on the work done on target groups and services and will normally make reference to both.

The mission statement is the simplest, shortest, most accurate expression of the organization's reason to exist. It should be used frequently in newsletters, press releases, advertisements, interviews and every other opportunity so as to link the name of the organization to its purpose.

This statement should be one short sentence that every board and staff member can memorize and use both frequently and naturally. Any mission statement that cannot be easily committed to memory and spoken as part of a natural conversation needs more editing.

Here is the mission statement of GovernanceMatters.com Inc.:

"The mission of GovernanceMatters.com Inc. is to enable not-for-profit organizations worldwide to balance the fulfillment of their customers' needs and the personal fulfillment of their staff and volunteers."

There is a tendency to put too much detail into a mission statement. When a mission statement has numerous points to explain the main one, the statement begins to overlap with the statements of services. People who hear the mission statement should be able to comprehend the purpose of the organization without getting lost in the detail.

8. Priorities

The challenge in setting priorities is to determine how resources will be allocated among competing target groups, services and places. Priorities may be expressed in the allocation of:

• human resources (staff and volunteer hours or fulltime equivalent)
• operational expenditures
• capital expenditures
• capital assets
• income.

This results in two or three matrix grids, one each for the target groups, services and places (if there is more than one place). In this way, the board gives clear direction to the CEO in developing the tactical plans and the financial plans (budget) that will support them.

These priorities do not include infrastructure costs. Those costs must first be subtracted from the total available financial resources before the balance is prioritized.

The amount that is spent on infrastructure (e.g., office expenses, systems, maintenance) may be a subject of a limitations policy. This limitation gives the CEO freedom to develop the infrastructure by placing a maximum percentage that can be used for those expenses.

Here is a sample matrix that demonstrates how one organization (a church) set its priorities in the first year of its new strategic plan.

Priorities

During the first year of this planning period, the allocation of resources will continue to follow current practice. Allocations will be recorded and priorities will be reviewed. Allocations in subsequent years will be modified to meet changing priorities. These allocations do not include administrative services and infrastructure, which shall not exceed 40% of the total financial resources during this planning period.

(Note: Infrastructure expenses (time and finances) are those required to maintain the facility and processes that cannot easily be allocated to a specific target group or service.)

Priority of Target Groups by Age Group

Age Group	Volunteer Time	Program Staff Time	Program Budget
Infants 0–3	2%	0%	14%
Children 4–12	17%	17%	16%
Youth 13–17	26%	30%	25%
Adults 30–65	17%	21%	15%
Senior Adults 65+	29%	16%	14%

Priority of Services

Services	Volunteer Time	Program Staff Time	Program Budget
Fellowship	6%	15%	7%
Learning	14%	31%	25%
Social Ministry	21%	6%`	20%
Spiritual Care	19%	10%	2%
Witness	21%	9%	23%
Worship	20%	29%	24%

If the organization has never formally set priorities in this way, it may seem like a challenge to know how to start. Following is the best way to approach the first effort:

- Prepare the two or three grids by placing the target, groups and places at the left of the rows in each of the grids. Then place the type of resource you choose from the above list at the top of the columns, as in the example. If income is largely unrestricted, it may be unnecessary to distinguish this resource from operational expenditures. For some organizations, however, priorities are set in part by the restriction of available funding.
- Analyze your current practice of allocating your resources in the categories you selected in the matrix. Use the operational, capital budgets and balance sheet from the last completed fiscal year. Analyze also the allocation of staff and volunteer time.
- Fill the grid with the actual allocation of resources that you are currently using.

The staff will have to complete this assignment so that the board can consider what priorities to set for the future.

The most likely first approach to setting priorities is to continue the present allocation for the next year. During that year, the board will be able to review the priorities in the light of:

- values of the people within the organization
- needs as expressed by the clients, staff and other stakeholders
- restrictions of available resources
- other factors that change the variables above (e.g., political and economic)

9. Strategic Goals

Strategic goals are the results the organization hopes to achieve in meeting the needs of its clients and staff. This is different from tactical measurements, such as the number of clients served and cost per client. Determining the strategic goals requires interaction with the clients and staff themselves.

This component of the strategic plan usually cannot be completed in the first year, since the organization will require:

- a process of identifying indicators of results
- an analysis of the results the organization (and similar organizations) are currently achieving.

Both of these are necessary before meaningful goals can be set for the future.

Since strategic measurement is part of the board's accountability process, a more complete explanation of this component is included in Chapter 13.

10. Critical Success Factors

Critical success factors form the bridge between the strategic plan developed by the board and the tactical plans prepared by the staff. Often overlooked, they are the missing link in the relationship between governance and management.

Getting these right will allow the board to be confident that it is dealing with the "How do we accomplish our mission?" question. Critical success factors allow the board to express its interest in management without becoming excessively involved in management itself. They do this by making 8 to 12 statements, each beginning with the words, "We must…" These indicate to the CEO what the board expects to see addressed in the organization's tactical plans for the year. This is vital for the board in monitoring the compliance of the tactical plans with the strategic plans.

Here is a list of areas that a board may consider "critical to the success" of achieving the mission. I encourage boards to select the "ten or so" areas they wish to address in the strategic plan, and thus control development of tactical plans without intervening directly in management. In your particular organization, there may be specific areas of concern (e.g., safety, evacuation, medical care, maintenance).

Before working only with the suggestions below, spend some time brainstorming.

- Ask each person to write ten sentences that begin with "We must…".
- Share them within the group to identify common issues.
- Select those that the group agrees are critical to your success.

Critical Success Factors – Suggested Topics

Relationships

- Relationships with members/donors/funding sources
- Relationships with regulatory authorities
- Relationships with staff/volunteers
- Relationships between board/staff volunteers
- Strategic alliances
- Staff/volunteer recruitment, retention, development
- Values

Processes

- Governance
- Management
- Planning – strategic/tactical
- Services/programs/products
- Communication
- Marketing/fundraising
- Monitoring and measuring

Finance/Infrastructure

- Operating funding
- Financing (operating credit)
- Financial management
- Capital needs
- Reserves
- Buildings and property
- Systems/equipment

Keeping the Strategic Plan Current

Completing the first formal and documented strategic plan is the beginning of a wonderful journey for the board that wants to monitor the present, measure the past and *focus on the future*!

It is against this common understanding of values, vision and mission that governing board members can build a challenging and rewarding future for the entire organization, including themselves.

This important board policy document is not to be put on a shelf. It contains the strategic direction for the CEO and the staff. It is the dynamic foundation for all that happens to benefit the clients.

We live in a constantly changing world. Some changes are dramatic—even devastating. More often, however, change occurs so gradually that considerable time goes by without our realizing that our strategic plans for the future are gradually losing their relevance.

The Planning Horizon Keeps Moving

The term "long-range plan" has given way to the "planning horizon" and "window of opportunity." The strategic plan outlined above is intended to look forward only three to five years.

As I have said before, the wise governing board will spend at least half of its time educating itself to the changes that are impacting the clients and, therefore, the organization itself. This time is used to listen to stakeholders, including clients and their families, staff and volunteers, funding sources, regulatory agencies and government planning departments. Every stakeholder has something to add to an understanding of the environment's impact on the organization.

I suggest preparing an annual calendar of invitations to stakeholders who, over the course of an annual planning cycle, can give a balanced view of the future.

The board may also wish to visit the geographical areas in which service delivery takes place, particularly if that involves a different culture than that of its members. Where time, distance and cost prevent the entire board from visiting the service delivery area, the CEO and a rotating number of board members may make an exploratory trip.

The purpose of visiting stakeholders and site visits is not simply to hear the stories that reinforce our wisdom. Rather, the challenge is to learn how to make a good thing better and more relevant to a changing environment.

Revising the strategic planning document should be done at the end of that annual cycle. It will take far less time than the first time, but the quality of the document and its relevance will increase with each revision.

The indicators of results will gradually change and the accuracy of measurements will improve, as the board gains experience with the success of its mission.

In the next chapters on delegating management authority to the CEO and monitoring and measuring, we will see how the governing board can make the time available for strategic planning without forgetting the past or losing control of the present.

◄

Completing the first formal and documented strategic plan is the beginning of a wonderful journey for the board.

Summary

This chapter is a presentation of the strategic planning process. Defining the ten essential components of the strategic plan allows the board to keep the strategic plan short and clearly focused on strategic issues. They are:

- historical context
- values
- target groups
- services
- places
- vision
- mission
- priorities
- strategic goals
- critical success factors

The critical success factors build a bridge from governance to management, allowing the board to give management direction without intervening directly in management. The tactical plans are management's response to the board's strategic direction.

Next, we discuss what may be the most critical relationship within the organization, the CEO/board relationship.

Delegating CEO Authority and Responsibility

Delegating Authority and Responsibility to the CEO

Every relationship in an organization is of great importance. One particular relationship, however, exemplifies the overall health of the organization, the CEO/board relationship. It will determine, more than any other, just how the relationship between governance and management functions in practice.

When designed properly, this relationship can have a very positive effect on both board and staff. When operating effectively, the board will concentrate on strategic issues without losing control of management. The CEO will have the freedom to design the management structure and process, yet receive clear strategic direction and input into future target groups, services and priorities. Such a healthy relationship creates a win-win situation for both governance and management, board and staff.

Hiring a Chief Executive Officer

Selecting a CEO is probably the most important decision any board will make. I believe it is even more important than the design of a governance model or the process of strategic planning. That's because the CEO/board relationship impacts those two responsibilities, as well as everything else that happens in the organization.

The quality of the hiring process among faith-based not-for-profit organizations varies widely. At one extreme, board members rely completely on what they refer to as "the Lord's choice" in which they have no role other than prayer and surrendering to God's will. At the other extreme, they may default to outside consultants, convinced that they have taken a thoroughly professional approach. In both cases the board underestimates the importance of its own due diligence.

The CEO and Board Membership

It is common in public corporations for the CEO to be a voting member of the board. The term for that position is "inside director." It is also common for the CEO to be the board chair as well. As a result, the same person who receives authority from the board leads the governance process that grants the CEO authority. This obvious conflict of interest has led to many inefficiencies and abuses. This same practice is not unknown in not-for-profit organizations.

Having the CEO as a voting member of the board is completely unnecessary and should not be permitted. The roles of governance and management are far too likely to become blurred, with the CEO having more influence in strategic issues than appropriate. What is worse is the potential for outright abuse of authority.

Should Only One Person Report to the Board?

Conventional wisdom suggests that only one person should report directly to the board. All other reporting should be through the CEO. All expectations of strategic results are negotiated through the CEO. In this way all authority and responsibility for management flows though one person, the chief executive officer. For staff there is no confusion about who is in charge and accountable for everything that happens.

Wherever possible, this is the design that a not-for-profit organization should follow. But every rule has an exception.

Some organizations may benefit from having two persons reporting directly to the board. In an educational institution we may see a president and an academic dean (a director of administration and a director of education). In an arts organization we may see an executive director and an artistic director.

In a hospital we may see a chief executive officer and a chief medical officer. In a church we may see a senior pastor and an administrator.

Selecting a CEO is probably the most important decision any board will make.

Three vital elements make this arrangement work:

- shared values
- mutually exclusive responsibilities
- strong competencies.

If any one of these is absent, the organization will suffer from confusion, perpetual conflict and ultimately dysfunction. Because one or more of these elements are so often lacking, conventional wisdom advises against having more than one person report to the board.

Shared Values

We have said repeatedly that the values with which we manage authority (power) are more important than the design of structure and processes. Nothing is more important than being on the right part of the values continuum.

If both the chief executive officer and the specialized professional affirm, involve and demonstrate servant leadership to one another, there is likely to be a smooth working relationship. They have a natural tendency to find a balance between productivity and their personal fulfillment. Most of us have seen relationships work well because of this value alignment even though structure and processes may be informal or poorly designed. But what if this value alignment is off?

Some organizations may benefit from having two persons reporting directly to the board.

It's easy to understand what will happen if both leaders are working from authoritarian values. There will be an ongoing power struggle. If both take a *laissez-faire* approach to their work, there is likely to be sloppiness in all aspects of management and service delivery. If one is authoritarian and the other *laissez-faire*, it's not hard to see which one will dominate and control the relationship.

The wise board will ensure that when the time comes to replace one of these leaders, the one remaining is involved in the selection process. The board can then assure itself that the new leadership works from the same relationship-oriented value system.

Mutually Exclusive Responsibilities

A carefully designed relationship description is required for each leader. The key is for each person to have mutually exclusive responsibilities. The board and the two leaders must know specifically what each is accountable for to the board. In cases where the volume of work is such that two people are needed to manage, a clear division of responsibility will be too difficult to attempt. Where there are clearly specialized administrative functions, (e.g., education, art, medicine), it is possible to design working relationships where both parties know what is expected of them.

Naturally there is some overlap. Poor administration may prevent efficient and effective service delivery. Unwillingness to document expenditures by the specialist will result in a weak infrastructure. At least it will be apparent to the board where the weakness lies. Where overlap makes accountability difficult, the common value system will enable the two leaders to work out any problems.

Strong Competencies

There must be a balance in the level of competencies of the two leaders. When both are carefully selected for their specialized competencies and experience, the dynamic duo can do amazing things for the organization. Occasionally, they may pick up the slack for one another in minor matters or for a short term. But when the artistic director has to reschedule the concert because the CEO forgot to book the concert hall, there is going to be a problem with effectiveness, and tension in the relationship.

It is the board's responsibility to assure itself that all three of these elements are in place before adding either leader to the team.

It is not likely that three or more leaders can report to the board. Some crucial elements need to be in place for two to work well. Adding a third leads to complexity beyond what is practical. (We have prepared governance manuals and relationship descriptions for organizations with two leaders.)

We will now explore the five components of a single CEO/board relationship as set out in the Relationship Model™. To remind you, they are:

1. Authority
2. Limitations of Authority
3. Responsibility
4. Expectations of Responsibility
5. Accountability

1. Authority

In most not-for-profit organizations the members delegate to the board the authority to initiate and terminate the employment of the CEO. It's true that in Christian churches it is common for the members to "call" a pastor. The members choose not to delegate that authority to choose a spiritual leader to their governing body. That practice is rare in not-for-profit organizations. Members rarely choose their CEO, because there is no process in place for them to do that.

▶

This means that the CEO has no authority to be the CEO unless it comes from the board by delegation.

This means that the CEO has no authority to be the CEO unless it comes from the board by delegation. By the same token, it also means that the CEO is accountable to the board as a whole, not to any committee of the board or the chair. There is more than a little confusion on this point.

Board Chair and CEO Are Peers

In the Relationship Model™ no authority flows directly between the board chair and the CEO. The role of the chair is to lead the board governance process. This process constitutes the authority transmitted to the CEO. When the chair informs the CEO of a board decision, s/he is informing the CEO on the board's authority, not authorizing the CEO personally. The chair may relay only those decisions that are documented in board minutes or board policy. The role of the CEO, on the other hand, is to lead the process of management.

I was having a quick lunch by myself in a crowded café. Seated at a table next to me were two men in heated debate. It was animated to put it mildly. I couldn't avoid being distracted by their conversation, particularly when I heard the words "board chair" in the conversation. At that point I actually started listening.

One said to the other, "I don't report to you. I report to the board."

"Yes," the other replied, "but you report to the board through the chair."

"I will continue to report directly to the board," came the reply.

They were debating the flow of authority from the board to the CEO and the accountability back to the board. It didn't sound like a happy relationship. I don't remember what I had for lunch.

The board chair and the CEO are peers. One focuses on the governance process, the other on the management process.

It is not uncommon to hear that "the CEO is accountable to the board *through the chair.*" This expression is confusing at best and dysfunctional at worst. The CEO has the authority to address, as well as to make written communication to the full board. The chair may be a conduit for that information flow as a normal process. The chair, however, has no authority to interrupt that flow or require that it pass through the chair. For example, the insistence of one board chair that the CEO submit a report to the chair 72 hours before releasing it to the full board is indicative of the dysfunction that can occur in this relationship.

The CEO/board chair relationship is critical to the success of the governance and management processes. Both parties and the board must be very clear on how authority flows between the board and the CEO. In the Relationship Model™ this is documented in the CEO/board relationship.

Authorization

Having said that all the authority delegated by the board is delegated to the CEO, the board's only employee, just what does that include? It means that the CEO has access to all the human and financial resources, as well as the information and time needed to achieve the results expressed in the strategic plan and other governance policies.

In order to achieve the results the CEO has the freedom to:

- design the management structure
- create and fill the senior management positions
- manage the human and financial resources.
- manage the operation of service delivery.

That freedom does not include delivering new services to existing target groups or existing services to new target groups not included in the strategic plan. It does, however, include developing new programs that will be efficient and effective in delivering the services to the target groups that are in the strategic plan.

Resources

Here we are faced with an important anomaly—perhaps even a paradox. We have said that the board (as the source of authority) is accountable to the CEO for providing the authorization and resources required for success. The reality is, however, that the board itself has no development or human resources departments, so the CEO is authorized to develop the financial and human resources on behalf of the board. This is the anomaly in the otherwise straightforward delegation of authority.

CEO Competencies

According to our research, it is vital that a CEO possess the 20 *most important* competencies listed in the box that follows. Those in italics are new competencies from those identified in Chapter 8 for board members. One is an achieving competency. The other four are all leadership competencies. We will expand on these new competencies in detail.

CEO Competencies

Achieving Competencies

These generally lie above the iceberg water line and are, therefore, possible to improve by training:

- Communication
- Conflict resolution
- Commitment to the organization
- Initiative
- Objectivity
- Process orientation
- *Results orientation*

Thinking Competencies

Often below the surface, there is a limit to how much they can be changed by training. They reflect a person's cognitive ability:

- Conceptual thinking
- Effective judgment

Leadership Competencies

Often below the surface, these may be improved through increased knowledge and experience. They are affected by a person's attitudes and self-image:

- Accountability
- *Concern for excellence*
- *Delegation*
- *Desire for staff fulfillment*
- *Leadership*

Personal Competencies

These mostly lie well below the surface and are, therefore, hard to change by training. Although all competencies are personal, these particularly reflect individual attitudes, traits, motives and self-image:

- Ambiguity tolerance
- Empathy
- Open-mindedness
- Personal integrity
- Self-awareness
- Self-esteem

Achievement Competency – Results Orientation

Structures and maintains an organization that meets client needs in the most effective and efficient way

An organization exists to meet the needs of an identified client market through the provision of services or products. This is often focused on a particular location and may include the establishment of priority needs.

Whether profit or not-for-profit, clients or customers generally focus on whether they get a quality product or service for the money they pay or donate. Achieving quality outcomes is costly; the higher the quality, the greater the cost.

The CEO is generally the one who must balance the quality or effectiveness of the product or service with the cost of producing it. The cost/benefit ratio, both for the organization and the client, will determine what results can be achieved and how they are to be achieved. This in turn identifies the most efficient way to produce the product or service at the quality level required by the client or customer.

Staff fulfillment is very important, but should not occur at the expense of achieving results. An effective CEO aims to hold both fulfillment and productivity in balance in order to achieve success in an organization. Neither goal is ignored at the expense of the other.

Achieving results is usually implemented through the setting of S.M.A.R.T. goals (Specific, Measurable, Achievable, Relevant to the mission and Time-limited). To measure effectiveness it is helpful if the organization's results or outcomes are compared with external standards. These standards may need to be gathered from similar organizations, then adapted to measure the organization's success.

Whether clients' needs are met satisfactorily or not cannot be assumed or guessed. Only the clients themselves can indicate a true level of satisfaction, and, therefore, an accurate measure of the organization's success.

In a not-for-profit organization the benefit is often experienced by a third party. This requires the CEO to lead the staff in listening and responding to what clients, customers and third parties say about their satisfaction with the services they receive.

Leadership Competency – Concern for Excellence

Sets and maintains the highest standards while achieving a balance between organizational productivity and staff fulfillment

A clear model of excellence set by the CEO encourages excellence throughout the organization.

Excellence is achieved when organizational productivity and staff fulfillment are both accomplished without sacrificing high standards of operation.

Concern for excellence is about balancing these two facets. Productivity is not achieved at the expense of certain values, attitudes and behaviours that fulfill staff. Neither is staff fulfillment the sole focus of attention at the expense of productivity. Both are necessary and interrelated.

The CEO is required to use the entrusted financial and staff resources wisely. With financial resources under constant outside scrutiny, s/he must decide where monies should be directed in order to achieve the best balance between increasing effectiveness or improving efficiency.

Staff, as the other key resource, need even more safeguards to ensure their proper treatment. Setting and monitoring standards of excellence at all stages of their working life is critical to their fulfillment. Independent research increasingly confirms that staff who are treated well are more likely to produce well. Thus, staff fulfillment has a direct consequence on an organization's productivity.

◄

Staff fulfillment is very important, but should not occur at the expense of achieving results.

A CEO who is concerned about excellence, balances these multiple facets, recognizing the tension that exists between them. S/he uses this tension to build an organization that creates value equally for both clients and staff.

Leadership Competency – Delegation

Multiplies the capacity of the organization by dividing the workload

Any organizational leader has to learn to delegate responsibilities together with the authority (authorization, resources, information and time) required to fulfill them.

Delegation multiplies the capacity of an organization. Staff motivation is increased as people feel empowered, valued, affirmed and, therefore, fulfilled.

When senior staff feel secure and enjoy the freedom that comes from being clear about their responsibilities and the extent of authority from the CEO to fulfill them, they are encouraged to take risks, especially if those limits are set as wide as possible. Efficiency and fulfillment increase since staff do not have to seek permission each time they need to achieve something.

A CEO who attempts to do everything him/herself, or continually meddles in the responsibilities of others, has a significant, negative impact on the organization. Rather than multiplying the capacity of the team, senior staff become disempowered and demotivated as the CEO holds on to responsibilities and authority that should be delegated. A CEO who is motivated by achievement is particularly at risk here.

Delegation by the CEO brings freedom, motivation, empowerment and affirmation. The CEO is free to fulfill other responsibilities and the overall capacity of the organization is magnified by the range and number of skills employed.

Leadership Competency – Desire for Staff Fulfillment

Structures and maintains an organization in which staff members are fulfilled and successful

This competency is foundational to the release of untold potential throughout the organization. It starts with a belief that people are inherently valuable, that work is intended to be enjoyed and that through enjoyment, people will be fulfilled and their productivity increased.

There is now measurable evidence that giving due regard to staff fulfillment has an effect on the bottom line. It has come about thanks to clear structures and policies as well as "softer" elements, such as changing values and attitudes in our organizations.

Fulfillment begins when the strengths and weaknesses of a person are correctly evaluated and taken into account when matching that person with a job. Failure to match appropriately is unfair to the individual and has negative implications for the organization.

Fulfillment comes from a work context that balances the available resources with mutually agreed expectations. In the case of senior staff, expectations are agreed upon with the CEO to ensure that staff do not feel that goals have been dumped on them or that expectations are unrealistic compared to the resources available.

It seems paradoxical, but an organization may be deemed successful in terms of its services to customers and yet have a very poor record of staff fulfillment. The major reason is that it's easy for CEOs to focus on productivity at the expense of fulfillment. Boards who demand results are often productivity-oriented. They usually consider the organization's finances the prime measure of "success," and omit the all-important people resource from the measurement.

CEOs who demonstrate this competency have a genuine desire to enable others to build confidence and develop as successful individuals.

Leadership Competency – Leadership

Inspires and energizes others to work together, sharing commitment and confidence in achieving success

What makes a good leader? The common denominator is probably that good leaders focus primarily on others rather than themselves. That is the meaning of servant leadership.

Sir Adrian Cadbury, the chocolate manufacturer and philanthropist from Britain, said, "Good leaders grow people, bad leaders stunt them; good leaders serve their followers, bad leaders enslave them."

In many ways the leadership competency can be described as an amalgam of all the CEO competencies.

Leadership ignites the spark in each staff member— empowering, inspiring, motivating, enthusing and energizing them; capturing their abilities and gifts to enhance the success of the organization while enabling them to reach their full potential.

Leadership is living by life values with consistency and integrity.

Leadership inspires trust because the leader demonstrates trustworthiness.

◄

CEOs who demonstrate this competency have a genuine desire to enable others to build confidence and develop as successful individuals.

Leadership commands respect because the leader keeps promises despite any problems or difficulties that arise.

Leadership is resilient in maintaining a balanced outlook on life when the unexpected happens.

Leadership inspires confidence and draws others to participate in a shared vision. The organization is energized as staff experience a CEO who values them as people, not just for the product or service they produce.

Leadership knows what priorities should take up the leader's time, not wasting it on unimportant issues or distractions.

The difference between a CEO and other staff is that a CEO cannot display leadership on erratic, one-off occasions. It must be demonstrated consistently, day in and day out.

This competency brings confidence and hope in the future at all times, building an effective and united team. It characterizes a CEO staff can believe in.

2. Limitations of Authority

The most empowering action that a board can take in its relationship with the CEO is to make clear the limits of the authority it delegates to that person. These limitations allow the CEO to take action with confidence 100% of the time, not just 1% when the board is in session.

A board may delegate as much authority as it wishes. The principle is that it is easier to give ten limitations than a thousand permissions. Thus, the number of limitations is small, but they are clear and comprehensive. Both board and CEO understand that if the answer isn't "no" in the limitations policies, the CEO is free to act.

Some limitations originate with the board. They include the strategic plan and the limitations policies in the governance manual. Others originate from an authority beyond the board. These include limitations imposed by regulatory agencies and national bodies of which the organization is a member.

You may review the CEO/board relationship description later in this chapter and also in the governance manual in Appendix B for specific limitations recommended for this important relationship.

3. Responsibility

With the CEO, the board focuses on broad areas of responsibility. If a list of responsibilities has more than six items, it likely includes tasks as well as responsibilities. The sample CEO/board relationship description later in this chapter includes the five primary areas of CEO responsibility.

The emphasis is on the CEO's freedom to develop the structures, processes, management policies and procedures necessary for the organization to realize its mission.

The board must also delegate to the CEO its responsibility for providing the human and financial resources needed for success. The anomaly is that these are tactical issues, not strategic. They deal with how the organization achieves its mission, not the mission itself.

The organization does not exist to raise funds or to hire staff, yet both are critical to the success of the mission. The CEO becomes the one responsible for fundraising and for recruitment of staff and volunteers.

4. Expectations of Responsibility

Expectations come in two forms:

- goals (quantifiable)
- standards (qualitative)

Strategic Goals

The CEO is expected to achieve the strategic goals negotiated with the board of directors. The goal process (part of the annual strategic planning) is a matter of balancing these goals with the available human and financial resources, information and time. To be fair to the CEO, accountability for the expected responsibilities must be negotiated in terms that are S.M.A.R.T.:

- Specific
- Measurable
- Achievable
- Relevant to the mission
- Time-limited.

The expectations negotiated with the CEO should measure strategic results, not the tactical means by which those results were achieved.

The CEO will learn from experience what programs fail to achieve the results required by the strategic goals. S/he will have to make adjustments to tactical plans regularly during the year, sometimes abandoning one program altogether in order to meet the strategic results negotiated and agreed to with the board.

◀ *The most empowering action that a board can take in its relationship with the CEO is to make clear the limits of the authority it delegates to that person.*

▶ *The expectations negotiated with the CEO should measure strategic results, not the tactical means by which those results were achieved.*

The only tactical exception relates to fund development and staff recruitment. The board will also want to negotiate expectations of these responsibilities, since it must be satisfied that the goals are achievable. Fundraising goals should never be based on need but on realistic resource development for the organization to reach its strategic goals (quantity and quality of service delivery).

Standards

Standards must be achieved for whatever areas are appropriate for the organization. These standards will vary widely and include quality, behaviour, safety, risk management, etc.

Standards should be defined carefully and then expressed in measurable terms. "Best possible" is not an appropriate standard since it cannot be measured without additional definition.

The Key Word is Negotiation

The way to ensure the CEO's success is to be specific in the definition of goals and standards (quantity and quality), then set them at a level agreed upon as achievable by the CEO.

Sometimes, however, expectations are imposed by authorities beyond board control. For example, quality or safety standards for maintenance or construction are mandated by regulatory authorities. Where this is the case, resources must be negotiated to meet the required expectations. The CEO cannot be put in the position of having to attain standards impossible to achieve with the staff and budget currently available. In other words, negotiation will always be required to balance the circles of authority and responsibility acceptable to both the board and the CEO. Normally, the responsibility is adjusted by negotiating expectations. Sometimes changes in the authorization or resources have to be negotiated in order to achieve the balance.

5. Accountability

We have stated several times throughout this book that accountability is a neutral concept. It consists of monitoring performance—including personal behaviour —and measuring results. That measurement is affirming, involving and demonstrates servant leadership when applied to the negotiated goals and standards. If these are not achieved, both board and CEO need to learn from the experience and determine how each can adjust the limitations and expectations for success in future.

Accountability is also mutual. Notice how it is addressed in the CEO/board relationship description that follows. The board is accountable to the CEO for providing the authorization and resources required for success. The CEO is accountable for achieving the goals and standards without violating the limitations of his/her authority.

CEO/Board Relationship Description

The CEO/board relationship description contains a general expression of the five components of this relationship. There may be some specialized responsibilities, depending on the nature of the organization. Notice, too, that there are references to other documents where more detail is to be found.

Normally, the limitations of authority are found in another section of the governance manual, as you will see in Part 3, Appendix B. Goals are normally found in the strategic plans. In the case of fundraising and staff recruitment goals, these are found in the tactical plans. Other expectations are in the governance manual.

CEO/Board Relationship Description

1. Authority

The CEO functions with authority from the board of directors to be the chief executive officer of the organization.

The board shall provide budgeted resources required for the successful fulfillment of the responsibilities of the position.

Resources delegated to the CEO include paid and volunteer human resources, financial resources for operations and a personal compensation package.

(Some organizations wish to list the competencies (qualifications) required for the position. Since they are a part of the circle of authority, they would be listed here.)

2. Limitations of Authority

The CEO operates within the parameters of the CEO limitations of authority policies, the strategic plan agreed by the board of directors, and the limitations of legal and regulatory authorities.

3. Responsibilities

It is the CEO's responsibility to lead the processes of planning, resource development and management of the organization. Specifically s/he shall:

- provide the board with the organizational information it needs for its governance responsibilities, including strategic planning, infrastructure, resource development, monitoring performance and measuring strategic results
- develop and maintain healthy relationships between the board of directors and the stakeholders, including members, staff and volunteers, clients and regulatory authorities
- prepare tactical and financial plans in compliance with the strategic plan and CEO limitations and expectations policies
- develop the human and financial resources needed for the success of the mission
- manage the human and financial resources of the organization and its infrastructure to achieve the strategic goals of the organization.

4. Expectations

The expectations of the responsibility for this position are contained in:

- the governance manual
- the strategic plan
- the CEO's tactical goals.

The CEO is also expected to:

- model and promulgate the organization's values
- maintain and develop teamwork at all levels of the organization
- ensure that the relationships between the organization and its stakeholders are open and co-operative.

5. Accountabilities

Accountability in this relationship is mutual. The board is accountable to the CEO for providing the authorization, resources, affirmation, involvement and servant leadership required for the successful realization of the responsibilities of the position.

The CEO is accountable to the board for performance with respect to the negotiated expectations of the position within the limitations of authority of the position and for behaviour consistent with the values of affirmation, involvement and servant leadership.

The components of this working relationship shall be reviewed annually at the initiation of the board of directors and shall include:

- a review of the authorization and resources provided and values expressed to the CEO
- a review of the CEO's performance towards expectations of the responsibilities of the relationship including the progress towards strategic goals and the CEO's personal tactical goals
- a negotiation of tactical goals and other expectations for the next year
- a review of the authorization and resources required for the next year, including plans for personal development.

Summary

In this chapter we dealt with the policies that relate to delegating authority and responsibility to the CEO and with the accountability processes of the board.

Normally, there is only one person accountable directly to the board, namely the chief executive officer. In some organizations such as educational, medical or arts organizations it may be possible to have two persons accountable to the board—one for the specialized professional role and one for the infrastructure. In order for this to work effectively, the two individuals will need:

- aligned values
- mutually exclusive responsibilities
- strong competencies.

The competencies required for success in the CEO position are a unique blend of 20 competencies that fit into four categories:

- achieving competencies
- thinking competencies
- leadership competencies
- personal competencies.

A complete list, with their definitions, is included in Part 3, Appendix D.

The CEO/board relationship description is the key to a successful and fulfilling relationship. The limitations of authority and the expectations of the CEO responsibilities do not all appear in this document, but there will be references to them in:

- the strategic plan
- the limitations and expectations policies in the governance manual
- legal and regulatory documents.

Notes

Monitoring and Measuring
(The Accountability Process)

Monitoring is the form of accountability that examines relationships and progress along the way. Measuring deals with final results.

Monitoring

Methods of Monitoring

There are three methods of monitoring compliance with limitations and expectations:

- internal report
- internal audit
- external audit and report.

The internal report is a CEO or designate report addressed to a specific limitations or expectations policy.

The internal audit is an examination of management documentation, e.g., income and expense reports, cash flows and balance sheets (financial policies).

The external audit and report is the engagement of an objective third party to examine internal reports and documents related to the subject of the audit and to report its findings in writing. The financial audit of the organization's accounts is the most common of these.

Monitoring CEO Authority/Responsibility Balance

Every person has primary responsibility for his/her personal health and fulfillment in the workplace. The CEO is no exception. Rare is the CEO who doesn't have more than enough to do, so this is an ongoing monitoring challenge. Prioritizing is usually necessary, since s/he can't do everything as soon as someone else would like it done. Even with strong time management and delegating skills, work pressure often exceeds available time and other resources.

The CEO may not be able to maintain the balance between authority and responsibility. Because of this the board may wish to consider the following:

- Maintaining a balance between authority and responsibility is critical to the personal health and fulfillment of the CEO.
- Only the board has the authority to adjust the CEO's authority or responsibility when necessary.
- The board should monitor the CEO's responsibility and available resources at least at every meeting.
- Between meetings the board chair may monitor the CEO's load.

The annual relationship review is the one formal opportunity to monitor this balance. The first of the four parts of this relationship review deals with the authorization and resources provided to the CEO by the board. It provides an excellent opportunity to assess this balance and to discuss means by which it can be maintained or regained.

Monitoring CEO Compliance with Limitations and Expectations

For monitoring to be effective, the limitations and expectations must have been negotiated and documented. Normally they are documented in the governance manual, the strategic plan and the CEO's personal tactical plans.

The *governance manual* contains the limitations and expectations that remain relatively constant. Some additions and minor changes may occur along the way, but for the most part they are an ongoing component of the CEO/board relationship. The limitations of the CEO's authority and expectations of responsibility may include the following policies:

- Tactical and Financial Planning
- Financial Condition - Operational Funds

- Financial Reporting
- Critical Event Reporting
- Asset Protection
- Capital Expenditures
- Restricted or Donor-designated Funds
- Operation of Bank Accounts
- Values Modeling
- Stakeholder Treatment

The *strategic plan* contains limitations and expectations that are directly associated with the mission and its priorities. These do change over time and are normally revised annually. Limitations and expectations of this document include:

- services, target groups, places
- priorities of each of the above
- strategic goals
- critical success factors.

The CEO's *personal tactical goals* may also include expectations related to:

- fundraising targets
- staff recruitment and retention.

◀

For monitoring to be effective, the limitations and expectations must have been negotiated and documented.

When all limitations and expectations are negotiated and documented, the CEO is empowered to develop the management structure and processes to assure the success of the mission.

Monitoring the CEO's compliance is an ongoing accountability process. The schedule should be determined and documented under a separate policy in the governance manual. Some limitations and expectations need to be monitored at each meeting, e.g., the financial condition policy. Others may require only annual monitoring, e.g., the operation of bank accounts policy.

The tactical goal related to fundraising may need to be monitored as frequently as the financial condition policy, since it is an integral part of the financial condition in many organizations. Monitoring fundraising is in everyone's best interest. When the numbers are less than projected, adjustments can be made to expenditures to keep things in balance.

Monitoring Financial Issues

The titles of finance-related policies have been included in the list above. Here we deal with the nature of the board's involvement in financial matters.

Most boards spend an inordinate amount of time discussing financial matters. You might, therefore, expect to have read more about the board's role in financial matters in this book. The reason for not saying more is simply that financial management is just that—management. Monitoring management is a governance issue. It takes far less time than the normal management approach many boards still use.

It is vitally important, however, for the board to design and use a thorough process for monitoring financial issues. That process begins with designing acceptable limits and expectations for financial planning and conditions. This is different from the common practice of examining financial statements to determine whether they are acceptable, without first indicating to the CEO what the board is looking for.

The governance approach to monitoring means that the board has already thought through ahead of time what limits are acceptable and has negotiated expectations that are reasonable. When those are specific and clear, the board will know in short order the degree to which the CEO is in compliance. This approach will give the board more control and assurance than a management approach of examining financial statements that carry no policy requirements.

Measuring

Measuring Tactical Results

The CEO's fundraising goals are likely to appear in the tactical plans of another staff member, as may other sources of funding, e.g., per diem funding from government. Normally, these would be the only tactical plans of the CEO and his/her staff that the board would measure. As we have said, the board does this, because it is responsible for providing the resources the CEO requires. At the same time, the board realizes that it cannot do that without delegating the responsibility to the CEO.

Naturally, the CEO and other staff members will
all other tactical plans. This chapter deals only w.
accountability processes of the board.

Measuring Strategic Results

Measuring strategic results of services, that is, the difference the organization makes in the lives of people, is
difficult. Many organizations have measured tactical
goals instead of strategic goals. Those that do measure
strategic results sometimes measure them anecdotally,
using success stories to satisfy themselves and their
donors that the organization is making a difference.

For this reason, setting strategic goals will not be possible
in the first strategic plan developed for many organizations. Instead, the board will devote itself to identifying
what strategic results it wants to measure. The means by
which strategic results can be measured are called indicators of results.

What is the difference between strategic results and
tactical results? Organizations may measure the number
of people who participate in a given program. That is a
tactical measurement. The strategic measurement is
concerned with finding a way to measure the degree to
which the program delivered the service and met the need
of the client. In other words, what happened in the lives
of the clients who received the service, not just the
numbers of and cost per client.

The key to strategic measurement lies in finding effective
ways to learn the answer from clients themselves. No
attempt to measure strategic results will be complete
without this type of interaction.

As we have already seen, to measure strategic goals
properly, they need to be S.M.A.R.T. (Specific, Measurable,
Achievable, Relevant to the mission and Time-limited).
These goals can only be set after the indicators of results
have been identified and one year's strategic results have
been measured. There are three steps:

◀

*The governance
approach to
monitoring
means that the
board has
already thought
through ahead of
time what limits
are acceptable
and has
Inegotiated
expectations that
are reasonable.*

▶

*The key to
strategic
measurement
lies in finding
effective ways to
learn the answer
from clients
themselves.*

1. Determine what goals and indicators of results will be used.
2. Measure what results the organization is presently achieving. Sometimes it may also be possible to obtain benchmark results from other organizations.
3. Set goals for the future. By the beginning of the second year of strategic planning, this cycle should be complete and some goals can be put in place.

Exercising the Board's Accountabilities

Accountability to Stakeholders

The board has different accountabilities to different stakeholders:

Members: The board is accountable to report the strategic results of the organization's mission in clear, accurate measurements. It is also accountable for acting in good faith in all matters, particularly in the use of resources, both human and financial. The primary mechanisms for that accountability are the annual report and the annual general meeting.

Regulatory Authorities: The board exercises its accountability by filing the required reports to government agencies and to any national offices with which the organization is associated.

Internal Board Relationships: The only means by which members can hold the board accountable is by election. The board must, therefore, develop an accountability process to measure its own performance and that of its chair, officers and individual members. The sample governance manual in Appendix B includes policies to guide the board through this process.

Summary

In this chapter we dealt with the policies that relate to the accountability processes of the board.

The process of accountability consists of monitoring the present and measuring the past. Monitoring includes:

- the balance of authority and responsibility delegated to the CEO
- compliance with limitations and expectations policies.

Measuring normally takes place in the annual relationship review and consists of:

- comparing strategic results to goals
- comparing fundraising results to fundraising goals.

The chapter concludes with a presentation of the board's accountabilities to its members and other stakeholders, and its own internal accountabilities for performance.

The Chief
Executive Officer

Introduction

With this chapter we present the application of the Relationship Model™ to the management of a not-for-profit organization. It is a subject that would not normally appear in a book about governance. The Relationship Model™, however, is an operating system for the entire organization, not only its governance. The same design of healthy relationships—values, structure, processes—that balance the productivity and personal fulfillment within governance, delivers similar benefits to other relationships:

The corporate culture that grows out of the Relationship Model™ has the strength that only a single design for all relationships, consistently applied throughout the organization, can provide.

- between governance and management
- within management teams
- between the organization and its clients.

The corporate culture that grows out of the Relationship Model™ has the strength that only a single design for all relationships, consistently applied throughout the organization, can provide. It is neither a disjointed model nor a double standard to create misunderstanding and confusion between board and staff. This benefit distinguishes the Relationship Model™ from other governance or management models.

In Chapters 11 – 13 we dealt with the board's role in the Relationship Model™ for:

- strategic planning
- delegation of authority and responsibility to the CEO
- monitoring and measuring.

In this chapter we discuss the role of the CEO in these three processes, but from the perspective of management.

The position of the CEO is illustrated in the puzzle under construction on the previous page. S/he occupies the pivotal position at the top of the trunk of the organizational tree. All nutrients that flow from the board (the trunk) to the branches and leaves (staff and volunteers) must pass through this position.

The CEO has no operational authority except the board. Staff and volunteers have no operational authority unless it comes from the CEO.

Chief executive officers come in all shades and colours. Take a look at the box on the next page.

There are many kinds of organizations. All are at various stages of the organizational life cycle. All have different financial conditions. All have unique facets. To meet their needs during different phases of their life cycles, organizations may require different kinds of CEOs.

Leadership

This is a chapter specific to the CEO's *leadership position*, not a chapter about *personal leadership*. That comes in Chapter 16 when we climb to the top of the tree to meet the many personal leaders. Yes, the CEO must demonstrate personal leadership, but there is a distinction between personal leadership and the CEO's leadership position. Personal leadership is far more important.

When we speak about the personal leadership qualities of the CEO's leadership position, the subject takes on even more significance. Some of the differences among CEOs are in competencies—gifts, personalities, temperament and the like. Such a diversity of talent means that every organization can find the CEO they need, at the right place and time. Some differences, however, have a significant values component. Values also determine a person's competencies, and those we address here.

Types of CEOs

- big picture visionaries who can't remember details and those whose strength is managing the details of the present

- grizzly bears and teddy bears

- prima donnas and those who prefer a backstage role

- brilliant theorists who find difficulty dealing with the realities of the position and those who are solidly practical but who don't seem to have a frame of reference

- CEOs who talk too much and those who don't share their thoughts

- lions and lambs

- those who think the board is "a necessary evil" and ignore it as much as possible and those who are afraid to proceed without getting detailed approval

- CEOs whom the staff wishes would leave yesterday and those whose eventual departure is too awful even to imagine

- builders and wreckers

- computer experts and those who plan to retire before being forced to buy their first one

- orators who inspire and speakers who put you to sleep

- reckless and fearful

- natural fundraisers and those who wish it weren't part of the job

- bean counters and bean growers

- CEOs who wear their hearts on their sleeves and those who don't appear to have one

- lone rangers and team players

- and everything in between

CEOs who succeed in leading the delicate, dynamic balance of client satisfaction and staff fulfillment virtually all share the same core values. The successful CEO not only demonstrates strong personal leadership, but develops and celebrates the leadership of everyone else in the organization.

Organizational Culture

Why is it that some organizations are very productive but at the expense of staff and volunteer fulfillment?

Why is morale consistently high in some not-for-profits and chronically low in others?

We believe that values are of fundamental importance to the organization's culture and, therefore, its success. Because the CEO is the board's only employee and all authority delegated to the staff and volunteers passes through this single individual, the CEO's values will ultimately affect everyone in the organization, as well as its clients.

If there is an imbalance between client satisfaction and staff fulfillment that people within the organization feel, its origin may very likely be in the way the CEO values power. Where the CEO is positioned on the continuum of values related to power (Chapter 2), will have a major impact on the culture, often called "the way we do things here."

The CEO who consistently demonstrates behaviours that flow from affirmation, involvement and servant leadership will shape the culture of the organization in a beautiful way. The governance manual of one organization mandates the following policy on how stakeholders can expect to be treated.

"The CEO is expected to demonstrate the values of affirmation, involvement and servant leadership in all relationships with stakeholders, the board of directors, staff and volunteers."

The Role of the Chief Executive Officer

The chief executive officer is the link between governance and management. S/he spends time focusing on:

- strategic issues with the board
- tactical issues with staff and volunteers.

It is the CEO's responsibility to lead the processes of planning, resource development and management for the organization. Here again are the five broad areas of responsibility found in the CEO/board relationship description:

◀

If there is an imbalance between client satisfaction and staff fulfillment that people within the organization feel, its origin may very likely be in the way the CEO values power.

- provide the board with the organizational information it needs for its governance responsibilities, including strategic planning, infrastructure, resource development, monitoring performance and measuring strategic results

- develop and maintain healthy relationships between the board of directors and the stakeholders, including members, staff and volunteers, clients and regulatory authorities

- prepare tactical and financial plans in compliance with the strategic plan and CEO limitations and expectations policies

- develop the human and financial resources needed for the success of the mission

- manage the human and financial resources of the organization and its infrastructure to achieve the strategic goals of the organization.

The CEO's Role in Governance

The CEO's Role in Strategic Planning

▶

In almost all not-for-profit organizations, a volunteer board is only as close to the "service delivery to client" environment as the CEO can enable.

Although it is the board's responsibility to position the organization for the future, it cannot fulfill that responsibility without the CEO's involvement. In almost all not-for-profit organizations, a volunteer board is only as close to the "service delivery to client" environment as the CEO can enable. The rare exception would include a board made up of or including the managers and staff of the organization itself.

The CEO is vital to the process of strategic planning. S/he is the key to identifying stakeholders who can keep the board up-to-date with changes that shape client needs and the services that will meet those needs. Such stakeholders should enter the boardroom on a regular schedule. Changes in the target groups and service delivery locations can also be determined only by close interaction with stakeholders, whom the CEO is in the best position to identify.

In cases where board members are not normally in contact with clients, e.g., where services are delivered to target groups in another geographical area, the CEO may suggest holding a board meeting within the client's own culture. This presents a great opportunity for high quality input to the board's strategic planning.

Vision – Board or CEO – Whose Is It?

Vision is a component of the strategic planning process. Sometimes the word is used to refer to the entire strategic plan. The strategic planning relationship between the CEO and the board is a very delicate balance. In one sense, the vision that draws the organization into the future belongs neither to the board nor the CEO. It belongs to the entire organization, including the external stakeholders.

On the one hand, the board cannot develop the vision without the CEO. On the other hand, the CEO must not develop the vision for the board. It is a shared responsibility that they both accomplish for the entire organization.

Can or should the CEO be an influence in developing the vision for the future? Definitely! At the same time s/he should maintain the perspective that it is the board's responsibility to develop and maintain that vision on behalf of stakeholders. The CEO can do this by giving the board options rather than recommendations about whom the board invites into the boardroom to share needs and perspectives for the future.

It is very common for a board to depend on a CEO to develop the vision. We have probably all heard a board member say, "Our CEO is a real visionary." Or "Our CEO has a very clear vision of where s/he wants to take this organization." These sentiments suggest a board that has abrogated its strategic role. In such organizations one may observe a shift of services, target groups and priorities, because the vision changes with each CEO.

Climbing the Tree

The concept of "management by walking around" is about more than management. It is one of the most effective means of looking into the future.

One of my favourite childhood activities was climbing trees. From the top of my favourite tree, "my baby", as I called it, I could see the next small town, two miles away.

In the traditional top-down imagery of the organization, the CEO may be criticized for staying "in his ivory tower." In our organizational chart, however, climbing the organizational tree puts the CEO in close touch with staff and volunteers, the very people who deliver the fruit into the hands of clients. This point of service delivery or "moment of truth" is where the CEO can learn the most about strategic changes the board should consider. In this sense, it definitely isn't lonely at the top.

Observing Other Trees

◄

On the one hand, the board cannot develop the vision without the CEO. On the other hand, the CEO must not develop the vision for the board.

Like each tree, every organization is unique. Like all trees, all organizations share similarities. Forming relationships with other CEOs can be a very helpful way to learn more about the changing needs of clients. You can:

- have a sounding board to test ideas
- hear what others are experiencing
- discuss obstacles in developing approaches to meet client needs.

For-profit corporations may also offer an important perspective. They are sometimes closer to the changes in economic, political and social environment. They may have a larger research and development budget and other systems from which the not-for-profit CEO can benefit.

Other learning opportunities include seminars, leadership forums and membership in service clubs. All these give leaders important strategic insights.

Thinking in the Shade of the Tree

"What do you actually do with your time?" a CEO may be asked. Sometimes, the sense is that the answer "Nothing much," is anticipated. The reality is that the CEO should find time to lie in the shade of the tree doing "nothing much."

Taking time to think and to read, to put into perspective the infinite number of variables that the CEO observes, is a vital ingredient to his/her role in strategic leadership. Some leaders do this literally by "resting" in the shade of a tree, some by walking, jogging and cycling. Some wake up in the middle of the night with creative insights spelled "i-n-s-o-m-n-i-a." Others have a special retreat where they can be alone with their thoughts or with a book.

CEOs whose senior managers are well-empowered, or have organizations large enough to employ chief operating officers, really help give the CEO time to consider strategic leadership. This strongly supports the board in planning the future.

We mention these activities not because CEOs are unaware of them, but because we've observed that some leaders either feel, or are made to feel, that time for such activities is time they shouldn't be taking from their management functions. The point is that this kind of strategic leadership is vitally important to the future success of the organization.

The CEO's Role in Delegating

In the Relationship Model™ the CEO is very much involved in determining how much authority and responsibility the board will delegate to him/her. The CEO/board relationship review gives both the CEO and the board an opportunity to assess the quality of affirmation, involvement and servant leadership that the CEO has experienced from the board. It also permits both to consider the balance between the authorization and resources available on the one hand, and the negotiated expectations of the CEO's responsibility on the other.

In some organizations the board is more likely to focus on the CEO's management of resources than on its obligation to ensure there are enough resources to cover the responsibilities. Not so in the Relationship Model™.

Negotiating Expectations

As we said in Chapter 12, expectations take the form of goals (quantity) and standards (quality). The CEO's primary goals are the strategic goals in the strategic plan. They do not include the secondary, tactical goals except perhaps fundraising. In these cases, the board exercises its responsibility for supplying resources to the CEO by delegating these functions to him/her to develop on the board's behalf.

◄

Taking time to think and to read, to put into perspective the infinite number of variables that the CEO observes, is a vital ingredient to his/her role in strategic leadership.

Standards, on the other hand, are likely to be imposed on the entire organization by the regulatory authorities. In such cases they are not likely to be negotiable.

Thus, in the negotiating process, the CEO must be a full partner with the board in ensuring that there is balance— balance that allows the CEO to fulfill the expectations within the limits of what is available. Where expectations cannot be reduced, resources must be increased. In planning the operational year, both parties must be satisfied that the balance is in place.

The CEO's Role in Monitoring and Measuring

Monitoring Tactical Plans

When the CEO brings the tactical plans to the board before or just after the start of the operational year, the board will monitor two things:

1. That the plans reflect the strategic plan

- The operational aspects of the tactical plans are compared to the mission and priorities that the board has determined in the strategic plans.
- The allocation of resources should reflect the mission and its priorities.
- All factors deemed critical to the success of achieving the mission have been addressed adequately.

2. That the limitations and expectations policies dealing with financial planning give the CEO clear direction as to the parameters acceptable to the board

In this way the board indicates to the CEO *in advance* what it will find acceptable. This is very different from the traditional process of "approving the budget." It is in this difference that the board can make the greatest transition in its relationship with the CEO.

When meeting with the board, the CEO can assure the success of the tactical planning process by making clear references to the strategic plan, as well as the financial limitations and expectations policies. Once the board sees that operational and financial plans comply with approved strategic plans and financial planning policies, it can make that declaration in a motion recorded in the minutes. This is how the CEO can support the board in taking a governance approach to planning, versus the traditional "approving the budget" approach. Governance gives the board more control over the mission of the organization; the CEO is more empowered to manage the resources for the success of the mission.

Monitoring Performance

The CEO is responsible for the management of finances. During the operational (fiscal) year this will be monitored on a regular basis. Here, too, the CEO will work closely with the board in providing the data needed for responsible monitoring.

In my experience, monitoring of financial planning and managing policies should be done by a finance and audit committee of financially literate board members, plus any non-board members required for their financial expertise.

The CEO will have in place income/expense, cash flow and balance sheet documentation for all the organization's funds and accounts. The finance and audit committee must have regular and timely access to these important management documents so that they can monitor CEO compliance with governance financial policies…the *internal audit* referred to in Chapter 12. Careful scrutiny by board specialists of the actual documents is the only way for a board to be assured that the CEO/management team is exercising accountability for the organization's finances. The wise CEO will regularly provide the best possible displays of accurate information so that the committee and board feel confident that they exercise appropriate control without getting into time-wasting, detailed management issues.

I know of no single item that will make a grea~~t~~
ence to the transition from board management t~~o~~
governance than getting this part of the relati~~on~~
right. Once the governance manual is in place with ~~t~~he
relevant policies, and the board and committee chairs
follow these policies, it is the CEO who holds the key to
the success of this important aspect of the relationship.

Measuring Results

Strategic measurements are the responsibility of the
board. They cannot be done, however, without the full
involvement of the CEO and staff.

The CEO can add important momentum and commitment to the process of measuring results that are truly
strategic.

S/he can enhance the wisdom that an ever-changing
board acquires on the difference between (a) measuring
what the mission is and (b) *how* it accomplishes the
mission.

Ironically, this is the easiest contribution the CEO can
make and often the most needed. We still see organizations that measure program numbers instead of the
results of the services those programs provide, and organizations that rely on anecdotal measurements, particularly
stories included in newsletters and fundraising letters to
donors.

The least likely strategic measurement that an organization makes is the measurement of staff and volunteer
fulfillment. CEOs in many organizations still believe that
staff and volunteers are simply an important means to an
end, not target groups in themselves. The CEO can do a
lot to champion the measurement of this strategic result.

▶ *Strategic
measurements
are the responsi-
bility of the
board. They
cannot be done,
however, without
the full involve-
ment of the CEO
and staff.*

◀ *Governance
gives the board
more control
over the
mission of the
organization.*

The CEO and Management

When we spoke of the Default Model in Chapter 1, we suggested that there is a natural tendency for a board to focus on tactical management issues, leaving the CEO to handle strategic issues by default. Some CEOs may feel a sense of disempowerment by having to "give back" to the board the task of strategic planning, including "visioning." S/he may feel limited, not empowered, by having to manage *how* the organization delivers *what* the board has defined as its mission.

Some CEOs may need to make a paradigm shift in order to experience the enormous empowerment the governing board gives a CEO to manage the mission.

Services and Programs

One area in which CEO empowerment to manage can easily be seen is in the distinction between strategic services and tactical programs.

When we lead a board and senior staff through the strategic planning process, we usually include a brainstorming session designed for the group to accurately define its strategic services. Invariably, the flip chart is filled with a mixture of services and programs. In many organizations board and staff think of programs as the focus for their work instead of the services those programs provide.

The services the organization provides is a matter for the board to determine as part of its strategic direction. Which programs will deliver those services most effectively and efficiently is the management issue that the CEO and staff are empowered to develop.

For example, Hope Seeds, a not-for-profit organization based in Florida, identified the following services. (You will find their entire strategic plan in Part 3, Appendix C.)

"The services that Hope Seeds shall offer in this planning period are to:
- provide seeds
- acquire or produce seed stock
- provide agricultural advice
- teach/train
- research
- provide a Christian witness."

Michael Mueller, the Founder and Executive Director of Hope Seeds, has a strong background in the seed industry and has established programs to deliver these services. He is empowered by the Hope Seeds Board of Directors to develop other programs to deliver the six services included in the mission.

For example, in order to provide the service "acquire or produce seed stock," Michael Mueller has developed programs of:

- soliciting gifts of seed stock from other producers
- growing his own seed stock for plants that are not easily available in his area but which are planted in other parts of the world.

Thus, far from being disempowered by the board's limitations of which services the organization provides, the CEO is empowered to work creatively to develop tactical programs that will effectively deliver the strategic services.

Building on Strengths

▶

A luxury that nearly every CEO can enjoy in leading the management process is choosing to work in areas of interest and strength while delegating areas of weakness and lesser interest to others.

A luxury that nearly every CEO can enjoy in leading the management process is choosing to work in areas of interest and strength while delegating areas of weakness and lesser interest to others.

A CEO has many areas in which s/he has to be productive. They include:

- planning
- people management
- financial management
- fundraising
- expertise in the organization's mission
- speaking and writing.

As any organization grows, it becomes apparent that a CEO must make choices about how to prioritize limited time and energy. Some CEOs focus on management, some on fund development and communication, some on the professional element of the organization's mission, e.g., music, education, health care, etc.

In larger organizations a CEO must match his/her strengths to the changing needs of the organization. The same need that brought the CEO into the position may become the reason to leave. For example, a CEO who is known to be a "turn-around" CEO may have completed his/her leadership role when the organization has turned around. To stay longer than the personal areas of strength and interest prevents both the CEO and the organization from being effective in the next stage of their respective development.

Change doesn't usually lead to the necessity of departure but to the need for a more specialized role, adapting the CEO to his/her areas of strength and interest. Thus, while the CEO has the luxury of choosing what that contribution should be, the CEO must be able to identify both areas of strength and of weakness. This can be done in several ways:

- professional assessment tools
- personal introspection
- input from family, friends, board members, peers, staff and volunteers.

Governancematters.com Inc. has developed strength surveys that enable CEOs, managers, board members and board chairs to assess their relative strengths in the competencies listed in the chapters that discuss these various positions. Every CEO, however, already has some sense of his/her personal gifts and areas of strength. I think the easiest way to assess that is to recognize that "we like what we're good at" and "we're good at what we like."

A CEO is wise to acknowledge areas of disinterest and weakness relative to areas of strength. It doesn't help to deny disliking a task simply because it's part of the job and has to be done.

This kind of honesty flows naturally for a CEO who treats him/herself with the values of affirmation, involvement and servant leadership. These values produce self-esteem and self-awareness, two of the most important CEO competencies. The willingness to celebrate strengths and accept weaknesses also allows the CEO to hear what others have to say. There is a wealth of wisdom available to the CEO from the experience and perspectives of people with more authority, peers and staff. That's why the assessment tools we have developed include self-perception and the perceptions of these three groups.

Management Structure

The Relationship Model™ gives the CEO the freedom to design the structure of the organization's management. The CEO is in the best position to respond

◄

*The same need
that brought the
CEO into the
position may
become the
reason to leave.*

to changes in size, complexity, the effects of technology and many other factors. Changes in structure should not normally require board approval. That approval should already be given within whatever limitations the board has assigned. For example, the board may limit the maximum percent of the budget that can be allocated to infrastructure.

On the following page is the current organizational chart of The Good Samaritan Society in Edmonton, Alberta, Canada, a large and complex health care organization that uses the Relationship Model™.

Operational and Financial Management

In the tactical planning process of the Relationship Model™, the CEO and his/her senior management team receive the freedom to develop the tactical plans—both operational and financial. I prefer "tactical plans" to "the budget." The word "budget" focuses too much on the financial side of plans and not enough to the operational side, i.e., the management of the money rather than what the CEO and staff actually do with it.

Proper tactical planning is the key to receiving the board's empowerment for operational and financial management. Tactical planning includes:

- operational plans that reflect the strategic plan
- financial plans that reflect the financial planning policy.

You will see both elements when looking at a "budget," though the focus is often more on the numbers than on the words that describe the operational plans.

Financial management is what the name implies—management. The CEO is empowered within the strategic plan and the financial policies to plan, evaluate, change plans, and to allocate or re-allocate resources to achieve the mission.

The Good Samaritan Society Organizational Chart

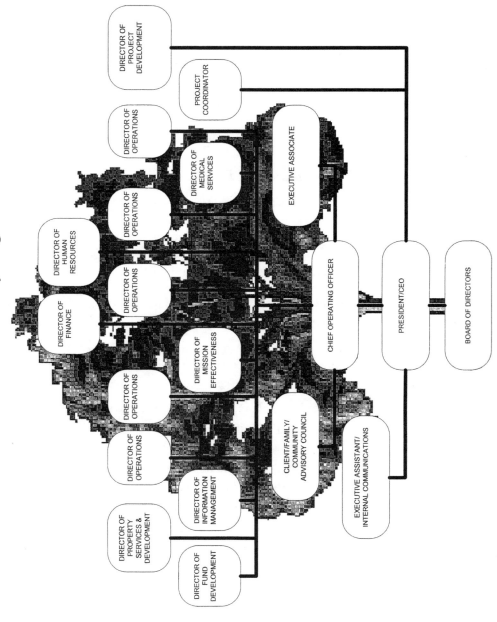

Summary

In this chapter we examined the role of the chief executive officer in governance and management.

We noted that the *personal leadership* qualities of the CEO are particularly critical because the CEO's *leadership position* spreads the values, which s/he models, throughout the organization. The personal leadership quality of the CEO is a primary factor in shaping the corporate culture, "the way we do things here."

We discussed the role of the CEO in governance. We examined that role in three processes in which the CEO interacts with the board:

- strategic planning
- delegation of authority and responsibility to the CEO
- monitoring and measuring.

We went on to cover the role of the CEO in management, highlighting the empowerment that the board gives to the CEO by keeping its focus on strategic issues and delegating tactical issues to the CEO.

Four illustrations of this empowerment to manage the organization are:

- freedom to develop the programs that provide the services
- freedom to focus on areas of strength and hire others in areas of relative weakness
- freedom to structure the management of the organization in order to achieve the mission effectively and efficiently
- freedom to develop operational and financial plans and to manage those plans and resources.

Management Structure and Processes

Introduction

Designing a management structure is significantly different from designing a governance structure because of the variables that make organizations different. The most significant variables are:

- size of the organization
- degree of geographical distribution
- type of services the organization offers
- type of infrastructure the organization requires
- national, cultural and linguistic complexities.

Because each organization is unique, we will deal with some of the general aspects of structure and process affected by the Relationship Model™.

Aspects of structure:

- CEO span of control
- senior management teams
- manager competencies

Aspects of process:

- decision-making by consensus
- tactical planning
- describing working relationships

Structure: CEO Span of Control

Today's designers of organizational structure recognize the need to reduce the height of hierarchical models. Stuart R. Levine and Michael A. Crom of Dale Carnegie & Associates, Inc., speak about this change in *The Leader in You*:

"Now this might come as a surprise to some people, but the pyramids are tumbling down...you can bet the future will be a whole lot more horizontal than in the past. All those rigid hierarchies, all those departmental lines, all those intricate chains of command—all of it stifled creative work. And who can afford that when the world is changing so fast?" (p. 98)

How flat can an organization become? How many people can any CEO manage effectively? 4? 12? 100? Is there any limit? There is a wide range in the CEO's span of control. Using a fully-developed form of the Relationship Model™ enables a CEO to increase the span of control and effectiveness at the same time. Factors that affect the CEO's effective span of control are:

- how the CEO values power
- how much the CEO is willing to delegate
- how clearly the working relationships are structured
- how the CEO uses a senior management team
- competencies of the CEO and the senior managers
- geographical distribution of the senior managers
- effectiveness of communication and information systems.

Some of these were discussed in the previous chapter. Others require more attention here, because they have an impact on how a CEO can design a management structure with a flatter hierarchy, larger span of control and increased effectiveness.

Structure: Senior Management Teams

Senior management teams are known by a variety of names. For the sake of simplicity we will abbreviate these to SMT.

The SMT: Decision-Making or Advisory?

CEOs may use the SMT as a decision-making team, an advisory team or both. The degree to which the team makes decisions depends largely on the success of the CEO in decentralizing decision-making. That, in turn, depends mainly on his/her values related to the use of power.

Authoritarian leaders are likely to favour centralized control, with significantly less authority and responsibility delegated to their SMTs. The SMT will primarily be an advisory group, even if they have decision-making authority "on paper."

Laissez-faire CEOs tend to want the SMT to make decisions. Poor clarity in delegation, however, often leaves the SMT wondering whether they are really a decision-making or an advisory body.

The CEO who works from relationship-oriented values at the centre of the values continuum, is the most likely to design a blend of advisory and decision-making functions. This is the type of SMT discussed here.

Advice or Decision?

In discussing each agenda item, it is vital that the CEO who values affirmation, involvement and servant leadership makes it clear as to whether s/he is requesting advice from the team or delegating the matter to them for a decision. It is frustrating, discouraging and disempowering for a team to think it is making a decision, then learn that the CEO was only asking for advice and has already selected a different option.

Team and Individual Responsibility

Each SMT member assists in group management of the entire organization, as well as managing his/her own department. Thus, every member works with two relationship descriptions:

- senior management team/CEO relationship
- senior manager/CEO relationship.

Later in this chapter we will offer examples of both.

The most effective use of the SMT is to coordinate organization-wide issues that involve planning, monitoring and measuring. The SMT is not the immediate source of authority for its members and, therefore, does not manage the work of individuals on the team. Instead, the team coordinates plans and changes in management issues that all managers have in common.

The SMT's responsibilities are to:

- assist the CEO with strategic planning and measurement of strategic results
- coordinate the tactical and financial planning of SMT members to comply with the strategic plan and the CEO limitations and expectation policies
- monitor SMT members' operational and financial management to maintain compliance with CEO limitations and expectations policies
- coordinate changes in operations that affect other managers
- develop and maintain the management manual including all processes.

The direct management of the individual's work remains a matter between the CEO and the individual manager. The CEO remains the immediate source of authority of the team and the individual members.

The responsibilities of the individual members are contained in the unique description of the working relationship each has with the CEO. You will notice that part of that responsibility is to participate in the SMT.

Senior Management Team Matrix

An SMT is made up of managers from both operations and support systems. These two groups combine to form a matrix of managers. Each support manager supports every operating manager and each operating manager is supported by every support manager. A basic matrix is displayed on the opposite page.

In this matrix all members are peers. No single individual has more authority or responsibility than any other. Group decisions require the discussion and debate of all individuals. To illustrate, let's examine the relationship of the manager of financial information to other members of the team. In some organizations the chief financial officer controls all expenditures. In that role s/he can instruct another senior manager that s/he may not make a certain purchase. It may not be in "the budget."

In this structure the chief financial officer is the source of information, not the source of control. Each member of the team has already negotiated with the rest of the team the amount of funding to be allocated to his/her position. It is the chief financial officer (or a member of that person's staff) who can provide information about how much of that financial resource is still available.

	Human Resources	Fund Development	Financial Information	Information Services	Maintenance Services
Manager					
Manager					
Manager					
Manager					
Manager					
Manager					
Manager					
Manager					

Team Leadership

As with any team, a leader must guide the core processes. The CEO could be this leader, and in many cases does fill that role. In larger organizations the chief operating officer (COO) often fills the position. There are important advantages, however, to assigning leadership to someone within the team. They include:

- greater sense of empowerment for the SMT
- greater sense of responsibility for the SMT
- opportunity to practice accountability within the team
- strong environment for consensus building
- practice in leading group process by rotating leadership.

The next pages display a sample SMT/CEO relationship description.

Senior Management Team/CEO Relationship Description

1. Authority

The Senior Management Team (SMT) functions by the authority of the Chief Executive Officer.

Resources delegated to the SMT consist of all financial resources, restricted and unrestricted, operational and capital, and include human resources of staff and volunteers.

The members of the SMT are the:

- Chief Executive Officer
- Managers of Services
- Manager of Human Resources
- Manager of Fund Development
- Manager of Financial Information
- Manager of Information Services
- Manager of Maintenance

2. Limitations of Authority

The limitations of authority for the SMT are determined by God's laws, civil laws, strategic plans and priorities, CEO limitations and the limitations specific to the SMT.

In carrying out its responsibility, the SMT or any of its members may not:

- hire, terminate or change the conditions of the employment of any member of the SMT
- restructure the SMT
- cause the board or the CEO to be in violation of any limitations or expectations policies.

3. Responsibility

The primary responsibility of the SMT is to assist the CEO with the management of operations and finances and other matters that impact the entire organization, including to:

- assist the CEO with strategic planning and measurement of strategic results
- coordinate the tactical and financial planning of members to comply with the strategic plan and the CEO limitations and expectation policies
- monitor its members operational and financial management to maintain compliance with CEO limitations and expectations policies
- co-ordinate changes in operations which affect other managers
- develop and maintain the management manual.

4. Expectations of Responsibility

The expectations of the responsibility of the SMT are expressed in the strategic plans (reviewed annually by the Board of Directors) and the operating and financial tactical plans (developed annually by negotiation with the CEO).

The SMT and its individual members are expected to:

- model the organizational values and the relationship values of affirmation, involvement and servant leadership in all relationships with staff, volunteers, clients and other stakeholders
- communicate or share relevant information with the CEO, within the SMT or between any of its members in a timely manner
- disclose to the CEO and the SMT any violation of their limitations of authority.

5. Accountability

Accountability is mutual. The CEO is accountable to the SMT for providing the authorization, resources, affirmation, involvement and servant leadership required for the successful realization of the responsibilities of the position.

Primary accountability of the SMT is to the CEO for performance and for compliance with the CEO limitations and expectations policies.

The working relationship is reviewed annually as part of the annual review.

Structure: Manager Competencies

An important part of the working relationships with managers is identifying the competencies of a manager. Some of the 20 manager competencies identified are shared with the board, board chair and CEO.

Two competencies are unique to managers—*team orientation* and *endurance*. (See Chapters 8 and 12 to review details of the other competencies. You will also find a table in Appendix D that illustrates how the competency sets of the board, board chair, CEO and managers compare with one another.)

Achieving Competencies

These generally lie above the water line and are therefore possible to improve by training. They are:

- Communication
- Commitment to the Organization
- Initiative
- Objectivity
- Process Orientation
- Results Orientation

Thinking Competencies

Often below the surface, there is a limit to how much thinking competencies can be changed by training. They reflect a person's cognitive ability. They are:

- Conceptual Thinking
- Effective Judgment
- Independent Thinking

Leadership Competencies

Often below the surface, these may be improved through increased knowledge and experience. These competencies influence other. They are affected by a person's attitudes and self-image. They are:

- Accountability
- Concern for Excellence
- Delegation
- Leadership
- *Team Orientation*

Team Orientation

A manager generally works with others in a team context. To be successful, the team needs to work in harmony, collaborating and cooperating as a united whole.

Team orientation by all members enables a team to work as one, overcoming any tendency to form subgroups or cliques. Personal agendas and domination by an individual or subgroup have no place on the team.

Group identity and commitment are built through a desire to cooperate and participate in reaching outcomes together.

Commitment does not smother independent thinking or imply mindlessly following the crowd. Decisions are made by consensus because there is a commitment to finding an outcome that the whole team produces and owns, even when there is genuine disagreement over the best course of action.

Teamwork may be built in many ways, including physically challenging outdoor activities where participants learn to trust their colleagues in difficult circumstances. Such pursuits may help develop certain skills. They may not necessarily induce a positive attitude towards teamwork, however, particularly if a manager prefers to work alone.

Sharing the same corporate values, vision and mission strengthens the bond where managers grow to guard and promote their reputation as a team, building foundations for mutual trust. Managers are not motivated by self-interest but share authority in order to reach common goals.

Team orientation usually has a harmonizing influence. Managers show support for each other and are better able to handle any conflicts that arise.

Personal Competencies

These mostly lie well below the surface and are, therefore, hard to change by training. Although all competencies are personal, these particularly reflect individual attitudes, traits, motives and self-image. They are:

- Empathy
- *Endurance*
- Open-mindedness
- Personal Integrity
- Self-awareness
- Self-esteem

Endurance

In the course of his/her work, a manager usually has to cope with situations that s/he would not necessarily choose. They may stretch and challenge the manager and create stress individually or in the team as a whole.

The obstacles may come from within the team or function or as a result of the wider internal or external environment. A manager needs the ability to overcome such obstacles, seeing them as opportunities to increase skills and develop character.

If a manager faces such difficulties with adequate personal resilience, then s/he is in a position to provide support and direction for those in the team. Others will look to him/her as role model. Seeing a manager drawing on personal resources, such as faith or family support and not caving in under the stress, increases self-belief and an ability to overcome. Whether spoken or unspoken, a manager, who shows such endurance, motivates and challenges others to endure.

Athletes provide a good example of stamina – not giving up at the first hurdle, but sticking with the challenge despite weariness and pain. The challenges at work may be different, but tenacity and endurance remain the same. Athletes, whether in individual or team events, are not distracted but keep pressing towards the goal, determined to reach it at any cost.

A certain amount of pressure is needed to keep individuals focused and motivated. When pressure turns to stress, it can debilitate, and in extreme cases, paralyze. Managers are unable to think clearly or make decisions.

The down side of endurance is stubbornness. Stubbornness is the inability to change your mind regardless of evidence to the contrary. Thus, the difference between endurance and stubbornness is often determined by the presence or absence of a logical argument to support the position.

The ability to overcome difficulties and complete tasks with a spirit of tenacity and endurance separates an ordinary manager from a successful one.

Process: Decision-making by Consensus

The SMT is not legally bound to make management decisions. In this regard their work is different from boards who are legally obligated to govern. When a board cannot decide an issue by consensus, it must decide by majority vote.

The SMT, however, has been established to assist and support the CEO in his/her obligation to manage. Where the SMT cannot make a decision, the matter may default to the CEO. This gives the SMT the luxury of making decisions by consensus instead of by majority vote. I recommend that CEOs require SMTs to make decisions by consensus. The advantages are too numerous to miss.

What Is Consensus?

Consensus occurs when the majority agrees on a certain course of action and everyone else in the group is willing to proceed for the sake of the group, even though some may not have chosen that course of action and would prefer another. Consensus does not occur if even one member of the group is unwilling to proceed with a decision that s/he cannot support.

Consensus can be unanimous, strong, medium or weak depending on the number of group members who agree with the course of action the majority wishes to follow.

A *unanimous consensus* occurs when the whole group is in agreement regarding the decision. This unanimous consensus is sometimes erroneously thought to be the only form of consensus. But consensus can occur without unanimity.

A *strong consensus* occurs when 75% or more of the group agrees and the rest are willing to proceed with the decision.

A *medium consensus* occurs when 50 – 75% of the group agrees and the rest are willing to proceed.

A *weak consensus* occurs when there are several viewpoints but no group has more than 50% support. If the group is still determined to decide by consensus, the majority may be willing to proceed with a minority viewpoint.

Consensus offers several distinct advantages over deciding by majority vote:

- There is much more involvement in and therefore ownership of the decision.
- It is easy to "test" the consensus with an unofficial poll or "straw vote" to see if consensus has been reached. If not, the group continues the discussion until the poll indicates that consensus has been reached or that consensus is not possible.
- Everyone in the group wins. Since consensus is a matter of freedom of expression, no one is forced to proceed against his/her will. There are no "losers" when there is no coercion, either blatant or subtle.

Reverse Consensus

I remember the time I was working with a group of 40 members of an organization, trying to achieve consensus on a bylaw revision. All but two people were willing to support the change in wording of a bylaw. It would have been an easy majority, but there would have been no consensus. I decided to ask the other 38 people if they would be willing to support the wording that the two preferred. To my amazement all 38 people were willing to agree for the sake of consensus. And the consensus became unanimous!

Consensus increases unity and commitment within a team. The process of reaching consensus, however, must be clearly understood and agreed upon by the entire team before the process begins.

Consensus Required – a Limitation of Authority

In one senior management team, the CEO, using the Relationship Model™, gave the team the freedom to make all management decisions within clearly defined limits. One of the limitations was that all the team's decisions must be made by consensus. If consensus was not possible, the decision automatically defaulted to the CEO. This leader reported that in four years, the team has never failed to reach consensus. He explains that the team is so committed to its management responsibility, the team is willing to take the time required to reach consensus, even when it isn't unanimous.

Process: Tactical Planning

The concise and comprehensive strategic plan discussed in Chapter 11 is the key to tactical planning. Earlier, we said that the basic tactical question that the CEO and senior management team must answer is, "How shall we achieve the mission within the limits of the available resources?"

In answer to that question, the SMT is responsible for developing the tactical programs to deliver the strategic services. In practical terms, think of a six-page strategic plan supported by a 100-page set of tactical plans.

In many organizations, however, the concept of programs and services is blended. Such an organization may produce a 100-page strategic plan that's mostly about tactical planning.

Organizations with no strategic plan run into trouble. Programs get designed without any clear understanding of the services they are to provide. If the programs "succeed" in practical terms, they are considered worth continuing. However, without clear strategic measurement of success, the organization has only tactical results to guide them in the planning process.

To emphasize the importance of distinguishing between services and programs, we need to recognize that what is tactical for one organization may be strategic for another. For example, an organization that provides humanitarian services in developing countries will require transportation, communication and logistics in order to fulfill its mission. For this organization, those services are tactical.

Mission Aviation Fellowship Europe (MAFE), on the other hand, is a consortium of national organizations organized specifically to provide transportation, communication and logistics to many national churches, international missions and relief and development agencies. For MAFE these services are strategic. The "how" for the humanitarian organization is the "what" of MAFE.

The humanitarian organization may, in its tactical plans, allocate resources to MAFE to provide transportation. MAFE, in its tactical planning, will address different issues. For example, the leaders will decide whether to create their own training and maintenance programs or to outsource those programs.

The Role of the SMT in Planning

The SMT adds enormous value to the organization in terms of tactical planning. Team members are all leaders of operating and support departments. Virtually all resources flow through their "branches" to fuel the programs bearing fruit for clients.

If the SMT understands the strategic plans and priorities, it is in a far better position than the CEO to prepare tactical plans. In turn, each SMT member will involve the managers, staff and volunteers in his/her department to create efficient and effective programs that form the management matrix of operations and support.

Departmental tactical planning begins in the treetop. Those plans flow back down the tree and converge in the SMT where they are coordinated with:

- strategic plans and priorities
- compliance with limitations and expectations.

SMT members should limit themselves to no more than six broad tactical goals, preferable three or four. To do this, the senior manager will organize the endless tasks that s/he must monitor and manage into specific broad goals. Every important activity will become a component of one or more of the goals.

Plans will be checked during the year, since changes invariably occur, sometimes affecting every goal. Senior managers may have to renegotiate additional resources or the goals themselves with peers or their source of authority.

Any change in the financial plan will have been preceded by a change in the plans themselves.

At the end of the planning period/fiscal year, the senior manager will discuss the results with staff and volunteers. The successes, failures and changes along the way will enable the team to refine the goals and plans for the next year.

Tactical Planning Simplified

Here is an outline for a goal-setting exercise that forms the heart of the annual tactical plan. On a single page (two at the most) address the following outline by describing the specifics of your plans. Keep it short and clear. Each goal statement will include:

- a goal statement
- objectives
- action steps
- resources required
- measurement of results
- risk assessment

Goal Statement

The tactical, operating goal is stated in a sentence that is S.M.A.R.T. (Specific, Measurable, Achievable, Relevant to the mission and Time-limited). The goal statement will likely state the broadest expression of the expectations of your responsibility.

Objectives

Objectives are a more detailed expression of the larger goal. Sometimes the goal will be the general statement that becomes S.M.A.R.T. only when the objectives are added. For example, if the new manager of fund development has a goal to establish a fully functioning department of development, the objectives may include:

- designing fundraising programs
- developing public relations programs
- recruiting paid staff and volunteers
- establishing a database.

Action Steps

Action steps are specific actions that must be completed in order to achieve the goals and objectives. They are usually sequential. Include only the most significant steps, not every single action you will be making. For example, action steps for establishing a database may include:

- researching available software programs
- selecting hardware

- finding a consultant to assist with the project
- installing existing records on the new system
- designing reports.

Resources Required

Financial resources should include a statement of the total operational cost of a particular goal. It should be set out in the financial planning format that the SMT has developed with the help of the chief financial officer.

Human resources should include the number of full or part-time staff and volunteers required to complete the goal successfully. These may be grouped with other goals.

Measurement of Results

In this section you will identify what measurement indicators will be used, the "M" in S.M.A.R.T. They may be expressions of quantity or the completion of a project, such as:

- number of people served
- people recruited
- dollars raised.

It may also be an expression of quality that will require a description of how quality will be measured, perhaps from a survey of clients.

Risk Assessment

The S.W.O.T. analysis is a proven means of assessing risk. Each goal should have been assessed. However, only the most significant strengths, weaknesses, opportunities or threats need mentioning here.

Process: Describing Working Relationships

Every organization is in a constant state of flux. For example, it's rare to find an organization where everyone has a current, written job description. Positions are constantly evolving due to:

- changes in staff
- specific talents that people bring to positions
- changing requirements
- changes in strategic plans and priorities
- changes in funding restrictions
- changes in the economy.

Few organizations keep up with these changes by reviewing and revising job descriptions. It is not uncommon for a person to be hired into a senior position and learn that no job description exists. "We'll do that as soon as you get acquainted with the position," we might hear the employer explain. Because of the confusion this lack of documentation causes, it is common for people to wonder:

- to whom they report
- how much authority they have
- how many resources they have and who decides
- what the boundaries of their authority are
- what their responsibilities are
- what is expected of them
- how their work will be assessed.

Assumptions get made often, but they differ, based on who happens to be making the assumption. It's a recipe for ineffectiveness, inefficiency, frustration and eventually brokenness.

The easiest thing a CEO can do within the management structure is to document all working relationships. Assuming that the values the board and CEO express have created a healthy organizational culture, designing and documenting working relationships will have a greater effect on achieving results and fulfilling staff than any other single factor.

Describing the Entire Working Relationship

If you began reading this book with Part 2, you may want to review the full concept of relationship descriptions in Chapter 6 (Delegating Process). In this section of this chapter we discuss the application of those concepts to the design of the management structure.

The traditional approach involves writing "job descriptions." Normally, this focuses on responsibilities, which are often expressed as detailed tasks. At the end of the list you may see words to this effect: "The position may involve other responsibilities not included here." In other words:

- "We may have forgotten something else that we want you to do."
- "We may have changes."
- "We don't want to alter the job description every time there's a change."
- "We want someone to pick up the pieces that fall off other people's tables."

It's not uncommon for the list of tasks to go on for two or three pages. Little is said about authority, let alone limitations of authority or expectations. The only reference to accountability is the common expression, "reports to the CEO."

The Relationship Model™ replaces the traditional job description with a relationship description. Introducing this model into the management structure, where every staff member and volunteer has a relationship description, will have a significant and positive impact on the organization. This should happen within the first year, because it can make such a difference for good.

To accomplish what seems like an insurmountable task, the CEO will begin with the senior management team. Following a training session on how to write a relationship description, s/he invites the team members to write a draft description of their working relationships with the CEO. An experienced staff person can usually do a more accurate job of describing the four or six broad areas of responsibility than the source of authority can. When the negotiation process of agreeing on limitations and expectations with the CEO has been completed, the draft becomes a final relationship description. Remember, the document itself is meaningless without the negotiation.

Senior managers are then able to take the process to the next level of the organizational tree. Finally, the process will reach the top where those staff and volunteers closest to the clients describe, negotiate and document their working relationships.

When complete, everyone in the organization will be able to understand the structure and their specific role in making it successful and fulfilling.

Here is a sample relationship description for a senior manager. Notice the reference to participation on the senior management team. In addition to the person's own areas of responsibility, s/he is responsible for participating in the senior management process. CEOs and senior managers should be aware that this may take up 10 – 20% of the total work load.

Manager of Fund Development /CEO Relationship Description

1. Authority

The Manager of Fund Development functions with authority from the Chief Executive Officer.

Resources delegated to the Manager include the department staff, financial resources for operations and a personal compensation and benefits package.

2. Limitations

The limitations of the authority for the Manager of Fund Development are determined by the:

- laws of (state, province, country)
- organization's strategic plans and priorities
- executive (CEO) limitations policies
- limitations of the Senior Management Team
- management manual
- limitations specific to the manager's position.

---

3. Responsibility

The responsibilities of the position are to:

- manage the organization's fund development programs, including the management of operational giving programs, capital campaigns, and endowment fund programs
- manage the organization's public relations programs
- develop and maintain a donor database
- contribute to effective organizational management including participation in strategic and tactical planning, policy development and decision-making through membership in the Senior Management Team.

4. Expectations

The expectations of responsibility are expressed in the tactical plans of the Manager, which are reviewed and negotiated with the CEO in the annual relationship review.

The Manager is expected to display the organizational values expressed in the strategic plan and the relationship values of affirmation, involvement and servant leadership with staff, volunteers and other stakeholders.

Overnight travel will be required.

5. Accountability

Accountability is mutual. The Chief Executive Officer is accountable to the Manager for providing the authorization, resources, affirmation, involvement and servant leadership required for the successful realization of the manager's responsibilities.

Primary accountability of the Manager is to the Chief Executive Officer for performance and for compliance with the limitations of authority and expectations of responsibility.

The working relationship is reviewed annually.

Summary

In this chapter we have examined the challenge that every CEO faces in designing the management structure of the organization. The issues include:

- understanding the CEO's span of control
- role and responsibility of senior management teams (SMTs)
- competencies required in senior managers
- relationship descriptions for senior managers, other staff and volunteers.

With respect to adapting the core processes to the management of the organization, we highlighted:

- decision-making by consensus
- tactical planning
- describing working relationships.

Decision-making by consensus is the more favourable form of decision-making in management teams. It involves everyone in the process and results in greater ownership of the decision.

Tactical planning fulfills the mission by developing the programs to deliver the services and by allocating the resources in keeping with the strategic plan. The senior management team is empowered to coordinate this process and in return builds a strong sense of ownership in the successful delivery of products and services to the clients.

We included two relationship descriptions:

- senior management team/CEO relationship description
- manager of fund development/CEO relationship description.

Notes

Leadership
at the Treetop

From Here We Can See Forever

Gordon MacKenzie is the author of *Orbiting the Giant Hairball, A Corporate Fool's Guide to Surviving with Grace.* It is a delightfully creative and irreverent commentary on life in an organization, a book that this book would be honoured to cuddle up to on the desk of any leader.

In a chapter entitled "The Pyramid and the Plum Tree," Mackenzie contrasts the top-down values depicted in the pyramid with those that might be seen in an organizational chart of the plum tree. The "product creators," as he refers to staff members, are at the top of the tree. Supported by their managers, staff members are the leaders who can see the needs of clients. Allowed to make their unique contributions, they find fulfillment in their work and the organization thrives.

The Power of Personal Leadership

In this final chapter we explore the power of personal leadership. We envision the enormous benefits from affirming, involving and being servant leaders of every staff person and volunteer—right up to the top of the tree! Then we address the challenge of how to ensure this potential can be realized in your organization.

A great deal has been written and continues to be written about leadership. Business sections of bookstores may carry one book on governance, but at least 20 on leadership. In this chapter I want to affirm many excellent insights into personal leadership that other writers have shared, highlighting the benefits to the leaders themselves and to the organizations they lead.

What is Personal Leadership?

Leadership is the competency that enables a person to influence people to make the whole greater than the sum of its parts. Leadership can influence others to:

- create new ideas
- go in a new direction
- embrace change
- focus on relationships
- work together
- have confidence
- seek challenge
- persevere in difficult circumstances
- thrive under pressure
- achieve the mission
- become more effective
- become more efficient
- become more fulfilled.

In offering a definition of the leadership competency required by all leaders, we said that *"leadership competencies can be developed by training and experience. To the extent that any person has developed his/her innate leadership qualities, s/he has personal leadership."*

This competency is not related to the position a person occupies in the organization. Virtually everyone in an organization can be a catalyst for change. I have often said to clients, "A good idea can come from anyone – even the CEO." To be sure, when the person who demonstrates *personal* leadership also has a leadership position, the position of authority enables him/her to multiply those personal leadership qualities. On the other hand, the person in a leadership position, who realizes the potential for personal leadership in everyone in the organization, can multiply the benefits exponentially.

When we witness *personal* leadership in the behav
staff and volunteers, we are likely to observe
qualities:

- sensitivity to the feeling of others
- willingness to take time to listen
- attention to others instead of self
- servanthood (hence the term "servant leadership")
- positive perspective
- willingness to work together
- clear focus on the vision
- confidence in one's ability
- belief in one's own value and ideas
- creativity
- desire to make a difference
- celebrating success.

◀

Leadership is the competency that enables a person to influence people and deploy resources to make the whole greater than the sum of its parts.

Cultivating Personal Leadership

We can nurture the leadership competency within our
organizations and "unleash" its enormous potential in a
number of ways. The result is greater productivity and
personal fulfillment.

Making Staff and Volunteers a Target Group

Much of what we have said in this book is intended to
place a greater value on the fulfillment of the staff and
volunteers of not-for-profit organizations than many
people experience now. We have said several times that
providing personal fulfillment for people within the
organization is not simply a means to an end. People are
part of the strategic direction of an organization, and
beneficiaries of the organization's mission themselves.

The benefits of taking this position are so incredible for
an organization that some are still convinced that
empowering an organization's people is really for the sake
of productivity. They believe that staff and volunteer
fulfillment is a means to effective service delivery, not an
end in itself.

I am personally convinced that the original design of healthy relationships compels us to balance client and staff fulfillment by placing both into the strategic mission of the organization, not by making one the means of achieving the other. For me this is not a semantic nuance. Lifting the nutrients up into the treetop will produce healthy leaves and abundant fruit. Both fulfill the organization's mission.

In his outstanding book, *Relational Leadership*, Walter C. Wright, Jr. writes:

"Volunteers, paid and unpaid, have something to give. But there is also something that they want, a need that must be addressed....Volunteers—all workers—want something out of it. They cannot be taken for granted. Volunteers want a return on the investment of their time. This is a foundational principle for the management of people, paid or unpaid. Only when we recognize this truth can we begin to lead people in a way that grows them and accomplishes our shared vision and values." (p. 167)

"Give them an inch and they will take a mile." Some fear that it is simply too risky to have staff and volunteers think that their fulfillment is as important as that of clients. Yet the shift from viewing staff and volunteers simply as a resource to viewing them also as a target group may not be the dangerous leap it appears.

Consider marriage and family. When a couple marries, two people hope to find fulfillment for themselves in fulfilling one another. When children arrive, they realize that the children are not there only for the parents' fulfillment. The children also want and need to be fulfilled themselves. Because the parents have more authority, they have more responsibility for ensuring that their children get what the parents want for themselves. The parents spend much of their adult lives finding ways to enrich the lives of their children through discipline, education, travel, recreation and a life of learning. At the same time, the entire family makes a contribution to the society around them. They seek to balance what they can give as a family with their needs as a whole family, not simply as a couple.

Or consider an organization where the beneficiaries of the services are the same as those who provide the services. A voluntary daycare organization might be such an example. Parents rotate in volunteering their time to care for the children of others, so that they may also benefit when others care for their children. Maintaining a balance between client and staff fulfillment is natural and self-regulating.

In a more complex organization, the example differs but the principle is the same. The board must now extend its efforts by engaging a CEO, staff and volunteers. Because the board has primary operational authority delegated to it by election, it also has primary responsibility for its own fulfillment and that of their CEO, staff and volunteers. They may not take on more plans or projects that those for which they are able to provide resources. By the same token, the board must provide as much service to clients as the staff can deliver, given the available resources. The balance between client and staff fulfillment is the key.

This commitment to balancing the fulfillment of everyone within the organization with its beneficiaries is likely the most significant single factor in bringing personal leadership to its fullest expression.

A Culture of Leadership

Neither an authoritarian nor a *laissez-faire* value system will support the kind of culture that encourages personal leadership. Only when the core values in healthy relationships become the foundation for organizational culture will personal leadership be brought to full flower. We have filled the pages of this book with applications of these values. Other authors, from different backgrounds and experiences, pick up the same themes.

Affirmation

In *The Leader of the Future* produced by The Drucker Foundation, Gifford Pinchot, writes:

"Less direct leadership focuses on communicating an inspiring vision and inspiring values, on listening to and caring for followers, on leading by personal example.... When indirect leadership is at its best, the people say, 'We did it ourselves.' The more indirect the method of leadership, the more room there is for other leaders within the organization." ("Creating Organizations with Many Leaders", p. 26)

◀

Lifting the nutrients up into the treetop will produce healthy leaves and abundant fruit. Both fulfill the organization's mission.

▶

Only when the core values in healthy relationships become the foundation for organizational culture will personal leadership be brought to full flower.

Involvement

Wright, whom we quoted earlier, speaks about involvement in terms of empowering others:

"Leadership is the process of giving power away, not collecting it. It is moving the power to influence into the hands of the people we are leading so that they can pursue the mission." (*Relational Leadership*, p. 135)

Charles Handy takes this concept a step further in *The Empty Raincoat:*

"No longer do people believe that the centre or the top necessarily knows best; no longer can the leaders do all the thinking for the rest; no longer do people want them to." (p. 118)

The values of affirmation and involvement jump out from comments by Ed Oakley and Doug Krug in *Enlightened Leadership:*

"...virtually every study and all our combined years of experience show money has much less importance to employees than being appreciated and feeling in on things and participating in what is going on within the organization." (p. 132)

Servant Leadership

The core value of servant leadership is addressed well in The *Leader in You* by Stuart R. Levine and Michael A. Crom. They quote Richard Barlett, Vice-chairman of Mary Kay Corporation,

"My personal view of the world is that there is no need for a president or chairman unless he is dedicated to serving the needs of others and to providing resources to the people who are getting the job done." (p. 100)

Charles Handy uses the word *subsidiarity* in relation to servant leadership:

"Subsidiarity sounds like another ugly word—empowerment. There is a significant difference. Empowerment implies that someone on high is giving away power. Subsidiarity, on the other hand, implies that the power belongs, in the first place, lower down or farther out. You take it away as a last resort. Those in the centre are the servants of the parts. The task of the centre, and of any leader, is to help the individual or the group to live up to their responsibilities. . ." (*The Empty Raincoat*, p. 126)

What may feel like a loss of control to a person in a leadership position is really the empowerment of others in their personal leadership. William C. Steere, Jr. makes this contribution in his article, "Key Leadership Challenges for Present and Future Executives," in the Drucker Foundation's book, *The Leader of the Future:*

"Inviting this kind of participation means giving up some of what we traditionally think of as control, but the end result is one of lasting value, because people become energized to achieve more when given authority and responsibility." (p. 276)

Changing Structures

There are two ways in which I think a change in structure takes place:

- in the way authority flows
- in how many levels there are.

The Way Authority Flows

In *The Empty Raincoat*, Charles Handy has already made a shift from top-down thinking when he speaks of "the centre" and "farther out." I think we should take it the final step suggested by servant leadership. One client calls it "roots up" thinking. Do it and you upend the whole concept of how authority flows in an organization. It's a wonderful way to encourage personal leadership.

How Many Levels?

Hierarchy is a normal and healthy part of organizational life. While some people use the terms hierarchical and authoritarian as synonyms, there is a significant difference. One speaks of the flow of authority, while the other names a value system that "lords it over" staff and volunteers.

The issue is not whether there should be any hierarchy. Levels of authority cannot be avoided in an organization of any size. The issue of structure is how many levels there should be.

In *The Leader in You*, Stuart R. Levine and Michael A. Crom, write:

"Now this might come as a surprise to some people, but the pyramids are tumbling down.... All those rigid hierarchies, all those departmental lines, all those intricate chains of command—all of it stifled creative work. And who can afford that when the world is changing so fast?" (p. 98)

In *The Leader of the Future*, "Creating Organizations with Many Leaders," Gifford Pinchot put it this way:

"In the times to come, leaders must find ways to replace hierarchy with indirect methods of leadership that allow greater freedom, lead to more accurate allocation of resources, and provide a stronger force for focusing on the common good." (p. 29)

Working in Teams

There's no lack of support for the impact of teams. Here's Stuart R. Levine and Michael A. Crom in *The Leader in You:*

"Clearly, what's been needed is a structure that loosens up the old rigidity, that could let people do their creative best, that could fully develop the talent that's been lying dormant for years. In more and more well-led organizations, the answer is being found in teams. Increasingly often, people are being asked to work beyond their disciplines, outside their cultures, above and below their usual ranks." (p. 98)

William N. Plamondon wrote one of the articles in *The Leader of the Future*, "Energy and Leadership." Here's what he had to say:

"...it's time to reengineer them to support an environment that breeds energy. What does such an environment look like? It is one where:

- *The organization is open to environmental information from customers, employees, competitors, and the marketplace.*
- *The team is aware of its strengths and weaknesses compared to the strengths and weakness of the competition and plays within them.*
- *Employees have a sense of purpose beyond just making money, which is guided by a core ideology as well as compelling and challenging performance goals.*
- *Authority and accountability are decentralized so that the organization becomes a collection of small, interchangeable units working toward a common goal.*
- *There are many leaders."* (pp. 274 – 275)

Decision-making

Decision-making, like all the other core processes, is impacted by this shift in organizational culture. There is a change in *where* the decisions are made.

Instead of top-down decisions, decisions are made as close to where they are implemented. As Warren Bennis says in *An Invented Life:*

"The new leader does not make all decisions herself; rather, she removes the obstacles that prevent her followers from making effective decisions themselves." (p. 220)

There is a change in *how* the decisions are made.

In "The Puzzles of Leadership," an article in *The Leader of the Future,* Steven M. Bornstein and Anthony F. Smith write:

"Clearly, building consensus is increasingly a critical leadership skill, because leadership through influence is demonstrably more effective in building commitment and sustained performance than leadership through positional authority or outright fear and intimidation." (p. 268)

Recruitment

In our presentation of competencies we noted that some competencies are harder to develop than others. The personal competencies listed in Part 3, Appendix D, are the most difficult to develop, because they are associated with attitudes and values. It follows that these are the competencies that we should watch for in the hiring process. People who join the organization and are strong in these competencies provide the most fertile ground for development through training.

William Plamondon puts it this way:

"The first step to ensuring that your organization is committed to its core values is to find the right people. This starts with the recruiting process.... In selecting new employees—especially for customer-contact positions—it's

wisest to hire for attitude and train for skills." (The Leader in the Future, "Energy and Leadership", p. 277)

Staff Development

What can the leaders of an organization do about developing the people who are already employed?

In *An Invented Life,* Warren Bennis writes:

"Whatever shape the future ultimately takes, the organizations that will succeed are those that take seriously—and sustain through action—the belief that their competitive advantage is based on the development and growth of the people in them. And the men and women who guide those organizations will be a different kind of leader than we've been used to. They will be maestros, not masters, coaches, not commanders." (p. 107)

In the excellent collection of articles in *The Leader of the Future,* Steven M. Bornstein and Anthony F. Smith write in an article entitled "The Puzzles of Leadership":

"Leadership is now understood by many to imply collective action, orchestrated in such a way as to bring about significant change while raising the competencies and motivation of all those involved—that is, action where more than one individual influences the process." (p. 282)

Development of personal competencies depends largely on changing values and attitudes that result in changes in behaviour. The most effective means of accomplishing that is for people in leadership positions to model the core values of healthy relationships in their own behaviour. People have a natural tendency to copy their role models. Observing behaviour in their maestros and coaches, people will tend to behave in similar ways. Gradually values and attitudes change until the behaviours are driven from within. It's self-initiated training.

Yes, it is possible to train staff in new behaviours that over time will shift values. Unless those values are supported and modeled by managers and leaders, however, the efforts will be fruitless or short-lived. That's because the effect of the behaviours they observe in others is greater than the effect of training. Corporate culture is more easily caught than taught.

The competencies that are skill and knowledge based, the ones we call achieving competencies, can more easily be developed through training the staff and volunteers we already have.

Summary

In this final chapter we have reached the top of the organizational tree where personal leaders find fulfillment for themselves and clients. We defined personal leadership as the competency that enables a person to influence people to make the whole greater than the sum of its parts.

To share some insights about personal leadership we have chosen the wisdom of some of the many authors who have accumulated a wealth of personal experience and have shared their knowledge with us.

Personal leadership can be cultivated in organizations by:

- making staff and volunteers a target group
- developing a culture based on the core values
- changing structures
- working in teams
- our decision-making process
- recruitment
- staff development.

In the epilogue we explore the reasons why efforts to introduce new models of governance, leadership and management sometimes fail and how the Relationship Model™ can be incorporated successfully.

◀

*Corporate
culture is more
easily caught
than taught.*

Keeping the Tree Green and the Fruit Ripe

In this chapter we will explore the reasons why organizations choose not to adopt new models and programs of governance and management. We will also explore why some who do, soon fall back into old habits they had hoped to change. In light of this, we will review ways in which boards, CEOs and managers can overcome this tendency to regress.

Our goal, using the Relationship Model™, is to have organizations work more effectively and to see their staffs more fulfilled. That, however, takes more than simply talking about theory and preparing documents.

Causes for Wilting

What organization has not tried to change its organizational culture, its mission and priorities, its structure or processes? And what organization has not experienced real frustration in the change process? Here are some of the factors identified from our own experience and research on why efforts to change can wilt and wither:

- the values of those in power
- natural resistance to change
- inadequate keeper of the flame
- inadequate training of existing people
- inadequate orientation of new people.

The Values of Those in Power

How the board, board chair, CEO and senior managers view their own power is one of the most significant factors influencing the success of change.

When a person has an unrealistic view of his/her own importance and lacks appreciation of the worth of others, s/he soon realizes that power would inevitably be slipping away to be redistributed elsewhere in the organization. Instead of recognizing the positive effect of empowering others, this person sees only the loss of his/her own power. The tendency is to use his/her position to conclude that the model "wouldn't work in this organization." The change to relationship-oriented leadership isn't likely even to begin.

On the other hand, when the organization's leaders work from a *laissez-faire* value system, there is little threat and considerable support for the empowerment of others. Unfortunately, it takes more than a *laissez-faire* attitude to keep the winds of change moving. *Laissez-faire* leaders allow the organization to float directionless. The focus on what creates meaningful change is soon lost and the new model is displaced by the original.

To succeed, it takes leadership that affirms, involves and serves those struggling with new structures and processes, and perhaps new values. Leaders of change must stay with the values, structure and process, nourishing the tree with its new supply of organizational energy.

Natural Resistance to Change

There is a natural inertia that resists change, sometimes as a self-defense against an unpleasant experience. The gain of change must exceed the pain of change, or change will slow down or reverse to what is or was less painful.

Resistance to change may mean that people do not:

- feel involved in making the changes
- understand the need for change
- understand what the changes are or how they will help
- understand what is expected of them in the process
- have confidence in the leadership of change.

Inadequate Keeper of the Flame

The process of introducing any new governance manual and strategic plan is very challenging. It requires extra time and energy from the board, CEO and senior managers. When complete, there is a sense of accomplishment, a feeling of satisfaction at a job well done. In turn, that is usually followed by a period of rest.

Too often, the period of rest becomes extended because of a sense that the job is over. Few realize that the process is ongoing. Not only did documents need to be written, but changes also need to be incorporated into the organization's structure and processes. I wonder how many documents rest on the shelves of organizations, either never having been implemented or waiting patiently to be used. Some eventually get transferred to archives as an important memory of the past.

What sometimes occurs is that the organization fails to appoint someone to monitor the change process. The board chair and CEO go back to their normal routine. People wait for someone else to make things happen.

The reality is that the process of implementation takes as much effort as the time to prepare it. The work is not as intense, because it must take place over a longer period of time, but the total effort is the same.

Inadequate Training for Existing People

For complete integration of the governance model and the strategic plan, everyone up to the managers near the treetop needs to understand:

- how governance and management relate to one another
- how the strategic plan provides direction for the development of their own tactical plans.

Sometimes the process of change slows to a stop because not everyone in management understands how they fit into the plan. This lack of involvement will result in confusion, discouragement and possibly the feeling that all this talk about involvement was just a tantalizing puff of air, not a sustained wind of change. Like leaves, they respond with an energetic flutter, only to be stilled again by inaction.

Inadequate Orientation for New People

New people continually enter the organization—and the parade of people who move in and out of organizations is amazing. Since the new people weren't part of the early development of change, they have no way of understanding how the past led to the changes that took place and why. Instead, they bring their own traditions and expectations of what the organization's culture should be. The result is frustration. They don't know what is expected of them or sometimes don't even understand the words they hear.

The need for a comprehensive orientation program for new people is essential, particularly in larger, more complex organizations. Unfortunately, this takes time and energy. Instead of mobilizing these new workers, who are ready and willing to fulfill their roles in a renewed organization, even more momentum is lost in the process of change.

How can we keep change moving in the right direction?

There are specific things that leaders in organizations can do to keep change moving in the right direction and the tree green. They all come under the following heading.

Focus on Healthy, Balanced Relationships

Relationships are the operating system of every organization. The Relationship Model™ makes healthy, balanced relationships the first and most important principle of building and maintaining healthy organizations.

Focusing on this balance will result in relationships that meet the needs of the client and those of staff and volunteers. People work together. Relationships bring people into community. Without leaders being committed to that balance, the Relationship Model™ will fail.

Many books speak of being people-centred, community-focused, and caring for staff and volunteers. There is a sense, however, that this is a means to an end to create a productive organization, i.e., if we don't look after our people, service to clients will suffer. We believe, however, that staff and volunteers of every not-for-profit organization are target groups themselves. The strategic plan includes them. Services are directed towards them.

Some leaders fear that emphasizing staff and volunteer fulfillment will make people lazy and have a negative impact on productivity. This may happen if too much emphasis is placed on staff and volunteer fulfillment. What I'm speaking about is achieving a balance that both the source of authority and recipient are agreed upon.

We can be successful in keeping the tree green and the fruit ripe when we focus on relationships in three specific areas: values, structure and process.

Focus on Values

People demonstrate their values in their behaviour. You will always be able to assess your own values by observing the way you treat yourself and others. Thus, the values that shape our behaviour are where we need to focus. Understanding the continuum of how we value power will help us avoid being authoritarian or *laissez-faire*, concentrating instead on the three core relationship-oriented values. It helps if we regularly ask ourselves the following questions:

- Am I affirming this person?
- Am I involving this person in decisions that affect him/her?
- Am I acting as a servant leader to this person?

The checklists that appear under structure and process also reflect on the degree to which we express the core values in our relationships.

Affirm the Leaders

In the previous chapter I emphasized leadership from a personal perspective, not the position of leadership. I said that the personal leadership of everyone in this living tree empowers an organization, not just the personal leadership of those in positions of leadership.

Affirming the leaders is not only a plea to the board and staff to affirm the CEO and senior managers. It is more a plea for the board, CEO and senior managers to affirm the leaders represented by each leaf on the tree. First, however, it is a reminder to recognize our own worth and the value of our own leadership to the organization.

Affirmation isn't just a good idea and worthy of being a core value to a model of governance, leadership, management and service delivery. It's a value that requires regular expression. A focus on affirmation means thinking about the value and using the word in conversations at work. It means making the commitment to make affirmation a regular part of your contribution to the organizational culture. If the people you affirm still don't think of their workplace as being affirming, at least it isn't because you aren't affirming them.

Here are three questions to ask yourself:

- Do I affirm myself in my thoughts, in my words to myself and in the way I treat myself?
- Do I affirm my source of authority in my private thoughts, in what I say to him/her and to others about him/her? Do I follow through with actions?
- Do I affirm those who look to me as their source of authority in my thoughts, my conversations with them and in the actions that follow?

Involve the Leaders

Every manager can focus on involvement, making it a regular personal contribution to the organizational culture. Ask yourself these three questions as you interact with people who look to you as their source of authority. Note that the three are related directly to the first three core processes.

- Do I make an effort to verify that I understand what is said to me?
- Do I involve people in the plans and decisions that affect them?
- Do I hear the concerns of my staff and deal with conflict promptly?

Be Servant Leaders for the Leaders

I have tried to demonstrate the energy we release in others when we support them instead of "lording it over" them. We can focus on this important value by assessing our own thoughts, words and actions.

- Do I support this person?
- Do I express my support in words?
- Do my actions reflect the support that I feel and express?

Focus on Structure

Keeping the tree green and the fruit ripe requires a clear focus on the technical components of structure: authority (with limitations), responsibility (with expectations) and accountability (monitoring and measuring). Here is a simple checklist on how to be confident that you have an adequate and ongoing focus on structure.

- Does every staff person, volunteer, committee and work group have a relationship description completed and/or revisited in the last 12 months?
- Does everyone above have a clear understanding of the limitations of the authority delegated to him/her/them written in the relationship description or limitations policies in the governance or management manual? And has it been revisited in the last 12 months?
- Does everyone above have a clear understanding of the expectations delegated to him/her/them written in the relationship description, strategic and tactical goals, standards and other documentation? And has it been revisited in the last 12 months?

While this is a concise checklist, it is also comprehensive. Keeping these three things current requires commitment to the time and energy it takes.

Time passes quickly in every organization. Documents become stale while we still think they were reviewed "recently." I recommend that you maintain a list of the position of every staff member, volunteer and work group in a computer file that will allow you to record the appropriate dates for review of the relationship and its documentation.

Every group and individual delegating authority to another individual or group is responsible for ensuring that the three items in the checklist are complete and current. This is not a task that the CEO is responsible for, even though the CEO is singularly accountable to the board for seeing that it is complete and current throughout the organization.

This means that the number of relationship reviews to be completed and kept current by any individual is not greater than the number of individuals or groups reporting to that person.

Once the governance manual and the strategic plan are in place, it is my view that no organization, regardless of size, should require more than one year to complete a relationship description for every person and group working in that organization.

Focus on Process

If structure is like a snapshot of the tree, process is a time-lapse motion picture. It shows the tree growing and bearing fruit.

Focus on process can be monitored with the checklist that follows. This checklist may be part of the board's annual self-evaluation of governance performance, as well as that done by senior management teams. In addition, every person who delegates authority to another may find it helpful to use these questions in the first part of the relationship review. In this process the recipient of authority reviews the quality of performance of the source of authority in demonstrating the values by keeping the structure clear and by leading the six core processes effectively.

Each of the questions may be asked at any level of the organization. They begin with "I" where an individual is asking them and "we" where the board, committee or a management team is using them. They apply to the relationship with your source of authority and to the relationship with the recipients of your authority. The answers to these questions are valid when the perceptions of both parties in any relationship are the same.

- Do I reflect the core values of affirmation, involvement and servant leadership in the manner in which I lead the process of:
  - communication?
  - decision-making?
  - conflict resolution?
  - planning?
  - delegating?
  - monitoring and measuring?

Communication

- Does our *communication* demonstrate affirmation of one another?
- Do we listen to one another, clarifying until we understand what we hear?
- Do we support one another in the feelings behind our thoughts even when we disagree with the other's thoughts, points of view or conclusions?

Decision-making

- Do I *delegate* decisions clearly to my staff, negotiating the limitations of their authority and expectations of their responsibility?
- Do I make it clear to my staff when I'm delegating the decision to them and when I'm asking for input into a decision that I intend to make myself?
- Do I ask for input from my staff in decisions that affect them—decisions that I cannot or choose not to delegate?

Conflict Resolution

- Are we able to disagree and debate issues without those issues becoming destructive to our relationships?
- Do I go privately and without delay to individuals whom I believe have violated my values or offended me?

- Which of the three statements most accurately describes you and/or your organization's approach to conflict?
  - I/We usually avoid dealing with conflicts even though everyone knows they are there.
  - I/We usually deal with conflicts in a way that drives people further apart.
  - I/We usually deal with conflicts in a way that results in resolution and reconciliation.

Planning

- Do we have both strategic and tactical plans that were revised in the last 12 months?
- Has our board determined what factors are critical to the success of our mission? Does our staff know them and refer to them in the tactical plans?
- Do our plans have goals that are specific, measurable, achievable, relevant to the mission and time-limited?

Delegating

- Is there a balance between my authorization, resources and competencies and the expectations of my responsibility?
- Does my understanding of the limitations of my authority give me the freedom I need to succeed in my work?
- Have the expectations of my responsibility been negotiated and agreed upon by me and my source of authority?

Monitoring and Measuring

- Do I participate in regular monitoring of the limitations and expectations policies that affect my working relationships?
- Do I provide a review annually of my working relationship with all those who report to me?
- Do I receive a review annually of my working relationship with my source of authority?

You Are Not Alone

The mission of GovernanceMatters.com Inc. is to enable not-for-profit organizations worldwide to balance the fulfillment of their customers' needs and the personal fulfillment of their staff and volunteers.

The primary vehicle for our service delivery is the Internet. We also offer personal consulting and training where requested. We seek to offer practical tools of high quality at costs that Christian faith-based organizations can afford, accessible from any location in the world.

The Relationship Model™ is trademarked, copyrighted and available for use under license from GovernanceMatters.com Inc. The permanent license fee for the ongoing use of the model is included with the purchase of some of the workbooks and tools. All of our other governance and management tools, surveys and materials are copyrighted and available for use under license at nominal costs. This enables us to maintain quality control and to share updates and new developments with clients.

Boards, CEOs and managers may order materials easily on our website: www.governancematters.com. All prices are available at that site.

Here are some of the publications, tools, surveys and workbooks available in hard copy and/or downloadable files.

Governance Matters
by Les Stahlke with Jennifer Loughlin

You may purchase copies of this book in quantities for your board or management teams. Discounts for volume purchases are offered on the website. This is the basic text for any application of the Relationship Model™ in your organization.

Governance Manual Development

Support in the development of a governance manual based on the Relationship Model™ is available in three levels of support. Purchase of any of these options includes the license to use the Relationship Model™ in one organization in perpetuity at no additional cost. Details for price and ordering are on the website.

Basic

We can provide you with a workbook file that you may print and distribute to your board. Working as a group, you may make the changes and additions to the policies and then submit your completed workbook to GovernanceMatters.com Inc. for review, recommendations, and certification. The cost for this is also included in the purchase price.

Advanced

GovernanceMatters.com Inc. will adapt the workbook to incorporate your current bylaws and governance policies so that your group work will be much more straightforward, requiring less time and effort on your part. Working as a group, you may make the changes and additions to the policies and then submit your completed workbook to GovernanceMatters.com Inc. for review, recommendations and certification. As above, the cost for this is also included in the purchase price.

Personal, On-site Consultation

A consultant from GovernanceMatters.com Inc. will prepare the workbook as per the advanced option and meet personally with your board to facilitate your board retreat in learning the Relationship Model™ and completing the governance manual in a single day. The consultant will make the revisions and return a finished electronic file for your formal approval.

Strategic Planning

GovernanceMatters.com Inc. has developed a strategic planning process workbook that may be used in one of two ways:

Self-Directed Planning

We can prepare a strategic planning workbook based on your existing documentation and the Relationship Model™. Going through this workbook together in a day-long board retreat will result in material that we can review and edit for your formal approval. This book (*Governance Matters*) is required reading for the board's effective strategic planning. There is no additional cost for our review, editing and recommendations.

Consultant-facilitated Planning

This more intensive process will begin with a similar process – the preparation of a workbook based on your existing planning documentation. A trained consultant will facilitate your board retreat and a clear, concise strategic plan will emerge in one day.

Strategic Survey

This additional module may be added to either option above. It surveys stakeholders on the components that will be included in your strategic plan. It provides a clear expression of needs and priorities, allowing the board to plan with confidence and effectiveness. The cost will depend on size and complexity of the group. This module is highly recommended for the first effort at strategic planning.

Distance Learning

GovernanceMatters.com Inc. also offers distance learning via interactive Internet-based learning software for:

- board members
- board chairs
- chief executive officers
- managers
- clergy.

The courses may be selected as entire courses or modules. Courses are offered on an ongoing basis with small groups of enrolled students forming a "class." Mentoring by an on-line specialist and interaction with the other students provides a highly effective, low cost, training program. *Governance Matters* is required reading for full courses and recommended reading for modules. See the website for details of offerings, dates and prices.

Relationship Descriptions

The preparation of relationship descriptions is one of the modules of the distance learning program. Providing practical training in how to write a relationship description, this module includes a license to use the copyrighted format in your organization in perpetuity at no additional cost.

Relationship Reviews

An additional module trains you and your staff members in the process of reviewing the working relationships. The review forms are copyrighted and available for use in your organization in perpetuity for a nominal charge. The cost includes one review of the changes and additions you may wish to make to personalize the process to your organization.

Strength Surveys

Governance Matters.com Inc. offers comprehensive surveys that assess the strengths of the 20 competencies associated with board members, board chairs, CEOs, managers and clergy. Particularly useful when evaluating internal candidates for career development or additional responsibility, these surveys are the result of a 100-statement questionnaire completed by a person's source of authority, peers, recipients of authority and the person him/herself. Up to 12 reviewers may participate in each survey. The questionnaire is composed of behaviours that express the presence or absence of each of the 20 competencies. Reviewers are invited to assess the frequency of their observation of these behaviours in the person being reviewed. The survey indicates how strongly each competency is present.

Self-analysis

A low-cost, high-value version of the survey is emailed to the individual and to his/her source of authority. It includes tables of data for each of the competencies and for each of the reviewers (without names) and their average scores on each of the five statements evaluating the 20 competencies. Graphs show how perceptions of the various categories of reviewers compare with the perception of the person being reviewed.

This version comes with detailed instructions for interpreting the information provided in the data and the graphs. The survey provides a clear set of perceptions of the strengths of all 20 competencies and indicates where additional professional development may improve performance and fulfillment.

Consultant-analysis

Two additional elements are added to the more comprehensive, professionally assessed version of the same strength surveys.

Comments are solicited from all reviewers to add perspective to the scores given to each of the statements in the questionnaire. These are presented in the final documentation to amplify the perceptions of the reviewers.

A professional analysis by a consultant experienced in this particular assessment tool will provide a wealth of information about the strengths and the significance of the data and the graphs. The consultant also offers suggestions and recommendations for professional development. Two confidential hard copies are bound and mailed to the person in the organization authorized to receive one and to distribute the other to the person being reviewed.

Obtaining questionnaires for review, pricing and ordering may be done by visiting the website.

Newsletters

GovernanceMatters.com Inc. offers several newsletters to assist board members and managers stay current with governance and management issues. They include practical help, refinements and ideas that have proven effective by others using the model in their organizations.

The newsletters are sent to one email address for printing and distribution by you or for forwarding to your internal email list. The quality is high, the cost low, thanks to the Internet distribution system.

Tree Trunks – a Newsletter for Boards and CEOs

This newsletter is directed to boards and CEOs and deals with a wide range of governance issues. It features articles on strategic planning and all other governance processes addressed in this book. Each of the six issues per year includes a question and answer forum and the experiences of other boards using the Relationship Model™ of governance.

Tree Tops – a Newsletter for CEOs and Managers, Staff and Volunteers

This newsletter, also emailed six times per year, has the same format as *Tree Trunks*, but deals specifically with management structure and processes.

Log in to www.governancematters.com for price information and ordering.

Summary

In this chapter we dealt with the reality of keeping the structure and processes of governance and management alive and healthy, growing and producing fruit. In doing this we have to be prepared to make changes.

Change is challenging. Some of the blocks to continued growth include:

- the values of those in power
- normal resistance to change
- inadequate keeper of the flame
- inadequate training of existing people
- inadequate orientation of new people.

It is possible to keep the tree green by focusing on relationships, the operating system of all organizations.

We do this by paying close attention to:

- values
- structure
- processes.

The chapter includes a series of questions in a checklist that enables an organization's leaders to monitor organizational performance in the values, structures and processes that maintain productivity and staff fulfillment.

The chapter concludes with a list of resources available on www.governancematters.com. They include:

- *Governance Matters* by Les Stahlke with Jennifer Loughlin
- governance manual development
- strategic planning
- distance learning
- board governance assessment
- senior management team assessment
- staff fulfillment assessment
- relationship review forms
- strength surveys for board members, chairs, CEOs and managers
- newsletters for boards, CEOs and managers.

The Relationship Model™
Principles of Governance, Leadership and Management

1 The organization seeks a balance between the fulfillment of the needs of the clients and the personal fulfillment of the staff and volunteers.

2 The affirmation, involvement and servant leadership of every individual and group at every level in the organization are vital to the success of the organization.

3 Authority, responsibility and accountability are the primary components of all relationships. Limitations of authority and expectations of responsibility are the secondary components.

4 Circles of authority and responsibility are defined clearly and are maintained equal in size by placing limits on authority or by negotiating expectations of responsibility.

5 The board of directors, acting on information from all stakeholders, is responsible for governance: defining target groups, services/needs, vision, mission and priorities, monitoring performance and measuring results.

6 The CEO is responsible for managing the delivery of services to the clients in accord with board-stated priorities and for achieving the strategic goals within the limitations of the authorization and resources available.

7 Each individual has a share in responsibility for creating, owning, understanding and implementing the mission of the organization.

8 Decision-making proceeds from shared values, vision and mission, not unilaterally from the board or the CEO. Decisions are made as close as possible to where they are implemented.

9 The organization is results-oriented. Indicators of results are identified. Strategic and tactical goals are set in balance with available resources. Results are measured.

10 Accountability is mutual. The source of authority is accountable to the recipient for providing adequate authorization and resources. The recipient is accountable to the source for achieving results.

Appendices

PART *3*

Appendix A
Definition of Terms

accountability—the third primary component of a direct working relationship. It is a neutral process of monitoring progress and measuring results. Authority (with limitations) and responsibility (with expectations) are the other primary(and secondary) components.

authoritarian—the name given to the value system on the continuum of values related to the use of authority. With this value system, "might is right" and obedience produces rewards. An authoritarian value system can result in abuse of power and harm to healthy relationships.

authority—the first component of a relationship. Authority at any level in the organization is always limited by the person or group who is delegating authority to others. In the Relationship Model™ the circle of authority includes authorization, resources and competencies. Power, when used in a positive sense, is synonymous with authority.

authorization—one of three components of the circle of authority along with resources and competencies. Authorization may be thought of as having "the keys to the car." It is delegated by the source of authority at the point of hiring and ends when the working relationship ends.

board chair—a member of the board of directors, elected by the board primarily to lead the process of governance. The board chair may also represent the organization to other organizations, to the stakeholders and to the civil authorities. The board chair receives authority and responsibility from the board and is accountable to the board. The board chair normally has no authority or responsibility for management.

board governance manual—the name of the manual that describes the values, structure and process of governance for an organization. This manual is within the authority given to the board by its members to approve and revise as necessary.

board of directors—the highest governing body in an organization. Elected by its members, the board of directors receives its authority from its members and other stakeholders and the government. Responsibilities include designing and implementing its own structure and process, directing strategic priorities, delegating management authority and responsibility to the staff and determining results by measuring and monitoring.

charity—a charitable organization, sometimes called a not-for-profit or a non-profit organization. A charity exists by the authority and support of its stakeholders and the authority of the civil government of the country in which it is based.

committee—a group designated by the board of directors to assist the board with the development of governance policies and with monitoring the executive director compliance with the limitations policies of the board. Committees have a singular responsibility to assist with governance and have no responsibility for management except by special authorization from the board.

critical success factors—the factors that the board determines are critical to the success of achieving the mission of the organization. These form the final component of the strategic plan and form a bridge between the strategic and the tactical (governance and management) functions. The CEO is expected to address the critical success factors in the tactical plans, enabling the board to express its interests in management without becoming involved in managing as a board function.

directors—members of the board of directors. Directors have been entrusted by those who elected or appointed them with the direction and governance of the organization. The emphasis on the word "director" is on the authority component of governance. Directors are individually accountable to the stakeholders and civil governments for their personal behaviour and collectively accountable to them for their governance of the organization.

executive director—the chief executive officer of the organization, hired by the board of directors primarily to lead the process of managing the infrastructure, including strategic planning and achieving the strategic goals within the limits of the authority delegated by the board. The executive director receives authority and responsibility from the board and is accountable to the board. The executive director has no authority or responsibility for governance and is not a member of the board of directors.

expectations—one of two secondary components of a relationship. Expectations are associated with responsibilities and are usually expressed in the form of goals. The quality of expectations may be expressed as minimum standards and standards to which we aspire.

forgiveness—the expression of affirmation in a relationship that has become broken. It allows us to accept the offending party even though there is no hope of return of what was taken by the offending party: money, health, reputation, life. Forgiveness sets the forgiving person free from hate and the need for retaliation.

goals—an expression of the expectations of responsibility. Goals may be strategic or tactical and are always negotiated by the source and the recipient of delegated authority to assure the balance between authority and responsibility. S.M.A.R.T. goals are specific, measurable, achievable, relevant to the mission and priorities and time-limited.

governance—the process by which a board of directors maintains control of its responsibility. Governance involves designing board structure and process, directing strategic priorities, delegating authority and responsibility and measuring and monitoring results. Governance is a more effective method of control than management for larger and more complex organizations. The board of directors is accountable to the stakeholders for achieving strategic results and to the appropriate government agency or department for remaining within the limitations of civil law.

healthy relationship—a working relationship is healthy when a balance exists between the authorization, resources and competencies on the one hand, and the expectations expressed in goals and standards on the other. In the case of an entire organization, the relationship between the staff and the clients is healthy when client satisfaction (productivity) and staff fulfillment (satisfaction) are in balance.

justice—the acknowledgement by the offending party, or a third party with authority in the matter, of the wrong that was committed. Justice includes a fair compensation for what can be repaid. Repayment can take one or more forms of acknowledgment, apology, amends, restitution, fine, imprisonment or capital punishment.

laissez-faire—the name given to a value system on the continuum of values related to the use of authority in an organization where conflict tends to be avoided or denied. To varying degrees, this value system exhibits lack of clarity on roles and responsibilities. Traditions and assumptions are more common than policies and goals. In its extreme form, *laissez-faire* is identified by a complete abdication of authority.

leadership—the process of enabling individuals and groups to express their values, realize their potential for service and personal fulfillment. Leadership is characterized by being affirming, involving and supporting. All individuals in the organization have an opportunity to provide leadership to others.

limitations—the limiting and defining element of delegated authority. Limitations are normally expressed in negative terms to create the circle of authority, which defines clearly our freedom in fulfilling our responsibility. Defining limitations to authority eliminates the need for returning to the source of authority repeatedly for permission to act.

management—the process by which the staff transforms the strategic direction of the board of directors into services and programs that benefit the stakeholders. Management works within the defined circle of authority to fulfill the expectations of its circle of responsibility and is accountable to the board of directors both for strategic results and for remaining within the limitations of authority.

minutes—the official record of the board of directors, containing the result of the governance process in the form of policies and strategic decisions, as well as exceptional management decisions. The board minutes are the only way the board communicates its decisions and directions to the staff through the executive director.

mission—a term given to the statement that contains the core reason for the organization's existence.

model—a design that provides the framework for a board of directors and the CEO to develop the structure and process (form and function) of governance and management for the organization to fulfill its mission.

not-for-profit—a type of organization in which the purpose is to deliver products and services to clients, not for profit, but as an expression of the values of the members and stakeholders. Sometimes called "non-profit," the organization may generate a surplus even though that is not its mission.

organization—a generic name given to a corporate entity or charity. The term includes the entire organization including the membership, board and staff.

policies—Policies are the expression of the board decision-making process. There are four types of policies: 1.Internal Relationships, 2. Strategic Direction, 3. Board/Staff Relationships and 4. Board Accountability (monitoring and measuring).

reconciliation—is the restoration of a broken relationship, which can only be achieved after forgiveness, justice and repentance have been experienced by both parties in the broken relationship. It is the weld that unites brokenness.

Relationship Model™—a name describing a model focusing on the values, structure and processes of relationships in an organization. Usually used to distinguish from an authoritarian structure, a relationship-centred structure is based on the three core values of affirmation, involvement and support. The three core components of a relationship are authority, responsibility and accountability. Secondary elements of The Relationship Model™ are limitations of authority and expectations of responsibility. The model is realized through the processes of governance, leadership, management and service delivery.

repentance and amends—are the willing expressions of an offending party to "right the wrong." It may take the form of an apology, public acknowledgement, financial compensation, time. These expressions may precede or follow forgiveness.

responsibility—the second primary component of a relationship. Responsibilities within an organization are typically described in a committee terms of reference or an individual job description. Responsibility is further defined by expectations of the responsibility.

stakeholders—individuals and groups who have a "stake" in the organization, similar to the shareholders in a for-profit corporation. In a charity they include the donors, members, strategic partners and the clients of the organization. Stakeholders are the "owners" of the charity. The board of directors consults the individuals within these groups for strategic direction and is accountable to them for the strategic results of the charity.

strategic—describes the focus of the board's responsibility, the "what" of an organization by defining the values, target groups and the needs to be addressed, vision for the future, purpose and priorities and allocation of funds. The result of all the board's strategic direction to the staff is contained in the strategic plan of the organization.

tactical—describes the focus of management responsibility, the "how" of an organization, including the development and management of programs for delivering the services directed by the board, the process of budgeting and financial management and the management of staff and volunteers.

target groups—the groups of people whom the stakeholders, through the board of directors, choose to serve. Target groups may be described by their type and by their geographical location.

values—a complex set of convictions held by the members of a charitable organization. Values include many levels: core beliefs and personal values, strategic direction values, relationship values and personal preferences and interests. People display their values by their behaviour.

vision—a futuristic and idealistic view of what can result from realizing the purpose of the organization. A vision stays just beyond the strategic planning horizon, drawing, encouraging and challenging the organization towards its potential. The focus is on the difference that the organization will make in the world, not on the organization itself.

Appendix B
Board Governance Manual

Introduction

This basic version of a board governance manual written in the Relationship Model™ is included here for your evaluation. Even though it is copyrighted and requires a license for use in your organization, we hope that having a sample copy will enable you to determine whether the Relationship Model™ will benefit the governance, leadership and management of your not-for-profit organization.

Every organization, new or well-established, small or large, located in one community or widely-dispersed, will need to make additions and changes to what follows here.

This sample includes only those policies that may be common to all organizations, and even these will need some adjustment to fit your organizational environment.

The three levels of support that we offer you to install the Relationship Model™ in your organization are detailed at the end of the Epilogue. Each option includes the license to use the Relationship Model™ in your organization in perpetuity.

More information on applying the Relationship Model™ to your organization can also be found on www.governancematters.com.

THE RELATIONSHIP MODEL™
Board Governance Manual

Table of Contents

Board Governance Manual

1.0 RELATIONSHIPS

People live and work within relationships. Relationships are the human operating system. In order to make our lives and our work successful and fulfilling, we need to apply the natural principles of relationships by establishing the values, structures and the processes of relationships throughout our organization.

In the Relationship Model™, values, structure and processes form the basis of governance, leadership, management and service delivery. The roles of governance, leadership and management differ, but the principles that underlie them are the same. There is a continuity of design from the organization's membership to the point where the clients receive the services.

A successful working environment is one in which there is a balance between the fulfillment of the individuals doing the work and the fulfillment of the people for whom the work is done. The organization itself is like the fulcrum of a seesaw that supports the dynamics of the process of maintaining this delicate and dynamic balance of fulfillment benefiting both staff and clients.

Putting emphasis on healthy relationships means investing a great deal of attention on the values, the structures and the processes that make up relationships. We have all observed that healthy and fulfilled men and women are more productive than unhealthy, dysfunctional people.

Understanding how to build and maintain healthy working relationships is critical for successful management of human and financial resources. The basic design of relationships is disarmingly simple. Yet the application of these values, structures and processes is a lifelong experience, and a complex one at that. It is necessary to maintain a focus on the design of relationships in order to succeed at living out the Relationship Model™.

1.1 VALUES

Our values determine our behaviour. In order to have an effective organization, all who work together must share the same values. When values are shared there is a built-in tendency to be able to work with the same operating system—within the same structure and with the same processes. There are many categories of values and many values in each category. The list of our values is as long as we want it to be. In the Relationship Model™ we have identified three core relationship-oriented values. Together they form the foundation of successful working relationships.

1.1.1 Affirmation

Affirmation is fundamental to healthy and productive relationships. Affirmation is the most elemental of all values. It encourages, builds, enables, empowers and ensures the fulfillment of each individual in the organization. It encourages calculated risk. Affirmation enables mistakes to fuel a learning culture instead of a blame culture. Our affirmation of ourselves and others is the most significant factor influencing the structure and the processes of our relationships.

1.1.2 Involvement

The concept of involving people in the matters that affect them is a principle introduced by God at the time of creation. God chose to involve the first couple in the work of caring for the world into which God placed them. God also involved them in creation by giving them the authority and the responsibility to reproduce themselves. In the New Testament the Lord involved his disciples and each of us in the challenge of the great commission. Involvement produces a strong sense of ownership for those who have responsibility related to what they helped to shape and plan.

1.1.3 Servant Leadership

Servant leadership is a quality that characterizes those who are the source of authority to others in a relationship-oriented organization. Servant leadership includes such values as care, concern, valuing the worth of others, service, help and the like. Servant leadership can be demonstrated by anyone who is in a position of authority in an organization. In any organization everyone has some authority. We often think of authority in a "top-down" manner. Our organizational charts, which place the "highest" level of authority at the "top", suggest the opposite of the kind of authority that supports those above. A better organizational "chart" is the image of the tree where those with the most authority support those above.

1.2 STRUCTURE

1.2.1 Authority

Authority includes authorization, resources (human and financial resources, information and time) and competencies. As in a tree, nutrients rise to nourish the entire tree and its fruit, so authority flows upwards to the top of the organization to empower its people to produce services for the clients. Authority at any level in the organization is always limited by the person or group who is delegating authority to others.

1.2.2 Limitations of Authority

Limitations are the elements of a relationship that define the boundaries of authority and the extent of our freedom in fulfilling our responsibility. Limitations are normally expressed in negative terms. In an organization, defining limitations of authority eliminates the need for returning to the source of authority repeatedly for permission to act. Limitations may be adjusted to maintain a balance between authority and responsibility.

1.2.3 Responsibility

Responsibility is the broad description of the purpose for a position within the organization. It is usually contained in the relationship description of an individual or a group. Healthy relationships always balance authority and responsibility. Responsibility is further defined by the expectations of the responsibility.

1.2.4 Expectations of Responsibility

Expectations are the adjusting components of responsibility. In a relationship-oriented organization expectations are negotiated, not imposed, in order to achieve a balance with the authorization and resources that are available. They are usually expressed in the form of goals and standards. Goals may be strategic or tactical. Standards may range from the minimum quality we expect of one another to the quality to which we aspire.

1.2.5 Accountability

Accountability is the monitoring and measuring component of a relationship. The first role of accountability is to monitor the balance of authority and responsibility in each relationship and to monitor compliance with limitations and expectations. The second role is to measure strategic and tactical results. The annual relationship review is the primary opportunity for accountability. Often given a negative connotation, accountability in The Relationship Model™ gives an opportunity for recognition and learning as well as correction. It is a neutral concept.

1.3 PROCESS

Process is critical to the success of any group. The six core processes of governance are:

• Communication
• Decision-making
• Conflict Resolution
• Strategic Planning
• Delegating Authority and Responsibility
• Monitoring and Measuring

SUMMARY

The Relationship Model™ offers the most natural means of giving an effective design to our organization. No major paradigm shift is required. At the same time, we will realize how important it is to use the conceptual framework that this model offers when we build a governance structure and when we process information.

1.4 PRINCIPLES

The combination of values, structure and process may be synthesized into ten basic principles that define The Relationship Model™. Using these principles as a checklist can assist the board to verify that the values, structures and processes used within the organization are consistent with the Relationship Model™. The checklist can also assist the board to identify weaknesses and to give guidance toward making adjustments that will improve relationships and productivity.

1.4.1 The organization seeks a balance between the fulfillment of the needs of the clients and the personal fulfillment of the staff and volunteers.

1.4.2 The affirmation, involvement and servant leadership of every individual and group at every level in the organization are vital to the success of the organization.

1.4.3 Authority, responsibility and accountability are the primary components of all relationships. Limitations of authority and expectations of responsibility are the secondary components.

1.4.4 Circles of authority and responsibility are defined clearly and are maintained equal in size by negotiating limitations of authority or by expectations of responsibility.

1.4.5 The board of directors, acting on information from all stakeholders, is responsible for strategic planning: defining target groups, services/needs, vision, mission and priorities, monitoring performance and measuring results.

1.4.6 The CEO is responsible for managing the delivery of services to the clients in accord with board-stated priorities and for achieving the strategic goals within the limitations of the authorization and resources available.

1.4.7 Each individual has a share in responsibility for creating, owning, understanding and implementing the mission of the organization.

1.4.8 Decision-making proceeds from shared values, vision and mission, not unilaterally from the board or the CEO. Decisions are made as close as possible to where they are implemented.

1.4.9 The organization is results-oriented. Indicators of results are identified. Strategic and tactical goals are set in balance with available resources. Results are measured.

1.4.10 Accountability is mutual. The source of authority is accountable to the recipient for providing adequate authorization and resources. The recipient is accountable to the source for achieving results.

2.0 GOVERNANCE STRUCTURE

2.1 ROLES

2.1.1 Role of the Board

The role of the board of directors is to direct and control the entire organization through the process of governance. It designs its own governance policies, creates and maintains the strategic plan, delegates management authority to the CEO, monitors the present performance and measures results.

The main focus of the board is on strategic planning. The basic strategic question for the board of the organization to answer is, "What services shall the organization deliver to which people in what places and in what order of priority?"

Monitoring compliance with limitations and expectations policies, measuring strategic results achieved by management, satisfying regulatory requirements of the charity and fulfilling the board's responsibility to all its stakeholders completes the board's role in governance.

2.1.2 Role of the Committees

Committees are used sparingly in the Relationship Model™. The primary role of the committees is to assist the board with its governance, not to govern on the board's behalf.

The committees monitor management's compliance with the board's limitations and expectations policies. The committees also assist the board with planning and measurement in the areas of each committee's mandate.

To avoid having to take management responsibility for results, the committees advise when asked by management, but do not manage or direct management unless authorized to do so by the board.

The committees may assist the board in identifying indicators by which strategic results can be measured.

2.1.3 Role of the Chair, Vice-chairs, Committee Chairs

The role of the chair is to lead the process of decision-making. The chair shall be objective and impartial and shall not lead the discussion to a predetermined conclusion. The chair shall not make or second a motion, speak for or against a motion or vote on a motion.

For any agenda item where s/he wishes to express a personal opinion and vote, the chair may defer to a vice-chair before the agenda item begins. In such cases the chair shall not lead any portion of the decision-making process.

The chair shall ensure that each director has ample opportunity to give an expression of his/her own opinion and shall ensure that no director dominates the discussion or demonstrates inappropriate behaviour.

The vice-chairs and committee chairs shall follow these same principles of leadership in the decision-making process.

2.1.4 Role of Individual Board Members

The primary role of individual board members is to participate in the process of governance. Board members study information and decision-making materials, participate in discussion and debate and share in the decision-making process by reaching consensus or voting.

Individual board members have no authority to act on behalf of the organization as individuals except by specific delegation from the board.

2.2 RELATIONSHIP DESCRIPTIONS

2.2.1 The Board of Directors/Stakeholders Relationship Description

1. Authority

The ultimate support of all the board's authority is the body of stakeholders. Those stakeholders include primarily the donors, clients and strategic partners of the organization and various government authorities, which grant the organization its legal, operational and charitable status.

The board's sources of moral authority are the stakeholders of the organization and the appropriate government agencies and departments.

The board's sources of strategic/operational authority are the stakeholders of the organization—the members, the donors, the strategic partners and the clients.

The board's sources of legal/regulatory authority are the governmental authorities where the organization is registered and where its services are delivered. National organizations of which the organization is a member may also have regulatory authority.

2. Limitations of Authority

In exercising its moral authority and its legal and regulatory authority, the board may not violate the civil laws in the countries where it is registered and operates.

In exercising its strategic/operational authority the board may not violate the bylaws of the organization.

3. Responsibilities

The responsibilities of governance of the board are to:

- design the board's structure and governance processes
- provide strategic leadership by determining the organizations' values, target groups and services, vision, mission and priorities
- delegate management authority and responsibility to the CEO

- be accountable for strategic results and to ensure that the organization and each individual in it act within all the limitations of delegated authority.

4. Expectations

The expectations of the board are described in its strategic plans and in the annual strategic goals of the organization and in the annual tactical goals of the board.

In fulfilling its strategic and operational responsibility, the board shall seek and follow the counsel of its stakeholders in its strategic planning process and in its governance of the strategic mission and priorities.

5. Accountabilities

The board is accountable to the stakeholders of the organization and to the civil authorities.

The board's accountability will be exercised by the submission of required documentation to civil authorities and by clear and true reporting to all of its stakeholders: employees, donors, strategic partners and clients.

2.2.2 Finance and Audit Committee/ Board Relationship Description

1. Authority

The finance committee shall be appointed annually by the board of directors and shall function with the authority of the board within the terms of its relationship description. The board of directors may fulfill the functions of this committee itself.

Membership shall consist of not less than three (3) and not more than five (5) of the directors.

A quorum shall be a majority of members.

2. Limitations

Advising the board on matters of finance, the committee may not, without additional authorization by the board:

- manage the day-to-day operations of the organization

- give management direction to the CEO or his/her staff
- monitor management performance not covered in financial limitations policies
- request reports not required for the monitoring of financial limitations policies.

Advising the board on matters of financial audit and internal controls, the committee may not enter into conflict of interest.

3. Responsibilities

As a committee supporting the board in financial matters, the committee shall:

- review CEO financial limitations policies and recommend changes to the board of directors
- monitor financial limitations policies in accordance with the monitoring schedule
- receive action plans from the CEO when financial limitations policies are violated and report significant violations to the board
- consider and recommend to the board the appointment of external auditors and their remuneration
- review the external auditors' management letter and management's response
- review financial reports submitted to regulatory agencies.

4. Expectations

The committee shall meet not less than four (4) times per year, not later than sixty (60) days following the end of any quarter of the fiscal year.

Members of the committee are expected to attend all meetings of the committee.

The committee shall provide copies of the financial limitations policy-monitoring reports to each director in a timely manner.

5. Accountabilities

The committee shall report the following to the board of directors in writing at the first board meeting of the fiscal year:

- dates of meetings and committee member attendance
- summary of financial policy recommendations for the year

- summary of monitoring of financial limitations policies.

The board of directors and the committee shall confirm or renegotiate the committee/board relationship annually.

2.2.3 Board Chair/Board Relationship Description

1. Authority

The board chair receives his/her authority by the election of the board of directors.

The board chair is authorized by the board to provide the leadership of the process of governance.

The board shall provide the board chair with the resources required for that process.

2. Limitations of Authority

In the fulfillment of the responsibilities of this position the board chair may not:

- take any action not authorized by the board of directors
- direct the decision-making process towards any specific outcome
- give management direction to the CEO or his/her staff
- cause or allow the board of directors to be in violation of the limitations of its authority
- prevent any proposal from any director from being considered.

3. Responsibility

The responsibilities of the board chair are to:

- lead the governance process, including the preparation of the agenda, ensuring the flow of relevant governance information to the board of directors and chairing the meetings of the board
- lead the process of designing and maintaining board structure and process
- ensure that the process of strategic leadership is initiated and continued
- lead in the process of delegating authority and responsibility to the CEO
- lead in the process of board accountability, including an evaluation of the strategic results, the annual review of the performance of the board, the individual

directors, the CEO, and a process of evaluation of the board chair

- ensure that all decisions are documented accurately in minutes, policies and other documents
- ensure that the requirements of the board's accountability to civil government and the stakeholders are met
- act as the official spokesperson of the organization to the stakeholders and the public.

4. Expectations

The expectations of this position shall be negotiated in the annual review of the board chair and shall include:

- preparation for and attendance at every meeting of the board of directors
- flow of all relevant governance information to the directors
- conduct that is consistent with the values of affirmation, involvement and servant leadership.

5. Accountabilities

Accountability in this relationship is mutual.

The board of directors is accountable to the board chair for:

- providing all the authorization and resources required for the responsibilities
- providing an annual review of the board chair's performance
- negotiating reasonable expectations of the board chair's responsibility
- expressing affirmation, involvement and servant leadership in its relationship with the board chair.

The board chair is accountable to the board of directors for:

- performance with respect to the negotiated expectations
- compliance with the limitations of authority of the position.

Scheduled at pre-determined annual intervals, the relationship review shall be led by two members of the board appointed by the board and may include one additional person who is not a member of the board.

It shall include:

- a review of the authorization and resources provided and values expressed to the board chair
- a review of the board chair's performance towards expectations of the responsibilities of the relationship
- a negotiation of expectations for the next planning period
- a review of the authorization and resources required for the next period, including plans for personal development.

2.2.4 Vice-chair/Board Relationship Description

1. Authority

The vice-chair receives his/her authority by the election of the board of directors.

While serving as acting board chair, the vice-chair shall function within the board chair/board relationship description.

The vice-chair may become the acting board chair at the request of the board chair or the board itself.

The duration of service as acting board chair shall be determined at the time of the appointment.

2. Limitations of Authority

While serving as acting board chair the-vice-chair is subject to the limitations of authority for the board chair.

3. Responsibilities

While serving as acting board chair the vice-chair carries the responsibilities of the board chair.

When not serving as acting board chair the vice-chair shall assist and support the board chair in accomplishing his/her tasks.

4. Expectations

While serving as acting board chair the expectations to the-vice-chair are as for the board chair.

5. Accountabilities

While serving as acting board chair the accountabilities for the vice-chair are as for the board chair.

2.2.5 Board Secretary/Board Relationship Description

1. Authority

The board secretary receives his/her authority by the election of the board of directors. The board secretary shall be elected from among the members of the board.

The board secretary is authorized by the board to record the actions and decisions of the board in the official minutes of the board.

The board shall provide the board secretary with the material resources required for that process, including the authorization to appoint or employ a recording secretary for the purpose of taking minutes during the board meetings.

2. Limitations of Authority

In the fulfillment of the responsibilities of this position the board secretary may not:

- record any action not authorized by the board of directors
- give management direction to the CEO or the management staff
- cause or allow the board to be in violation of the limitations of its authority.

3. Responsibilities

The responsibilities of the board secretary are to:

- supervise the recording of minutes, notes and action lists at board meetings
- ensure that all decisions are documented accurately in minutes, policies and other documents
- distribute minutes, documents and notices of meetings to the board members in a timely manner
- ensure that the board's expectations of the board secretary are fulfilled.

4. Expectations

The expectations of this position shall be negotiated in the annual review of the board secretary/board relationship and shall include:

- preparation for and attendance at every meeting of the board
- timely flow of all relevant information to the board members, including board minutes and changes to the documents of the board.

5. Accountabilities

Accountability in this relationship is mutual. The board is accountable to the secretary for providing the authorization, resources, affirmation, involvement and servant leadership required for the successful realization of the responsibilities of the position.

The secretary is accountable to the board for performance with respect to the negotiated expectations and for compliance with the limitations of authority of the position.

The components of this working relationship shall be reviewed at predetermined intervals at the initiation of the board and shall include:

- a review of the authorization and resources provided and values expressed to the secretary
- a review of the secretary's performance towards expectations of the responsibilities of the relationship
- a negotiation of expectations for the next planning period
- a review of the authorization and resources required for the next period, including plans for personal development.

2.2.6 Committee Chair/Board Relationship Description

1. Authority

The committee chair receives his/her authority by the election of the board of directors.

The committee chair is authorized by the board to provide the leadership of the committee process.

The board shall provide the committee chair with the material resources required for that process.

2. Limitations of Authority

In the fulfillment of the responsibilities of this position, the committee chair may not:

- take any action not authorized by the board of directors
- direct the decision-making process towards any specific outcome
- give management direction to the CEO or his/her staff
- cause or allow the committee to be in violation of the limitations of its authority.

3. Responsibility

The responsibilities of the committee chair are to:

- lead the committee process, including the preparation of the agenda and chairing the meetings of the committee
- ensure that all decisions are documented accurately in minutes, policies and other documents
- ensure that the board's expectations of the committee are fulfilled.

4. Expectations

The expectations of this position shall be negotiated in the annual review of the committee chair board relationship and shall include:

- preparation for and attendance at every meeting of the committee
- flow of all information relevant information to the committee members
- conduct that is consistent with the values of the organization.

5. Accountabilities

Accountability in this relationship is mutual. The board is accountable to the committee chair for providing the authorization, resources, affirmation, involvement and servant leadership required for the successful realization of the responsibilities of the position.

The committee chair is accountable to the board for performance with respect to the negotiated expectations and for compliance with the limitations of authority of the position.

The components of this working relationship shall be reviewed at predetermined intervals at the initiation of the board and shall include:

- a review of the authorization and resources provided and values expressed to the committee chair
- a review of the committee chair's performance towards expectations of the responsibilities of the relationship
- a negotiation of expectations for the next planning period
- a review of the authorization and resources required for the next period, including plans for personal development.

2.2.7 Board Member/Board Relationship Description

1. Authority

The board member is authorized by virtue of his/her election to the board of directors. Once elected the source of authority is the board of directors.

The board of directors shall provide costs of board meetings, including travel and accommodation, directors' liability insurance, board materials and resources for orientation and training.

2. Limits of Authority

Without specific authority from the board, an individual director may not:

- speak officially on behalf of the board or organization
- enter into any legal or financial agreement on behalf of the organization
- give direction to the CEO or the management of the organization.

3. Responsibility

The responsibility of each director is to:

- participate in the governance process of the board

- share in the responsibilities of the board of directors as defined in the board/ stakeholder relationship description
- represent accurately and support the official positions and decisions of the board when interacting with the stakeholders and the public.

4. Expectations

Each director is expected to:

- participate in an orientation program in the Relationship Model™ and the bylaws, governance manual and strategic plan of the organization
- read reports and study materials provided for preparation of board meetings
- attend all board meetings and meeting of committees of which he/she is a member or to indicate to the board or committee chair the reason for his/her inability to attend
- participate actively in discussion and the decision making process
- display personal conduct that reflects the values of the organization.

5. Accountabilities

Accountability in this relationship is mutual.

The board is accountable to the director for providing the authorization, resources, affirmation, involvement and servant leadership required for the successful realization of the responsibilities of the position.

Each director shares in the board's accountability to the stakeholders for achieving strategic results and in governing the organization with due diligence and integrity and to civil governments for compliance with all relevant laws and regulations.

Each director is accountable to the board and to the civil government's regulatory body under whose laws the organization is registered, for handling the finances of the organization with integrity.

The director is accountable to the board for performance with respect to the negotiated expectations and for compliance with the limitations of authority of the position.

The components of this working relationship shall be reviewed at predetermined intervals at the initiation of the board and shall include:

- a review of the authorization and resources provided and values expressed to the director

- a review of the director's performance towards expectations of the responsibilities of the relationship

- a negotiation of expectations for the next planning period

- a review of the authorization and resources required for the next period, including plans for personal development.

3.0 GOVERNANCE PROCESSES

The governance processes are divided into four separate areas. They reflect the four distinct responsibilities of the board.

3.1 BOARD PROCESSES

In these processes the word "shall" means the action is required. The word "may" means the action is optional.

3.1.1 Election of Directors, Chair, Vice-chair, Secretary

The board shall appoint a nominating committee from among its members. The CEO shall be an advisory member of the committee. The committee shall bring names of nominees forward to the board at its first meeting of the fiscal year in sufficient number to fill all vacancies on the board.

The election of directors shall be held annually at the first board meeting of the fiscal year from among those nominated by the nominating committee or other directors. No director may be elected without having consented to his/her nomination.

Elections for the office of chair, vice-chair and secretary shall be held annually at the first board meeting of the fiscal year. All elections are for a one-year term, commencing at the end of the meeting at which the election took place. No officer

may be elected to more than three (3) consecutive one-year terms.

Nominations for officers may take place at the same meeting where elections are held. Nominees shall agree to their nomination. Where a nominee is absent from the meeting where the nominations and elections take place, that nominee shall have agreed to the nomination in writing prior to the meeting.

Elections shall be by secret ballot. The chair shall appoint two members of the board as scrutinizers. They shall report the election results to the chair who shall announce them to the board. Following the announcement of election results, the ballots shall be destroyed.

3.1.2 Election of Committee Chairs

Committee chairs shall be nominated and elected to one-year terms of office by voting at the first board meeting of the fiscal year. No committee chair may be elected to more than three (3) consecutive one-year terms.

3.1.3 Removal of Elected Officers

The chair, vice-chairs, secretary, and individual directors may be removed from office by a two-thirds majority vote of the remaining directors.

3.1.4 Board Meetings

The minimum number of board meetings is prescribed in the organization's bylaws. The dates, venue and duration of each meeting shall be determined by majority vote. Changes to dates, venue and duration may be made by majority vote at any time before the meeting being changed.

3.1.5 Board Meeting Preparation

The board chair shall prepare a proposed agenda, having consulted the CEO.

A complete information packet shall be delivered to each director not less than seven (7) days before the meeting.

3.1.6 Quorum

The quorum for meetings of the board is prescribed in the organization's bylaws.

3.1.7 Meeting Procedures

The chair shall determine the protocol for the presentation of information and for discussion by directors. In order to determine the need for and the content of the motion, discussion may occur on a subject before a specific motion is made and seconded. Motions shall be made and seconded before debate on the specific motion may begin. The motion shall be recorded by the recording secretary and read aloud before discussion commences.

Amendments or substitute motions or changes in wording require a motion and a second after the original motion has been seconded. The amendment, motion to substitute or to change wording shall be decided by vote before the amended, substituted or modified motion is put to the vote.

Agendas shall be structured to include major items of general information, monitoring information and decision-making information.

Unless otherwise specified in this governance manual, meeting procedures shall follow the most recent edition of Robert's Rules of Order. The board chair shall appoint a parliamentarian to monitor the meeting procedures.

3.1.8 Regular and Extraordinary Board Meetings

The board shall meet four (4) times per year. The schedule of the year's meetings shall be determined at the first meeting of the fiscal year.

The requirements for calling extraordinary board meetings are prescribed in the organization's bylaws.

3.1.9 Consensus and Voting

Decisions may be made by consensus. When consensus is not possible, decisions shall be made by voting. The majority required to pass a motion is prescribed in the organization's bylaws.

A show of hands is sufficient, but a director may call for a count.

3.1.10 Conflict Resolution

The board shall follow the guidelines for conflict resolution contained in Matthew 18:15 – 17 and 1 Corinthians 6:1 – 8. Thus, the principles of any conflict resolution process shall include the following:

a. A forgiving spirit on the board's part will be the foundation of any conflict resolution process.

b. The process shall begin with direct negotiation and proceed to mediation and arbitration as required.

c. The process shall be fair and transparent and shall seek to uphold the dignity of all persons.

d. The process shall seek justice first and reconciliation second, recognizing that justice is necessary in order to achieve reconciliation.

This policy addresses the following potential conflicts:

1. Conflicts in which the board is directly involved:

   a. Conflicts within the board

   b. Conflicts between the board and persons or groups within the organization (members/staff/volunteers)

   c. Conflicts between the board and persons or groups outside the organization

In cases where the board is one of the parties in the conflict, the board shall attempt to negotiate the conflict. Should those efforts fail, the board shall seek to resolve the conflict through mediation before submitting the conflict to arbitration.

2. Conflicts that the board is being asked to arbitrate:

a. Conflicts between persons or groups within the organization

b. Conflicts between persons or groups within the organization and persons or groups outside the organization

In cases where the board is not one of the parties in the conflict but is being asked to arbitrate the conflict, the board shall not become involved until all efforts at negotiation and mediation (whether described in policy or not) have been exhausted.

Where those efforts have failed and the board has agreed be the arbiter in the conflict, the following components shall be part of the board process:

a. The person or group making the allegation(s) shall be identified.

b. The person or group to whom the allegation(s) is/are directed shall be identified.

c. The allegation(s) shall be made in writing to avoid assumptions or misperceptions, hearsay or irresponsible criticism.

d. The allegations shall be accompanied by information that supports the allegation(s).

e. Both the allegations and the supporting information shall be shared with the person(s) or group to whom the allegations are directed.

f. At the discretion of the board the allegations shall be presented to the board in the presence of the person(s) or group to whom they refer.

g. The person(s) or group to whom the allegation is directed shall have an opportunity to request additional information in writing and respond to the allegations in the presence of the person(s) bringing them.

h. The board shall have an opportunity to ask both parties for clarification or information.

i. The board may meet *in camera* to consider the conflict. New information may not be considered in the *in camera* session.

j. The board shall report its decision to both parties in writing.

k. Under exceptional circumstances (e.g., sexual harassment, fraud) there may be delays in the conflict resolution process to allow for external investigation.

3.1.11 Governance Manual Reviews

The review of the governance manual, except for the strategic plan, shall take place at the first board meeting each year. The chair, vice-chair, secretary and CEO shall prepare the review at a meeting prior to this board meeting.

The strategic plan shall be reviewed and revised annually at the third board meeting of the year.

3.1.12 Expenses

Board meeting venue costs, director and staff travel costs and the cost of accommodation at board meetings or retreats are the responsibility of the organization.

3.1.13 Minutes, Recording, Distribution, Approval

The board minutes are the only official record of board action. Only decisions and actions recorded in the official minutes shall be considered as official action of the board.

The board secretary shall submit the board minutes to the board chair within one week following the board meeting.

The minutes shall be approved at the next board meeting and shall become the official record of action taken at the previous board meeting.

3.1.14 Staff and Guest Attendance

The board may invite any person to attend its meetings as a guest observer, presenter or participant. Normally, the chair shall approve such visitors.

Permission to speak or participate in discussion shall be the prerogative of the chair. The board may also approve the presence and level of participation of visitors by vote.

Normally, all visitors shall sit in a separate gallery reserved for them.

3.1.15 Communication with Staff

Individual board members are free to communicate with any members of the staff at any time. In doing so, the following guidelines shall be followed:

- Information may be requested provided no financial resources or significant time is required of the staff to provide the information.
- Advice may be freely offered provided that it is understood that such advice is not regarded as management direction.
- The CEO shall be copied in communication that may affect the management of his/her staff and volunteers.

3.2 STRATEGIC PLANNING PROCESS

Because of rapid changes in opportunity and in the cultural and political environment in which we work, the strategic plan shall be reviewed and revised each year at the third board meeting of the year.

Consultation with all stakeholders is the vital component to a strategic plan that will inspire donors, clients, staff, and volunteers to commit themselves to the success of the plan. That consultation shall remain a regular component of each annual planning process.

The components of the strategic plan that require annual review and possible revision by and approval of the board are target groups, services/needs, vision, mission, priorities, strategic goals and critical success factors.

The values that brought people together into the organization are the least likely to change and may be reviewed at longer intervals as determined by the board.

3.2.1 Historical Context

The significant events and milestones in the formation and development form the historical context in which strategic planning takes places and changes over time.

3.2.2 Values

The men and women of the organization share values that bring us together into a relationship. Organizational values may change slightly over time. The board may review and revise the values statement from time to time.

3.2.3 Target Groups

Target groups are the categories of individual or groups that form the clients who benefit from the services of the organization. They may be described by need, age, type of individual or organization or other categories that are mutually exclusive.

3.2.4 Services

A fundamental basis of the strategic planning process is identifying what services we shall provide to which people in which places. Because target groups, services/needs and places can change significantly and rapidly, the board shall review these variables annually in the strategic planning process.

3.2.5 Places

Places are the geographical references in which the services are delivered. They may be expressed by regions, countries or places within countries.

3.2.6 Vision

The vision is a statement of what we want the future effect of the services of the organization to be. It is challenging and expresses the hope for the future that lies just beyond the strategic planning "horizon". The board shall review the vision statement annually as part of the strategic planning process.

3.2.7 Mission

The mission statement is the most concentrated expression of what strategic purposes the organization exists to accomplish. The board shall review the mission statement annually. It may change from time to time to reflect changes in need and opportunity.

3.2.8 Priorities

The board shall review and revise its strategic priorities annually to determine how best to allocate limited resources to fulfill its mission.

3.2.9 Strategic Goals

Strategic goals are an expression of intent for the accomplishing of the strategic plan of the organization. They are based on the indicators of strategic results. The board shall set strategic goals annually as the final step in the strategic planning process. No strategic goals exist at the present time.

Note: Strategic goals refer to the S.M.A.R.T. goals that are specific, measurable, achievable, relevant to the mission and priorities, and time-limited. They deal with the "what" the organization seeks to do, rather than the tactical goals that deal with "how" management seeks to accomplish the mission and priorities.

3.2.10 Critical Success Factors

The strategic plan is completed with a list of those factors in the management of the organization's service delivery that are critical to the success of its vision and mission. These form the bridge between the strategic governance of the board and the tactical management of the CEO. Identifying the critical success factors allows the board to give management direction to the CEO without becoming directly involved with management. Critical success factors may address the following subjects among others.

> Capital needs
> Financing (operating credit)
> Financial management
> Fund development
> Governance
> Management
> Monitoring and measuring
> Operating funding
> Planning
> Public relations
> Relationships with members
> Relationships with government
> Reserves
> Risk analysis
> Services
> Staff and volunteer treatment
> Strategic alliances
> Values

(The actual strategic plan of the organization may be inserted here. The board may also choose to place the ten-part strategic plan into a separate document.)

3.3 DELEGATING AUTHORITY AND RESPONSIBILITY TO THE CEO

The board of directors shall delegate all authority and responsibility for management of the organization's infrastructure and for fulfilling the strategic mission and priorities to the CEO. The board shall instruct the CEO of all limitations of the authority being delegated in written limitations policies. No limitations may be assumed or implied. Limitations policies may be added, modified or deleted as required from time to time.

The board shall hold the CEO singularly accountable for all performance related to the management of the organization's infrastructure and for performance of strategic mission and priorities. S/he is also accountable for compliance with limitations of authority and expectations of responsibility. The CEO is the only person accountable directly to the board.

The board shall request all information for strategic planning, monitoring performance and measuring results for the organization's infrastructure directly from the CEO, who may delegate the requests to the appropriate staff members. The board may, with the CEO's consent, make such requests directly.

The board may, in exceptional circumstances, delegate temporary authority and responsibility to other staff members. In such cases the CEO shall be informed of the authority and responsibility being delegated and of its recipient and duration. The board may not hold the CEO accountable for management performance or strategic or tactical results in such cases.

3.3.1 CEO/Board Relationship Description

1. Authority

The CEO functions with authority from the board of directors to be the chief executive officer of the organization.

The board shall provide budgeted resources required for the successful fulfillment of the responsibilities of the position.

Resources delegated to the CEO include paid and volunteer human resources, financial resources for operations and a personal compensation package.

(Some organizations may wish to list the competencies (qualifications) required for the position. Since competencies are a part of the circle of authority, they would be listed here.)

2. Limitations of Authority

The CEO operates within the parameters of the:

- CEO limitations of authority policies
- strategic plan agreed by the board of directors
- imitations of legal and regulatory authorities.

3. Responsibilities

It is the CEO's responsibility to lead the processes of planning, resource development and management of the organization. Specifically s/he shall:

- provide the board with the organizational information it needs for its governance responsibilities, including strategic planning, infrastructure, resource development, monitoring performance and measuring strategic results

- develop and maintain healthy relationships between the board of directors and the stakeholders, including members, staff and volunteers, clients and regulatory authorities

- prepare tactical and financial plans in compliance with the strategic plan and CEO limitations and expectations policies

- develop the human and financial resources needed for the success of the mission

- manage the human and financial resources of the organization and its infrastructure to achieve the strategic goals of the organization.

4. Expectations

The expectations of the responsibility for this position are contained in:

- the governance manual
- the strategic plan
- the CEO's tactical goals.

The CEO is also expected to:

- model and promulgate the organization's values
- maintain and develop teamwork at all levels of the organization
- ensure that the relationships between the organization and its stakeholders are open and cooperative.

5. Accountabilities

Accountability in this relationship is mutual. The board is accountable to the CEO for providing the authorization, resources, affirmation, involvement and servant leadership required for the successful realization of the responsibilities of the position.

The CEO is accountable to the board for performance with respect to the negotiated expectations of the position within the limitations of authority of the position and for behaviour consistent with the values of affirmation, involvement and servant leadership.

The components of this working relationship shall be reviewed annually at the initiation of the board of directors and shall include:

- a review of the authorization and resources provided and values expressed to the CEO
- a review of the CEO's performance towards expectations of the responsibilities of the relationship including the progress towards strategic goals and the CEO's personal tactical goals
- a negotiation of tactical goals and other expectations for the next year
- a review of the authorization and resources required for the next year, including plans for personal development.

3.3.2 CEO Limitations and Expectations Policies

Limitations and expectations policies are the means by which clear limitations of the authority and expectations of responsibilities negotiated with the CEO are communicated to him/her and his/her respective staffs. Normally, these policies shall be prepared by the board or one of its committees with the involvement of the CEO and brought to the board for approval. The board may also prepare these policies directly whether or not they deal with matters covered by a committee.

The development of these policies shall be monitored annually by the board or one of its committees. They shall ensure that limitations to the authority and expectations of the responsibilities of the CEO are added, modified or deleted in such a way that the board remains in control of management through governance. All limitations and expectations policies shall be approved by the board and recorded in this manual. Limitations or expectations not documented in these policies may not be assumed or implied.

3.3.2.1 Tactical and Financial Planning

Limitations

With respect to tactical and financial planning, the CEO may not plan for the expenditure of more operational or capital funds than are reasonably projected to be received in the year(s) included in the plans.

Expectations

With respect to operational and financial planning, the CEO is expected to enable the board to fulfill its fiduciary responsibilities and maintain its integrity in financial matters. Accordingly, the CEO is expected to create a tactical or financial plan that:

- is complete within one month before the end of the fiscal year
- complies with the strategic plan and priorities in its allocation of resources
- contains enough detail to enable accurate monitoring, including accurate projections of income and expenditure, the

separation of capital and operational items, cash flow and audit trails
- includes a contingency plan equal to 5% of the cost of the tactical plans.

3.3.2.2 Financial Condition

Limitations

With respect to operating the organization in a sound and prudent financial manner, the CEO may not allow the organization to be put at risk financially, or cause the directors to be in violation of their responsibilities. Accordingly, s/he may not:

- expend more operational funds than have been received in any financial year
- expend funds on operations not included in the strategic plan.

Expectations

With regard to the management of the organization's finances, the CEO is expected to:

- maintain all of the organization's accounts in a timely manner in compliance with generally accepted accounting practices
- notify the board in a timely manner of any financial event which could affect the financial security of the organization
- provide a plan for regaining compliance at the same time that the violation of limitations is reported if the financial condition violates these limitations
- continue to comply with the tactical and financial planning policy in any revision of the plans.

3.3.2.3 Capital Expenditures

Limitations

With respect to proper control of capital expenditures, the CEO may not incur capital expenditures:

- in excess of funds specifically given as restricted funds
- for items that are not required for the normal operations
- which, while otherwise fulfilling the two forgoing, exceed $_____ per expenditure.

Expectations

The CEO is expected to report all purchases when this policy is monitored.

3.3.2.4 Capital Assets

Limitations

With respect to minimizing losses of the organization's capital assets, the CEO may not:

- allow the disposal of assets at less than market value
- sell or dispose of assets of a value in excess of $_____.

Expectations

Additionally, the CEO is expected to:

- maintain a reasonable level of property and liability insurance
- take all reasonable steps to minimize fraud, losses and liability claims
- maintain net assets above a level sufficient to meet the organization's liabilities
- plan for the replacement of depreciating capital assets.

3.3.2.5 Restricted or Designated Funds

With respect to the restricted funds and assets, the CEO may not:

- spend restricted funds for a purpose other than that for which they were restricted
- fail to consult the donor before disposing of or moving restricted assets outside of the restriction before the end of its normal economic life.

3.3.2.6 Banking Operations

In order that the board may comply with responsibility regarding the operation of bank accounts, the CEO may not:

- open, close or amend a bank account in the name of the organization, whether or not the process for opening, closing or amending requires a copy of a resolution passed by the directors to be presented to the bank prior to the account's being opened, closed or amended

- enter into a loan or overdraft agreement on behalf of the organization.

3.3.2.7 Stakeholder Treatment

Limitations

In relating to staff and volunteers, the CEO may not:

- impose work expectations on any staff that have not been negotiated, agreed and confirmed in writing
- allow acceptance criteria—gender, status or competencies (knowledge, skills attitudes, motives or attributes)—to be imposed on staff that have not been previously stated and agreed prior to selection.

Expectations

In relating to the board of directors, staff, volunteers and other stakeholders, the CEO is expected to demonstrate the values of affirmation, involvement and servant leadership.

In relating to staff and volunteers, the CEO is also expected to:

- respond to staff and volunteer concerns promptly
- provide adequate financial compensation for the level of responsibility the person holds.

3.3.2.8 Board Governance Support

In supporting the board's governance process, the CEO is expected to:

- attend all board meetings
- ensure that monitoring information is made available to the board or committee in a timely, accurate, understandable and comprehensive manner
- comply with the regulatory guidelines set out in current legislation.

3.4 BOARD OF DIRECTORS' ACCOUNTABILITIES

3.4.1 Measuring Strategic Results

As part of its duty, the board of directors shall measure the strategic results of its efforts to fulfill its mission and priorities.

3.4.1.1 Indicators of Results

The board of directors shall identify indicators of results that shall be the basis of setting strategic goals that are specific, measurable, achievable, relevant to the mission and priorities, and time-limited (S.M.A.R.T.).

The indicators shall be reviewed on an annual basis and revised where necessary as part of the strategic planning process.

(Here list the indicators or make reference to another document, e.g., a questionnaire that acts as the indicator of results.)

3.4.1.2 Measuring Process

The board shall measure the progress toward the strategic goals on an annual basis as part of the strategic planning process. On the basis of this measurement and evaluation of strategic results, the board may make revisions to priorities and strategic goals for the following year.

3.4.2 Monitoring Tactical Performance and Annual Relationship Reviews

As part of its accountability process, the board shall have its own performance reviewed and shall monitor the performance and shall complete annual relationship reviews for the CEO and the committees to which it has delegated authority and responsibility.

Accountability in all relationships is mutual. The source of authority is accountable to the recipient of authority for providing the authorization, resources, affirmation, involvement and servant leadership required for the successful realization of the responsibilities of the position.

The recipient of authority is accountable to the source of authority for performance with respect to the negotiated expectations and for compliance with the limitations of authority of the position being reviewed.

The components of this working relationship shall be reviewed at predetermined intervals at the initiation of the source of authority and shall include:

- a review of the authorization and resources provided and values expressed by the source of authority to the recipient
- a review of the recipient's performance towards expectations of the responsibilities of the relationship including the progress towards tactical goals
- a negotiation of tactical goals and other expectations for the next planning period
- a review of the authorization and resources required for the next period, including plans for personal development.

Copies of all annual relationship reviews shall be distributed to all members of the board.

3.4.2.1 Board Annual Review

The annual review of the performance of the board shall be assigned to two members of the board and one outside person appointed by the members of the board and qualified in reviewing the process of governance.

3.4.2.2 Chair, Vice-chair and Secretary Annual Review

The annual review of the chair, vice-chair and secretary/board relationship shall be delegated to three board members appointed by the board. The reviewers' annual appointment may be renewed.

3.4.2.3 Committee Annual Reviews

The annual review of the committee/board relationship shall be delegated to the chair and two board members appointed by the board and who are not members of the committee whose relationship with the board is not being reviewed. At least one of the reviewers shall attend one meeting of the committee being reviewed during the year under review.

3.4.2.4 Committee Chair Annual Review

The annual review of the committee chair/board relationship shall be delegated to the chair and the same two board members who have reviewed the relationship of the corresponding committee.

3.4.2.5 Board Director Annual Review

The annual review of the board director/board relationship shall be delegated to the chair, the vice-chair and the secretary.

3.4.2.6 Monitoring CEO Limitations and Expectations Policies

The board shall perform the monitoring of the CEO's compliance with the limitations of authority and expectations of responsibility, unless the monitoring is delegated to the committee in whose area the limitations of authority apply.

The board or the appropriate committee shall establish and maintain an annual schedule of this monitoring process for each of the limitations and expectations policies. They may be monitored monthly, quarterly or annually at the direction of the board.

(A monitoring schedule shall be established and placed here as part of this policy.)

3.4.2.7 CEO Annual Review

The annual review of the CEO/board relationship shall be delegated to the chair and two members of the board appointed by the board.

3.4.3 Accountability to Civil Authorities

The board shall ensure that all documents required by the government are filed in accordance with the laws of the civil authorities.

The board shall further ensure that the organization complies with all the laws of the state/country in which the organization is registered and works.

3.4.4 Accountability to Members

The board shall report fully and accurately the annual measurements of strategic results to each member of the organization in a timely manner in its annual report.

3.4.5 Accountability to Other Stakeholders

The board shall report fully and accurately the results of its annual measurements of strategic results to the donors and all sources of financial resources. The board shall also make available relevant information to the clients and primary beneficiaries of the organization services through an annual report that shall be made available in a timely manner.

Appendix C
Strategic Plan

Hope Seeds, Inc.
The Strategic Plan 2002-2007

1.0 Historical Context

- January 1998 – First seed sent to Haiti as part of a mission effort of Hope Lutheran Church.
- March 1999 – Hope Seeds, Inc. formed by Mike and Jean Mueller
- August 1999 – 501(c)3 status established with the IRS
- January 2000 – First meeting of the Hope Seeds Board of Directors
- April 2000 – First grant received for $45,000
- April 2000 – First open house & garden party at Hope Seeds - Public invited
- May 2000 – First agricultural seminar conducted in Haiti

2.0 Values

The values of Hope Seeds are:

- Providing a Christian witness
- Turning seed to food
- Feeding the whole person
- Helping people help themselves
- Securing a long-term solution

3.0 Services/Needs

The services that Hope Seeds shall offer in this planning period are to:

- Provide seeds
- Acquire or produce seed stock
- Provide agricultural advice
- Teach/train
- Research
- Provide a Christian witness

4.0 Target Groups and Strategic Partners

The target groups to whom Hope Seeds shall direct its services during this planning period are:

- Entrepreneurs
- Small Farmers
- Children

We will build strategic alliances with missionaries and mission organizations in the countries where we provide services.

5.0 Places

During this planning period Hope Seeds shall focus primarily on the humid and arid tropical areas of the world.

6.0 Vision

Hope Seeds' vision for the hungry people of the world is to be the source of a living hope, of seeds and of help in learning how to grow seeds into food through successful agriculture wherever seeds are planted.

7.0 Mission

The Mission of Hope Seeds is that hungry people may have appropriate seeds and knowledge to provide for the basic needs of body and mind and soul, as intended by God in heaven since the world was created.

8.0 Priorities

8.1 Priorities of Services

During this planning period we shall allocate approximately one-third of our resources to providing seeds. The remaining two-thirds of our resources shall be allocated more or less equally to the other five services.

Normally we shall provide seeds in the context of providing one or more of the other services.

8.2 Priorities of Target Groups and Strategic Alliances

The priority among target groups shall be determined by need as expressed in requests for services.

We shall provide between 80% and 100% of our services to our target groups through strategic alliances for greater effectiveness, efficiency and accountability.

During this planning period we may provide up to 20% of our services directly to one or more target groups.

8.3 Priorities of Places

Within the humid and arid tropical areas of the world the needs of the target groups and the strategic partners shall determine the specific countries where we will provide services.

9.0 Indicators of Results and Strategic Goals

At the present time we have not identified indicators of strategic results.

During the first year of this planning period we shall identify indicators of results that will allow us to measure the benefits that our target groups and strategic partners receive from the services we provide.

During the second year of this planning period we shall establish specific and measurable strategic goals based on the indicators of results when the latter have been identified.

10.0 Critical Success Factors

Critical Success Factors form the bridge between the strategic plan of the Board and the tactical plans of management. While they are tactical items from the Board's point of view, they may still require Board approval because they may go beyond the authority delegated to the CEO, e.g., capital projects. On the other hand while they are in the domain of management, they are critical to the success of the strategic plans and are therefore of strategic importance. For this reason the tactical plans developed by the Executive Director and his staff are directed towards one or more of the Critical Success Factors in the Strategic Plan. In this way the Mission expressed in the strategic goals will be realized.

10.1 We must ensure that our Christian values are the foundation on which our service is based.

10.2 We must plan, develop and provide programs that deliver our services to our target groups consistent with the priorities of this strategic plan.

10.3 We must develop relationships with our stakeholders that enable them to experience responsible stewardship through their relationship with us.

10.4 We must secure operating and capital resources in order to sustain and extend our Mission.

10.5 We must manage our financial resources for maximum effectiveness and efficiency.

10.6 We must recruit staff and volunteers and create and sustain a positive corporate culture and learning environment.

10.7 We must develop and maintain strategic alliances in each of the countries were we provide services.

10.8 We must ensure that buildings and equipment are maintained at an acceptable standard.

10.9 We must ensure continual organizational development at the governance and management level.

10.10 We must measure our success.

Appendix D
Competencies

Competencies	Board	Board Chair	CEO Member	Manager
Achieving Competencies - These generally lie above the iceberg water line and are, therefore, possible to improve by training.				
Commitment to the Organization	X	X	X	X
Communication	X	X	X	X
Conflict Resolution	X	X	X	
Initiative	X	X	X	X
Objectivity	X	X	X	X
Process Orientation	X	X	X	X
Results Orientation			X	X
Thinking Competencies - Often below the surface, there is a limit to how much they can be changed by training. They reflect a person's cognitive ability.				
Conceptual Thinking	X	X	X	X
Effective Judgment	X	X	X	X
Independent Thinking	X	X		X
Logical Thinking	X	X		

Competencies	Board	Board Chair	CEO Member	Manager
Leadership Competencies - Often below the surface, these may be improved through increased knowledge and experience. They are affected by a person's attitudes and self-image.				
Accountability	X	X	X	X
Concern for Excellence			X	X
Delegation			X	X
Desire for Staff Fulfillment			X	
Interdependence	X	X		
Leadership			X	X
Stewardship	X	X		
Team Orientation				X
Personal Competencies - These mostly lie well below the surface and are, therefore, hard to change by training. Although all competencies are personal, these particularly reflect individual attitudes, traits, motives and self-image.				
Ambiguity Tolerance	X	X	X	
Empathy	X	X	X	X
Endurance				X
Open-mindedness	X	X	X	X
Personal Integrity	X	X	X	X
Self-awareness	X	X	X	X
Self-esteem	X	X	X	X
Transparency	X	X		

Definitions of Competencies

Achieving Competencies

Commitment to the Organization—the attachment a person has to the organization when its values, vision and mission are aligned with his/her own

Communication—gives and receives information with clarity, attentiveness, understanding and perception

Conflict Resolution—ensures conflict is resolved with justice and fairness in order to restore healthy relationships

Initiative—pro-actively grasps opportunities and ensures that neither issues nor people are forgotten or overlooked

Objectivity—draws conclusions by impartial evaluation of other perspectives and views without prejudice or bias

Process Orientation—makes decisions and seeks outcomes by consistent application of a logical sequence of agreed steps

Results Orientation—establishes clear strategies and goals and draws conclusions, which achieve results that are both acceptable and effective

Thinking Competencies

Conceptual Thinking—makes connections between apparently separate issues, seeing patterns, trends or relationships and developing mental frameworks to explain and interpret information

Effective Judgment—applies commonsense, measured reasoning, knowledge and experience to come to a conclusion

Independent Thinking—maintains own convictions despite undue influence, opposition or threat

Logical Thinking—breaks issues down into their constituent parts and predicts cause and effect in a sequence of steps

Leadership Competencies

Accountability—welcomes giving and receiving objective evaluation of working relationships and performance of self and others

Concern for Excellence—sets and maintains the highest standards while achieving a balance between organizational productivity and staff fulfillment

Delegation—multiplies the capacity of the organization by dividing the workload

Desire for Staff Fulfillment—does not focus solely on productivity at the expense of staff fulfillment

Interdependence—works effectively with others, demonstrating commitment to the group decision or activity

Leadership—inspires confidence and motivation in others, sharing commitment and confidence in achieving success together

Stewardship—makes the best use of resources while striving for high standards and a balance between effectiveness and efficiency

Team Orientation—committed to group activities and decisions, working effectively in partnership with others

Personal Competencies

Ambiguity Tolerance—operates effectively when issues are unresolved or inconclusive and is willing to take a measured risk even when the outcomes are uncertain

Empathy—shows awareness and appreciation of the feelings concerns and needs of others

Endurance—draws on personal resources to cope with difficulties, demonstrating willingness and stamina to make repeated efforts to overcome obstacles and/or to complete tasks

Open-mindedness—maintains an open and flexible mind towards new information, thoughts and ideas, welcoming the opportunity to grow in knowledge and understanding

Personal Integrity—trustworthy and conscientious and can be relied on to act and speak with consistency and honesty

Self-awareness—accurately assesses own strengths and weaknesses and can manage them successfully

Self-esteem—respects and likes him/herself, confident in his/her self- worth and capabilities

Transparency—has no hidden agendas, but is open with information while maintaining the privacy of individuals

Appendix E
Bibliography

Bender, Peter Urs. *Leadership from Within*. Toronto: Stoddart, 1997.

Bennis, Warren. G. *An Invented Life: Reflections on Leadership and Change*. Reading, Massachusetts: Addison-Wesley, 1993.

Dale Carnegie & Associates, Inc. *The Leader in You: How to Win Friends, Influence People, and Succeed in a Changing World*. New York: Simon & Schuster, 1993.

Handy, Charles. *The Empty Raincoat*. Great Britain: Arrow Books, 1995.

Harvard Business Review on Change. Boston: Harvard Business School, 1998.

Harvard Business Review on Corporate Governance. Boston: Harvard Business School, 2000.

Hesselbein, Frances, Goldsmith, Marshall, Beckhard, Richard, Editors, The Drucker Foundation. *The Leader of the Future*. New York: Jossey-Bass, 1996.

MacKenzie, Gordon. *Orbiting the Giant Hairball, A Corporate Fool's Guide to Surviving with Grace*. New York: Viking Penguin, 1996.

Oakley, Ed., and Doug Krug. *Enlightened Leadership: Getting to the Heart of Change*. New York: Simon & Schuster, 1991.

Sande, Ken. *The Peacemaker*. 2nd ed. Grand Rapids: Baker Books, 1997.

Stevens, Susan Kenny. *Nonprofit Lifecycles*. Long Lake, Minnesota: Stagewise Enterprises, Inc., 2001.

Weisbord, Marvin, and Sandra Janoff. *Future Search*. San Francisco: Berrett-Koehler, 2000.

Wright Walter C. Jr., *Relational Leadership A Biblical Model for Leadership and Service*, Carlisle, Cumbria, UK, Waynesboro, GA: Paternoster Press, 2000.

GovernanceMatters.com Inc.

# Information Request

PHONE: (780) 433-9839 (Canada country code is "1") (GMT -6 hours)

FAX: (780) 433-9657 (Canada country code is "1")

EMAIL: info@governancematters.com

WEBSITE: www.governancematters.com

MAIL: GovernanceMatters.com Inc.
Suite 301
7905 – 96 Street NW
Edmonton, Alberta, Canada T6C 4R3

Please send me FREE information on:

☐ introductory presentation to our board/management team
☐ Relationship Model™ seminars
☐ *Governance Matters* volume discount
☐ board governance manual development
☐ strategic planning facilitation
☐ distance learning courses
☐ board governance performance assessment
☐ senior management team performance assessment
☐ staff fulfillment assessment
☐ relationship reviews
☐ strength surveys for: ☐ board members
  ☐ board chair
  ☐ CEO
  ☐ managers
  ☐ pastors
☐ *Tree Trunks*, a newsletter for boards and CEOs
☐ *Tree Tops*, a newsletter for CEOs and managers

Name: _____

Address: _____

City:_____Prov/State/County: _____

Country:_____ Postal Code/Zip: _____

Telephone: _____

Email address: _____